Who Gav the Bible?

MW01231742

The Canon: Why do we have the books we now do in the Bible?

Which are the actual books of the Old Testament?

Which are the actual books of the New Testament?

Are there 'lost books of the Bible'? What about the 'missing' gospels?

What about the Books of Enoch, Jasher, and Jubilee?

Which books did Jesus cite?

What about the Apocrypha?

Was the original apostolic canon formed in Asia Minor?

Who maintained the best 'chain of custody' of the knowledge of the books?

Are biblical manuscripts accurate? Which are best?

Is one translation inspired to be without any error?

Copyright © 2021/2022, Version 1.2 by *Nazarene Books*. ISBN 978-1-64106-093-6. Booklet produced for the *Continuing* Church of God and Successor, a corporation sole. 1036 W. Grand Avenue, Grover Beach, California, 93433 USA.

Cover photo: This is the Rylands Library Papyrus P52, also known as the St. John's fragment. It is believed to date from around A.D. 100.

Various translations of the Bible are used throughout this text; where no name nor abbreviation is given, then the New King James Version (NKJV) is being cited (Thomas Nelson, Copyright © 1997; used by permission).

CONTENTS

1. Introduction

The Bible is the written revelation of the Creator God for humankind.

Many people accept the Bibles that they see as authentic. Others do not believe the Bible at all.

Some Bibles contain books that others do not contain.

Which books are really inspired by God?

While religious people have argued about this for centuries, is there a way you really can know?

Most books about how we got the Bible *overlook scriptures* and certain early writings which help provide the answer. So, this book is intended to provide many details that are often overlooked or not emphasized.

Actually, of the many books on the canon checked by this author, not one of them included certain Arabic and Syrian preserved documents that shed a lot of light on what happened.

Yet this book has those and more.

Of course, theologians have debated which books should be in the Christian Bible for nearly two thousand years.

Because of debates and many less than faithful theologians, the modern scholarly consensus is that it took centuries to determine the biblical canon.

But are those scholars correct?

What if they have overlooked scriptures and misidentified some early writers as Christian who were actually apostate?

Could you accept such a dramatically different conclusion about the formation of the biblical canon?

Can you believe the truth over traditions of humans (Mark 7:9-13)? Should you rely on the Bible believing that you should "let God be true but every man a liar" (Romans 3:4)?

Can you be confident enough in the Bible that you will face tribulations that Jesus said would come (John 16:33) and "obey God rather than men" (Acts 5:29)? Christians should also be "avoiding the profane and idle babblings and contradictions of what is falsely called knowledge — by professing it some have strayed concerning the faith" (1 Timothy 6:20-21).

Some may find that approach is not 'scholarly' enough, whereas others may find citations and references supporting the truth in this book too scholarly. Yet, in an age where people often cannot identify truth, we need to look to the word of God to have a foundation for truth (John 17:17) — which the true Church of God does (cf. 1 Timothy 3:15).

Perhaps it should be mentioned that the word of God, itself, points out that unconverted experts and others who claim knowledge tend to have a veil of blindness (2 Corinthians 3:14-16) and many are "always learning and never able to come to the knowledge of the truth" (2 Timothy 3:7).

The Bible also warns "of men, who suppress the truth in unrighteousness" (Romans 1:18). And of those, "Professing to be wise" (Romans 1:22) "who exchanged the truth of God for the lie" (Romans 1:25). "And even as they did not like to retain God in their knowledge, God gave them over to a debased mind, to do those things which are not fitting" (Romans 1:28). Do not accept conclusions of "experts" who make statements in conflict with the Bible.

The Bible Text Itself

The Bible was written over a span of about 1500 years, by many writers. There are believed to have been forty men beginning with Moses.

The books in the Bible were originally written on parchments of animal hides or papyrus. These items tend to deteriorate over time. Writing by hand took a long time and was a costly process.

In ancient times, God commanded that anyone who became king of Israel would have to "write for himself a copy of this law" (God's law) and "read it all the days of his life" (Deuteronomy 17:18-19). This was not a task to be delegated to someone else as God wanted all the Israelitish kings to truly see His words. God's words are important to know.

Around 1454, Johannes Gutenberg produced the first machine-printed version of the Bible. Since then, the Bible has become the most printed and distributed book of all time. The *Guinness Book of World Records* estimates that more than 5 billion copies of the Bible have been printed (www.guinnessworldrecords.com/world-records/best-selling-book-of-non-fiction --- accessed 01/04/21).

Furthermore, the Bible, in various forms and versions is available in multiple electronic forms, many of which are accessible via the internet or screen-containing cellular telephones.

As of October 2020, the full Bible has been translated into 704 languages, the New Testament has been translated into an additional 1,551 languages and Bible portions or stories into 1,160 other languages, for a total of 3415 languages with at least a portion of the translated Bible (Scripture Access Statistics. Wycliffe Global Alliance. October 2020 www.wycliffe.net/resources/statistics/).

The Bible has been a popular, though often improperly maligned, book.

The Bible Contains the Truth

The truth about the Bible is important for Christians to understand as it helps them better to be able to determine which church is more likely "to contend earnestly for the faith which was once for all delivered to the saints" (Jude 3). The Bible provides certainty for our faith in Jesus (Luke 1:1-4)—thus Christians need to be certain it is true.

Consider something that Jesus prayed:

> [17] Sanctify them by Your truth. Your word is truth. (John 17:17)

The truth of God's word is important. That "word" for us is the Bible.

Similarly, the Apostle Paul was inspired to write:

> ¹³ For this reason we also thank God without ceasing, because when you received the word of God which you heard from us, you welcomed it not as the word of men, but as it is in truth, the word of God, which also effectively works in you who believe. ¹⁴ For you, brethren, became imitators of the churches of God which are in Judea in Christ Jesus. (1 Thessalonians 2:13-14)

Yes, we are to accept scripture as the word of the almighty God!

Pay close attention to the following:

> ² ... For You have magnified Your word above all Your name. (Psalm 138:2d)

> ² ... you have exalted your name and your word above everything (Psalm 138:2d, New Revised Standard Version Catholic Edition)

Notice how much God has exalted His word! Knowing what His word is, therefore, is extremely important.

Yet some wonder, is the Bible accurate?

Yes, it is.

The Bible is inerrant in everything that it affirms. What this means is that while the Bible teaches truth, it also contains errors that it points out. For example, the serpent told Eve, "You shall not surely die" (Genesis 3:4). That was stated by the serpent, but the serpent's statement was false—and the Bible was clear about that (cf. Genesis 2:17, 5:5).

Christians are not to rely on faulty logic above the Bible.

Jesus denounced those who relied on tradition above the word of God:

> ⁹ ... "All too well you reject the commandment of God, that you may keep your tradition. ... ¹³ making the word of God of no effect through your tradition which you have handed down. And many such things you do." (Mark 7:9,13)

As the Apostle Paul wrote, God's ministers are those who should be "rightly dividing the word of truth" (2 Timothy 2:15)—and thus need to know what books are truly inspired in order to be able to do that effectively.

As far as truth goes, notice some Old Testament scriptures:

> [5] Every word of God is pure ... (Proverbs 30:5)

> [4] For the word of the Lord is right, And all His work is done in truth. (Psalm 33:4)

> [160] The entirety of Your word is truth, And every one of Your righteous judgments endures forever. (Psalm 119:160)

The word of God is recorded in the book called the Bible. People are to treat the word of God actually as truth (1 Thessalonians 2:13). Christians are to live "by the word of truth" (2 Corinthians 6:7).

The Apostle Paul wrote:

> [20] Do not despise prophecies. [21] Test all things; hold fast what is good. (1 Thessalonians 5:20-21)

There is no other book like the Bible. No book has the amount of fulfilled prophecies that the Bible has. In the Bible, God declares He alone is God. ***Only God can predict the future and always make it come to pass*** (cf. Isaiah 42:8-9, 46:11). Notice what God states in the Bible:

> [8] "Remember this, and show yourselves men; Recall to mind, O you transgressors. [9] Remember the former things of old, For I am God, and there is no other; I am God, and there is none like Me, [10] Declaring the end from the beginning, And from ancient times things that are not yet done, Saying, 'My counsel shall stand, And I will do all My pleasure,' [11] Calling a bird of prey from the east, The man who executes My counsel, from a far country. Indeed I have spoken it; I will also bring it to pass. I have purposed it; I will also do it. (Isaiah 46:8-11)

Here, for example, are some details of one fulfilled prophecy:

> We read of Tyre in Ezekiel 26:1-3, the Moffatt translation, in a little plainer English:

"In the eleventh year, on the first day of the month" — now this was in 585 B.C. — "this word from the Eternal came to me." Ezekiel was writing this. … this man said that the very Word of God came to him, and he wrote it down.

Now this is what God is quoted as saying … :

> "Son of man, since Tyre has gloated over Jerusalem, 'AHA! this door into the nations is broken down! It lies open to me. I shall prosper, now she is laid waste.' Therefore, the Lord, the Eternal utters this sentence: 'Tyre, I am against you … I will bring many a nation against you, — as the sea brings many a wave.' "

… Let us begin with this third verse from the King James or the Authorized translation, and read on including the fifth verse:

> "Therefore, thus saith the Lord God; Behold, I am against thee, O Tyrus, and will cause many nations to come up against thee, as the sea causeth his waves to come up. And they shall destroy the walls of Tyrus, and break down her towers: I will also scrape her dust from her, and make her like the top of a rock. It shall be a place for the spreading of nets [fishers' nets] in the midst of the sea: for I have spoken it, saith the Lord Eternal: and it shall become a spoil to the nations."

Here is … one of the two greatest cities of the world, as great in the world in that day as New York or London is today. … He said that many nations would come up against this Tyre, and attack her.

For over 1500 years the armed forces of other cities and nations had attacked this proud city of Tyre, but never had any army been able to batter down its walls or actually to invade the city.

But let us read on, beginning with Ezekiel 26 — verse 7 on through verse 11:

> "For thus saith God Eternal [here is God quoted as speaking directly, and in the first person]; Behold, I will

8

bring upon Tyrus NEBUCHADNEZZAR, the king of Babylon."

This becomes quite a specific prophecy. Notice how this prophecy becomes even more specific, beginning with verse 12 on through verse 14. "And THEY" — no longer does God say, "and HE." It is speaking of "they." This would mean OTHER NATIONS to follow Nebuchadnezzar. "They shall make spoil of thy riches, and make a prey of thy merchandise: and they [that means other nations following Nebuchadnezzar] shall break down thy walls, and destroy thy pleasant houses: they shall lay thy stones and thy timber and thy dust IN THE MIDST OF THE WATER." There it is!

God says, "I will cause the noise of thy songs to cease; and the sound of thy harps shall be no more heard. And I will make thee like the top of a rock: thou shalt be a place to spread nets upon; THOU SHALT BE BUILT NO MORE: for I the Eternal have spoken it, saith the Lord God." ... Notice this prophecy said they would lay the stones, the timber, the soil in the Mediterranean, and after that, Tyre was to be completely destroyed and BUILT NO MORE, NEVER AGAIN TO BE BUILT! ...

Very soon after the prophecy was uttered there was a 13-year siege by King Nebuchadnezzar exactly as this had been foretold, as the One speaking and saying, "I am God," said it would happen! ...

Let me quote for you a little of the history of these events from the *Encyclopedia Britannica*, volume 22 ... under the article "Tyre." It says: "Tyre, the mistress of the seas, in the 6th century, B.C., endured a 13-years' siege from Nebuchadnezzar." During this siege, Tyre, as already mentioned, was demolished.

Nebuchadnezzar... did everything that was prophesied for him. But, he did not move the stones, the timber or the soil into the Mediterranean. For about 250 years after Nebuchadnezzar had invaded Tyre, it seemed improbable that that prophecy ever would be completely fulfilled. ... Then, after two and one-half centuries, Alexander the Great came down ... The CITY of Tyre was completely destroyed. (Armstrong HW. The Proof of the Bible. Ambassador College, 1958, pp. 4-10)

The above source also provided information about nearby Sidon which demonstrated that the prophecy Ezekiel wrote was prior to Tyre's destruction (some skeptics have falsely claimed otherwise). Note: "Some say Tyre was rebuilt, and even exists today, but they are confusing Phoenician Tyre with Alexandrian Tyre" (Was the Tyre prophecy fulfilled: Ezekiel 26? Belief Map). "The original site is still basically a bare rock, even today. ... The rock Tyre stood on lies just off the coast. The causeway which led to the city which Alexander used to destroy it is now gone. There is a city called Tyre, but it is not at the site which was destroyed by Alexander."

To see hundreds more biblical predictions that have been fulfilled, check out the free book, online at ccog.org, titled *Proof Jesus is the Messiah*; see also the free online book *Is God's Existence Logical?* The former book exposes errors of objection to scriptural positions put forth by prominent atheists, so we will not deal with those here. The Bible is accurate as originally inspired and does not have contradictions that the ill-informed have claimed.

Books from other religious traditions simply are not in the same category as the Bible.

Christians are sometimes said to be 'the people of the book.' That 'book' being the Bible.

The Apostle Paul wrote of "the word of truth, the gospel of your salvation" (Ephesians 1:13) and "the word of the truth of the gospel" (Colossians 1:5).

But many wonder, what really are the books of the Bible? Are there missing gospels? Are any human translations totally perfect?

This book has proofs, scriptures, and facts about which are the true books of the Bible, who maintained the proper chain of custody of the knowledge of those books throughout history, and which manuscripts best contain the true words of God for those who wish to believe the Bible.

2. What is the Canon?

The sum of the books which constitute the Bible is generally referred to as the canon. The Greek term 'kanon,' which is called 'canon' in English, originally meant 'measuring rod.'

The main theological use of the term canon now has to do with a body of 'accepted' scriptures (i.e. those writings that passed the measure).

From a biblical perspective, the canon of the Old Testament consists of the books considered to be inspired. These books were predominantly originally written in Hebrew (with some Aramaic). The canon of the New Testament consists of books considered to be inspired that were originally predominantly written in Greek (including some Aramaic language quotes).

But there are many questions people have. Such as, who preserved the books of the Old Testament? What are the books of the Hebrew scriptures? When did Christians know what they were?

Where did the term Old Testament come from? What about the New Testament?

Who knew? Did something change?

Which books were part of the "faith once for all delivered to the saints" (Jude 3)?

All the faiths that claim to be Christian claim to get some or all of their doctrines from the Bible.

Many are confused as to why certain books are in the Bible and why some books are not in it.

Before going further, pay particular attention to the following that the Apostle Paul wrote:

> [16] All Scripture is given by inspiration of God, and is profitable for doctrine, for reproof, for correction, for instruction in righteousness, [17] that the man of God may be complete, thoroughly equipped for every good work. (2 Timothy 3:16-17)

The biblical definition of 'scripture' is writings that God inspired to be given to humans to read (cf. Matthew 21:42) for the reasons including those that the Apostle Paul was inspired to write. Those who believe the Bible accept Paul's writings as true (cf. 2 Peter 3:15-16).

Yet, many fail to consider how *the man of God may be complete, thoroughly equipped for every good work* once the original apostles were dead and the books that compose the sacred scriptures were not determined until centuries after the apostles died. Did God intend for humans to not be equipped for centuries until councils of men figured it out?

What are all the scriptures that God inspired?

As far as the books of the New Testament go, understand that the true Church of God, Church of Rome, Eastern Orthodox, and traditional Protestant faiths accept the same 27 books as inspired. Mainly they differ on who determined this and when this was determined (the New Testament will be covered in more detail later), as well as which ancient manuscripts are the most reliable.

As far as the books of the Old Testament go, this a subject of debate between faiths.

Basically, most of the Protestants and the true Church of God point to what are considered now to be 39 books of the Old Testament, whereas the Church of Rome and the Eastern Orthodox point to 46 books. Some Coptics and others have even more. Then, there is also the Church of Jesus Christ of Latter Day Saints (Mormons) who accept the books that the Protestants and Church of God accept, but then add 15 books that are included in the Book of Mormon, that other faiths do not accept.

Various ones also point to 'lost books of the Bible' and claim that other books should be considered on the same level as the accepted books.

How do we know who could be right? Or when the canon was known?

Well, we need to look to the Bible and the available records of early church history to properly determine this.

The Widely Accepted View

But before doing so, let us first consider that the most common and widely accepted view held by Roman Catholic, Eastern Orthodox, and most Protestant scholars is that there were debates over the centuries about which books should be considered as part of the Bible.

That view essentially says that the true Christian church did not really know the sacred books and it took councils a very long time to decide the full list.

Some have claimed that because a 2nd century apostate named Marcion had his own, very limited canon, that this forced the Christian church to eventually develop one (such as perhaps one by Irenaeus in the latter portion of the 2nd century) and that this did not happen in full until at least the 4th century.

We in the *Continuing* Church of God have a different view on when the true canon was known and do not believe it was the result of any post-apostolic human council (cf. Psalm 119:89). We believe the entire canon was known at or near the time the Book of Revelation was finalized.

Which view is the only one that makes theological sense?

Is there any historical evidence that supports the view that the canon was known at an early stage?

Certainly there is, and this is something that the reader is challenged to explore and consider.

Catholic Questions and Answers

At this stage, let us consider some explanations from Roman Catholic perspectives.

Catholic Bible 101 put forth the following question and answer:

> Does the Bible come from the Church, or does the Church come from the Bible?
>
> The answer is that the Church gave the world the Bible. The Bible does not exist apart from the church, nor does the Church exist apart from the Bible. The Church was established by Jesus Christ around 33 AD, and the New Testament was not finalized in its present form until 382 AD, about 350 years later. Pope St. Damasus I, at the Council of Rome, in 382, proposed the current

canon of scripture with 73 books (46 OT + 27 NT). Subsequent councils at Hippo in 393 AD, and at Carthage in 397 AD, ratified this canon as being inspired and complete. Pope Innocent I sent a letter out in the year 405 AD that listed all 73 books as being the total and complete canon of the Christian Bible. The Catholic Bibles of today still have all of these 73 books. …

Jesus Himself created the Church, about 350 years before the Bible in its present form was canonized by the Church at the Councils of Rome, Hippo, and Carthage. (The Role of The Church According to the Bible. Catholic Bible 101 www.catholicbible101.com/theroleofthechurch.htm accessed 04/13/17).

So, the above claims that after Christians lived for over three centuries, the Bible was determined by Greco-Roman Catholic Church councils. (It, perhaps, should be pointed out that the Bishop of Rome did not take the title Pope until the time of Damasus' successor Siricius and that 31 A.D. is a closer year as to when Jesus' established the church than 33 A.D.).

Here is something, unedited, from the Roman Catholic EWTN (Eternal Word Television Network):

Question from Bill Pick on 01-04-2005:

This is a question that was asked of me by a member of the church of christ can you please help with a {sic} answer? If the Roman Catholic church gave the world the Bible, being infallible, then why did Rome reject or question the inspiration of James and Hebrews, then later accept it? Conversely, Rome accepted as scripture books that were later rejected. If the Catholic church really is illuminated by the Holy Spirit so that men can trust her as 'God's organization', why was she so wrong about something so simple? Should not the 'Holy See' have known?

Answer by Fr. John Echert on 01-06-2005:

The recognition of the canon of Sacred Scripture was not accomplished in an instant and by an audible voice of declaration from Heaven, but over time and in light of what the

Church universally recognized as the works of the Bible. Over time and under the authority of the Church the canon became solidified, and knowing the promise of Christ to Saint Peter and the Church to bind and loose, once the canon was formally declared, we had assurance thereafter that it comprised the whole of the inerrant Word of God.

Thanks, Bill

Father Echert

PS. Never was the Church 'wrong' on such a matter, as She never infallibly declared a 'wrong' canon. It is one thing to discern over time prior to making an infallible declaration, it is another to declare that which is wrong, which the Church has never done. (Bible and the Church. Question from Bill Pick on 01-04-2005. EWTN Catholic Q&A. www.ewtn.com/v/experts/ showmessage_print.asp?number=424051&language=en --- accessed 04/14/17).

This author would not agree with Priest Echert's position that his church was never wrong on the canon matter. The FACT is that the Church of Rome admits that it taught that some non-inspired books were scripture, plus, for a time, it taught at least seven inspired books were possibly not scripture: "the Epistle to the Hebrews, that of James, the Second of St. Peter, the Second and Third of John, Jude, and Apocalypse" (Reid G. Canon of the New Testament. *The Catholic Encyclopedia, Volume III.* Copyright © 1908 by Robert Appleton Company. Nihil *Obstat, November 1, 1908.* Remy Lafort, S.T.D., Censor. *Imprimatur.* +John Cardinal Farley, Archbishop of New York). Thus, Priest Echert's assertions suggesting otherwise are misleading.

Furthermore, the length of time for the Church of Rome to make an 'infallible declaration' on the canon was excessive by all reasonable theological standards.

The New Catholic Encyclopedia specifically states that the dogmatic canon list was not finalized for the Church of Rome until the Council of Trent in the 16th century:

According to Catholic doctrine, the proximate criterion of the Biblical canon is the infallible decision of the Church. This decision was not given until rather late in the history of the Church (at the Council of Trent). Before that time there was some doubt about the canonicity of certain Biblical books, i.e., about their belonging to the canon. (The New Catholic Encyclopedia, McGraw Hill, Copyright 1967, Volume 3, 'Canon, Biblical', p. 29)

Although most Protestants do not accept the canon approved by the Council of Trent, their scholars essentially tend to agree that it took centuries to determine the canon (e.g. Bruce FF. The Canon of Scripture. InterVarsityPress, 1988).

Yet, consider something God promised:

> [5]... I will never leave you nor forsake you. [6] So we may boldly say:
>
> "The Lord is my helper; I will not fear. What can man do to me?" (Hebrews 13:5-6)

Would God have forsaken His church by not letting it know what His word was for centuries?

If so, God was not then acting as a "helper" that way.

The true canon was known much earlier than the Greco-Roman-Protestant-Secular scholars often tend to believe.

Even some non-Church of God scholars have realized the truly canonical books were always the word of God:

> Although it is out of vogue in some critical circles today, Christians have traditionally believed that the canon is a collection of books that are given by God to his corporate church. And if the canonical books are what they are by virtue of the divine purpose for which they were given, and not by virtue of their use or acceptance by the community of faith, then, in principle, they can exist as such apart from that community. After all, aren't God's books still God's books—and therefore still authoritative—prior to anyone using them or recognizing them? (Kruger MJ. Question of Canon, InterVarsity Press, 2013, p. 39)

One thing must be emphatically stated. The New Testament books did not become authoritative for the Church because they were formally included in a canonical list; on the contrary, the Church included them in her canon because she already regarded them as divinely inspired, recognizing their innate worth and generally apostolic authority, direct or indirect. (Bruce FF. The New Testament Documents: Are They Reliable? Wm. B. Eerdmans Publishing, 2003, p. 27)

Yes, it is correct to conclude that councils of men did not change books to be inspired by God. Those that God inspired were always inspired, despite the fact that various Greco-Romans were confused about them.

Chapters and Verses

Although almost all Bibles have numbered chapters and verses, it should be pointed out that the Bible was not written with inspired chapter breaks, unless you count the individual Psalms in the Book of Psalms.

In the Middle Ages, various ones came up with chapter breaks and numbered verses. By the 13th century much of what is now commonly used was standardized.

While chapter and verses assignments do make research and finding scriptures much easier, they were not inspired by God. Chapter and verse breaks are not canonical.

That is something to keep in mind when you read or study the Bible.

As far as Bible study goes, the Bible is the only book inspired by God, but with many parts. Therefore, it should be read reverently and in multiple places to better understand what it truly teaches in terms of doctrine (cf. Isaiah 28:10; Acts 20:27b).

As God intended (Ephesians 4:11-16), true Christian ministers have long been available to assist in the understanding of the scriptures (Nehemiah 8:1-7; Acts 8:26-35). They also know the true canon that has been passed down since the time of the Apostle John.

3. The Hebrew Scriptures

The original language for nearly all of what is often called the Old Testament was Hebrew.

The first five books of the Bible were mainly written by Moses. Notice the following:

> [4] And Moses wrote all the words of the Lord … (Exodus 24:4a)

> [24] … Moses had completed writing the words of this law in a book, when they were finished, [25] that Moses commanded the Levites, who bore the ark of the covenant of the Lord, saying: [26] "Take this Book of the Law, and put it beside the ark of the covenant of the Lord your God (Deuteronomy 31:24b-26)

After writing, Moses wanted them protected.

Since the time of Moses, the Jews and Levites preserved and copied them. They knew what the other inspired books were and taught from them. Later those books, and later canonical books, were placed in the Temple (which was destroyed in 70 A.D.).

Jesus said:

> [46] For if you believed Moses, you would believe Me; for he wrote about Me. [47] But if you do not believe his writings, how will you believe My words? (John 5:46-47)

Jesus declared therefore that Moses did write the books, which of course means that Moses could write in the 15th century B.C.E. Those who believe Jesus accept this.

Secular scholars, however, generally do not believe that Moses wrote the books. They basically claim that ancient Hebrew (sometimes called Paleo-Hebrew) did not exist before the 10th century B.C.E., hence it was not possible. Those of us who believe the words of Jesus must agree that somehow Moses did write what Jesus said he did, hence there was some type of written 'Hebrew' language.

Some less secular scholars believe that Moses wrote in something like Proto-Sinaitic, also referred to as Proto-Canaanite (Aschmann R. When Was Hebrew First Written? © Richard P. Aschmann. Last updated: 25-Apr-2019), a language that was related to Phoenician which had 22 consonants and no vowels, like ancient Hebrew did (Sáenz-Badillos A. A History of the Hebrew Language. Cambridge University Press, 1996, pp. 16-17).

Some others, like Dr. Doug Petrovich, assert that the alphabetical Hebrew language essentially was derived from Egyptian hieroglyphics and was the earliest prototype of modern languages, perhaps initially developed by Israel's son Joseph (Petrovich D. The World's Oldest Alphabet: Hebrew As The Language Of The Proto-Consonantal Script. Carta Jerusalem, 2016, pp. 28-33; Berkowitz AE. Did Moses Really Write the Bible? Breaking Israel News, February 28, 2019). This is consistent with a finding from Yale's Egyptologist John Coleman Darnell about the timing of the earliest alphabetic writing (Darnell JC. Egypt Carvings Set Earlier Date for Alphabet. The New York Times, Nov. 14, 1999).

Furthermore:

> Proto-Sinaitic texts discovered in the ancient Egyptian turquoise mines of Serabit el-Khadem in Sinai—are generally dated to the 19th century B.C.E., ... are thought to have been written by Canaanite workers, adapted Egyptian hieroglyphs to serve as written symbols for distinct alphabetic sounds. (Early Alphabetic Writing Found at Lachish. Biblical Archaeology Society, April 20,2021; Goldwasser, O. How the Alphabet Was Born from Hieroglyphs." Biblical Archaeology Review, March/April 2010)

According to Dr. Petrovich's translation of certain inscriptions found in Egypt, one dating to 1842 BC., includes the phrase, "Hebrews of Bethel, the beloved." He also asserts there were three inscriptions naming three biblical people. These, he said, were Asenath, the wife of Joseph (Genesis 41:45), Ahisamach, the father of one of the craftsmen who would build the Tabernacle (Exodus 35:34), and Moses. Dr. Petrovich says that the Moses related one dates to 1446 BC, a possible year of the Exodus.

Some critics claim Dr. Petrovich misunderstands aspects of Hebrew grammar, and have denounced his conclusions.

That being said, Dr. Petrovich wrote:

> Sinai 115 ... called the Renefsheri Stele ... Sinai 115 ... indeed mentions six Hebrews, as has been argued here, the oldest extrabiblical reference to Hebrews/Israelites (*ca.* 1842 BC) ...
>
> Sinai 377 is a rock inscription ... Sinai 377 holds the honor of being the oldest extant, fully Hebrew, proto-consonantal inscription yet known. Dating precisely to 1840 BC, thanks to the accompanying ME inscription (Sinai 46) ...
>
> Hebrew has the distinction of being the world's first alphabet, the one from which Phoenician and every other alphabetic script in the history of the world has been derived. (ibid, pp. 15, 28,29,35,192)

Whether or not Hebrew was the world's first alphabet, the dates of Sinai 115 and Sinai 377 were several centuries before Moses was born (cf. Genesis 50:24-25; Exodus 7:7; 12:40-41, 13:19)—which would have been around 1526 B.C. (based on an Exodus date of c. 1446 B.C. and Moses being 80 years old at the time per Exodus 7:7).

Consider that Moses was considered the educated son of Pharaoh's daughter (Exodus 2:10). Stephen the martyr declared:

> [22] And **Moses was learned** in all the wisdom of the Egyptians, **and was mighty in words** and deeds. (Acts 7:22)

Since Moses was educated in Egypt, he would have been able to read hieroglyphics, but likely also was trained in other scripts, like perhaps some proto-Canaanite or proto-Phoenician and/or proto-Hebrew.

Either way, Moses did write the books in some type of Hebrew or proto-Hebrew/Phoenician script that Jesus and biblical writers said he did, irrespective of scholarly disputes (cf. Romans 3:4). Those books were preserved by the Levites and the Jews (cf. Deuteronomy 31:25-26; Romans 3:1-2).

What about Jesus, Christians, and the Bible?

Jesus, quoting Deuteronomy 8:3 (which Moses wrote), said:

> [4] It is written, "Man shall not live by bread alone, but by every word of God." (Matthew 4:4)

Since it was 'written' that humans are to live by every word of God, is it not theologically improper to state that the true Church would not have the finalized canon until centuries after Jesus was resurrected?

Also, consider that Jesus often referred to various passages in the Old Testament as scripture (e.g. Matthew 12:18-21; Luke 4:21; John 7:38; 13:18; 17:12).

Does anyone really think that Jesus did not know which books of the Old Testament were inspired?

Not only did Jesus know the canon of the Old Testament (e.g. Luke 4:21), He essentially taught that the Jewish leaders in His area knew what the Hebrew scriptures were as well (cf. Matthew 12:3,5; 19:4; 22:29). And, of course, His disciples, and the Apostle Paul would have known them as well.

Why Don't We have the Originals?

When Jesus read scripture in the synagogue He read from scrolls (e.g. Luke 4:17, YLT/NIV/ESV/AFV). Those scrolls were copies transcribed by hand, from copies that were copies of the original manuscripts. Writing in Old Testament times was a difficult, painstaking, and long process.

Original manuscripts are referred to as *autographs*. We do not have any of these for neither the Bible nor nearly all literature of its time on this earth. However, perhaps it should be pointed out that since the Bible is the word of God, that God has all of His words preserved perfectly in heaven (Psalm 119:89). A location in heaven looks to have been associated with the reference to the "Scripture of Truth" (cf. Daniel 9:21) stated by the angel Gabriel (Daniel 10:21).

Some may wonder why we no longer have the originals that were penned through inspiration on the earth.

There are several reasons, but deterioration and human error are the main ones. Ancient manuscripts were usually written on ancient papyri (a paper-like material referred to in 2 John 12) or animal skins (referred to in 2 Timothy 4:13). In time, these materials decay to the point where what is written on them is no longer readable. Physical handling of them for many years could also ruin the manuscripts. Natural humidity also would tend to destroy them. The burning of the Jewish Temple in 70 A.D. destroyed many as well. The main physical reason we have some of the oldest manuscripts is because they were found in desert areas with very low humidity — not because they were necessarily superior to others.

Since natural deterioration, as well as deterioration from use was known, a process of copying the biblical manuscripts was implemented by the children of Israel. Because they considered the Bible as the word of God, many safeguards were put in place in order to try to avoid copying errors. Back in ancient times, there were no electronic copiers, and all the letters had to be written out by hand by scribes. They checked their copying work to the number of letters, etc. that were to be in each book and had other forms of what we would now call 'quality assurance.'

Because of their concern, the Jews and Levites precisely copied the scriptures, consistent with the following:

> [6] The words of the Lord are pure words,
>
> Like silver tried in a furnace of earth,
>
> Purified seven times.
>
> [7] You shall keep them, O Lord,
>
> You shall preserve them from this generation forever. (Psalm 12:6-7)

So, yes, God's word is preserved forever. And that has certainly been done in heaven (Psalm 119:89).

It should be pointed out that not all later translators were as careful as the Jews and Levites when they made copies. That is why there are concerns about what is commonly called 'the Alexandrian texts,' which the Greco-Romans and many modern Protestants mainly rely on (more on that later).

Jews Understood the Old Testament Canon

When considering questions of the books that are in the canon, it is important to not overlook what the Bible shows and teaches.

Internal (biblical) evidence should take precedence over external evidence (historical reports). Yet, that does not mean that historical evidence is not valuable, but that it is not as valuable (or trustworthy?) as 'word of truth' evidence in the Bible itself.

It is widely accepted by scholars and others that the Jews/Levites preserved the books of the Old Testament. This is based not only upon historical evidence, but also from scripture (cf. Deuteronomy 31:9-11, 31:24-26; Psalm 119:89, Romans 3:1-2).

The fact that there were numerous inspired books of the Old Testament was known and referred to in Daniel's time:

> [1] In the first year of Darius the son of Ahasuerus, of the lineage of the Medes, who was made king over the realm of the Chaldeans — [2] in the first year of his reign I, Daniel, understood by the books the number of the years specified by the word of the Lord through Jeremiah the prophet, that He would accomplish seventy years in the desolations of Jerusalem. (Daniel 9:1-2)

Daniel's reference to Jeremiah looks to be from the books/scrolls containing 2 Chronicles 36:21, and possibly Jeremiah 25:11-12 and/or Jeremiah 29:10. Daniel had access to the books of the Bible.

A little over a century after Daniel's writing, the last book of the Old Testament was written (Malachi) and the Jews preserved all of the books.

The Apostle James confirmed this when he stated:

[21] For Moses has had throughout many generations those who preach him in every city, being read in the synagogues every Sabbath. (Acts 15:21)

Moses could not have been READ unless the Jews had preserved the scriptures.

Notice something that the Apostle Paul taught in the New Testament:

[1] What advantage then has the Jew, or what is the profit of circumcision? [2] Much in every way! Chiefly because to them were committed the oracles of God. (Romans 3:1-2)

The Greek term in the New Testament for oracle, means inspired writings. And based upon historical records this was so, as the Jews in Palestine preserved what we call the Old Testament.

Jesus, of course, grew up in Palestine/Judea, and scholars have normally rightly concluded that He used the same books of the Old Testament as were preserved by the Jews in Palestine.

It should be noted that the New Testament, itself, makes it clear that the original disciples were Palestinian Hebrews and not from the Hellenists (Jews mainly from the Greek-speaking dominated areas, e.g. Acts 6:1-2).

The Apostle Paul was not a Hellenist either (Acts 9:26-29, Philippians 3:5).

Hence, it is also reasonable to conclude that the apostles were using the same books as the Palestinian Jews, not the Hellenists.

The Jewish Encyclopedia

What do the Jews teach?

The Jews do not call the Hebrew scriptures the 'Old Testament.' They will often refer to their accepted scriptures with the acronym TaNaKh.

In the Jewish tradition, this consists of three groups of books: the "Ta" stands for Torah, the first five 'Books of Moses' - Genesis, Exodus, Leviticus, Numbers, and Deuteronomy. The second division, "Na," stands for "Nevi'im" (prophets). The third division, "Kh," stands for "Ketuvim", the remaining sacred writings.

Here is some information from the *Jewish Encyclopedia* about the Jewish 'canon' and the 'books':

> The oldest and most frequent designation for the whole collection of Biblical writings is סְפָרִים, 'Books.' This word, which in Dan. ix. 2 means all the sacred writings, occurs frequently in the Mishnah, as well as in traditional literature, without closer definition. The expression סִפְרֵי הַקֹּדֶשׁ ('Holy Books') belongs to later authors. ...

> **Outside Books**

> The canonical books, therefore, needed no special designation, since originally all were holy. A new term had to be coined for the new idea of non-holy books. The latter were accordingly called סְפָרִים חִיצוֹנִים ('outside' or 'extraneous books'); that is, books not included in the established collection ...

> **Contents and Divisions.**

> The Jewish canon comprises twenty-four books, the five of the Pentateuch, eight books of the Prophets (Joshua, Judges, Samuel, Kings, Isaiah, Jeremiah, Ezekiel, the Minor Prophets), and eleven Hagiographa (Psalms, Proverbs, Job, Song of Solomon, Ruth, Lamentations, Ecclesiastes, Esther, Daniel, Ezra, and Chronicles). Samuel and Kings form but a single book each, as is seen in Aquila's Greek translation. The 'twelve' prophets were known to Ecclus. (Sirach) as one book (xlix. 10), and the separation of Ezra from Nehemiah is not indicated in either the Talmud or the Masorah. A Bible codex written in Spain in 1448 divides Samuel, Kings, and Ezra into two books each (Ginsburg, *l.c.* p. 586). These books are classified and arranged into three subdivisions, 'Torah,' 'Prophets,' and 'Hagiographa'; Greek, νόνος καὶ προφῆται καὶ βιβλία (Ecclus. [Sirach]). In Yalḳ. ii. 702

they are styled as abstracts, 'Law, Prophecy, and Wisdom,' תורה נבואה חכמה; compare Yer. Mak. 31d, below, and Blau, *l.c.* p. 21, note. The division of the Prophets into נביאים ראשונים ('Earlier Prophets') and נביאים אחרונים ('Later Prophets) was introduced by the Masorah. ...

Epiphanius' division of the number 94 into 72 + 22 ('De Ponderibus et Mensuris Liber,' in Lagarde, 'Symmicta,' ii. 163) is artificial. Josephus expressly puts the number at 22, as does Origen (Eusebius, 'Hist. Eccl.' vi. 25); while Jerome (Preface to Samuel and Kings) mentions 22, but nevertheless counts 24. Since both of these church fathers studied under Jewish teachers, it is probable that some authorities within the synagogue favored counting 22 books; and the hesitation between 22 and 24 can be explained by a Baraita (B. B. 13b), according to which each book of the latter two divisions (Prophets and Hagiographa) had to be written separately as *one* roll. Since Ruth with Judges or with Psalms (Jerome, and Baraita B. B. 14b) might form one roll, and Lamentations with Jeremiah another, the rolls would be counted as 22, while the books were actually 24. That there were 24 books will be apparent from the classical Baraita on the question (see § 5 of this article). ...

New Testament.

The New Testament shows that its canon was none other than that which exists today. None of the Apocrypha or Pseudepigrapha is ever quoted by name, while Daniel is expressly cited in Matt. xxiv. 15. Matt. xiii. 35 (= Luke xi. 51) proves that Chronicles was the last canonical book. The statement, 'That upon you may come all the righteous blood shed upon the earth, from the blood of righteous Abel unto the blood of Zacharias,' contains a reference to II Chron. xxiv. 20. The three chief divisions are enumerated in Luke xxiv. 44— 'Law,' 'Prophets,' and 'Psalms'—as they are in Philo. Usually, however, only the Law and the Prophets are mentioned (Matt. v. 17; Luke xvi. 16); but by them the three divisions are intended just as the Talmudic teachers include the Hagiographa under Prophets ...

Josephus (c. 38-95) enumerates 22 books, ... It is evident that Josephus, instead of counting Ruth and Lamentations as separate books, combined them with Judges and Jeremiah, respectively. (Hirsch EG, et al. Jewish Encyclopedia, Funk and Wagnalls, 1906, Volume 2, 'Bible Canon')

So, while the Jews, because of how they combine them, count 22 or 24 books of the Old Testament, they correspond with the 39 books of the Old Testament as found in Protestant and Church of God Bibles.

The Jews recognize the three chief divisions as enumerated by Jesus in Luke 24:44 as the 'Law,' 'Prophets,' and 'Psalms.'

Partially because of taking the admonition to "not add to the word which I command you, nor take from it" (Deuteronomy 4:2), the Palestinian Jews did not accept the Apocrypha.

Josephus and Other Sources

The first century (AD) Jewish historian Josephus wrote there were only a specific number of books that were justly considered to be divine:

> For we have not an innumerable multitude of books among us, disagreeing from, and contradicting one another: [as the Greeks have:] but only twenty two books: which contain the records of all the past times: which are justly believed to be divine. And of them five belong to Moses: which contain his laws, and the traditions of the origin of mankind, till his death. This interval of time was little short of three thousand years. But as to the time from the death of Moses, till the reign of Artaxerxes, King of Persia, who reigned after Xerxes, the Prophets, who were after Moses, wrote down what was done in their times, in thirteen books. The remaining four books contain hymns to God; and precepts for the conduct of human life.

> 'Tis true, our history hath been written since Artaxerxes very particularly; but hath not been esteemed of the like authority with the former by our forefathers; because there hath not been an exact succession of Prophets since that time. And how firmly we have given credit to these books of our own nation, is

evident by what we do. For during so many ages as have already passed, no one has been so bold, as either to add any thing to them; to take any thing from them; or to make any change in them. But it is become natural to all Jews, immediately, and from their very birth, to esteem these books to contain divine doctrines; and to persist in them: and, if occasion be, willingly to die for them. For 'tis no new thing for our captives, many of them in number, and frequently in time, to be seen to endure wracks, and deaths of all kinds, upon the theatres; that they may not be obliged to say one word against our laws, and the records that contain them. (Josephus. Against Apion 1:8. Kregel Publications, 1960)

Josephus, and others, have properly concluded that the canon of the Old Testament was fixed by the first century A.D.

Again, those 22 books Josephus referred to correspond with the 39 books of the Old Testament as found in Protestant and Church of God Bibles (though listed in a different order). Interestingly, the 119th Psalm has 22 sections which progress alphabetically through the Hebrew with each of the consonants. It may be that the Jews decided to count the Hebrews scriptures as 22 books since their Hebrew had 22 consonants.

Ezra (Ezra 4:7) and Nehemiah (Nehemiah 2:1) lived at the time of Artaxerxes (5th century BC). 1 Maccabees 9:27 (a non-inspired book) teaches that there had been a cessation of prophets — apparently the same cessation that Josephus referred to. Thus, books during the period of the Maccabees were not considered to be inspired by God.

Changes and Preservation

Here is something regarding scribal edits:

"Emendations of the scribes" ... part of ... Jewish tradition holds that even some of the oldest Hebrew manuscripts had been edited in several places. Third-century rabbi Simon ben Pazzi referred to these instances as "emendations of the scribes."

These scribal edits have been used to argue that the Masoretes were working from flawed texts, which explains some of the discrepancies. However, this doesn't lend credibility to the Septuagint, and while Jewish tradition readily admits these edits exist, it also attributes them to biblical writers (such as Ezra and Nehemiah) and scribes who were members of the Great Synagogue, where the canon was allegedly established in 450 BC. (Nelson R. What Is the Masoretic Text? The Beginner's Guide. © 2018 OverviewBible. September 28, 2018)

The late Church of God evangelist John Ogwyn explained some of the details of what happened with the Jews:

> The portion of the Bible that we commonly call the Old Testament was completed in the days of Ezra the Priest and Governor Nehemiah, about 420bc. Ezra was sent by King Artaxerxes of Persia to Jerusalem in 457bc with the temple scrolls and other treasures which had been kept in Babylon since the days of Nebuchadnezzar (Ezra 7:14). Ezra came back to teach Scripture to the people (v. 10) and to institute religious reform for people who were on the verge of losing their very identity and absorbing the syncretistic paganism of their neighbors. About thirteen years after Ezra's return, Nehemiah returned as governor and had the authority to insist that Ezra's reforms be carried out. The first century Jewish historian and priest, Flavius Josephus, recorded the history of the Hebrew Scriptures and contrasted them to the Greek writings extant in his day … Josephus went on to state that the Jewish scriptures had been compiled in their final form in the days of King Artaxerxes, who reigned in the days of Ezra and Nehemiah. He emphasized that, while many books had been composed among the Jews since that time, they were not considered to have divine authority, because there had not been a succession of prophets since the time of Malachi, a late contemporary of Ezra and Nehemiah. In addition to Josephus, the book of 1 Maccabees (second century bc), writings by the first century ad philosopher Philo, and traditions preserved in Seder Olam and the Talmud (ancient commentaries) all testify to a fixed canon since the time of Ezra. The 22 books mentioned by Josephus correspond to the books of our Old Testament—normally counted as 39 books in modern translations. The difference in number is because of a difference in the way the books were

counted. The 12 Minor Prophets, for instance, were kept on one scroll in Hebrew, and were counted as simply one book, not as 12 separate ones. There are several other combinations as well'. (Ogwyn J. How Did We Get The Bible? Tomorrow's World. January-February 2002)

God obviously had someone add to the ending of the Book of Deuteronomy as Moses could not have added about his own death. There were also clarifications of geographic locations (names sometimes change). Furthermore, since it is not believed that Moses wrote with the Hebrew characters that came later, this would be why someone like Ezra would have made edits for understanding.

But the Hebrew Bible was well preserved. Melito of Sardis later came up with the same '22' books.

A 20th century Catholic scholar, priest Bellarmino Bagatti, confirmed that it was widely believed during the 2nd-4th centuries that the preservation of the Old Testament was given to the Jews in Palestine:

> The preservation of the texts among the Jews gave occasion to the anonymous author of *Exhortations to the Greeks* to draw this conclusion (PG 6, 268): "Today also the Jews guard the books that belong to our religion. This was a work of Divine Providence for our advantage, so as not to give rise to suspicion of any falsity to those who wish to speak ill of us, when we bring them from the church; and therefore we wish to bring them to the synagogue of the Jews, so that from these books, guarded also by them, it may be evident that the laws written by holy men for teaching clearly and evidently belong to us". (Bagatti B. Translated by Eugene Hoade. The Church from the Gentiles in Palestine, Part 1, Chapter 1. Nihil obstat: Ignatius Mancini. Imprimi potest: Herminius Roncari. Imprimatur: +Albertus Gori, die 28 Februarii 1970. Franciscan Printing Press, Jerusalem, p. 19)

So, as late as perhaps the fourth century (*Exhortations to the Greeks* was seemingly written between the second and fourth centuries), even the Greco-Roman churches tended to accept that the Jews preserved the books now called the Old Testament.

Priest Bagatti, himself, also acknowledged that when Church of God Pastor/Bishop Melito went to verify the list/canon of Old Testament books, that he went to the Jews in Palestine, not the Hellenists in Egypt (Ibid, pp. 18-19). Protestant scholars have essentially recognized this as well (e.g. Bruce, The Canon of Scripture, p. 71).

Here is something from an Anglican priest and scholar:

> It is also of interest that Melito traveled to Palestine, and is thus an indication that this is the Old Testament canon known by Palestinian Christians, and perhaps Jews. (Stewart-Sykes A. Melito of Sardis On Pascha. St. Vladimir's Seminary Press, Crestwood (NY), 2001, p. 72)

The Jews and true Christians in Palestine/Judea knew what the books of the Old Testament were and so did Jesus and His original disciples.

Sequence and Approximate Dates Written

The *Jewish Encyclopedia of 1906* teaches:

Sequence.

> The classical passage for the sequence of the books is the Baraita in B. B. 14b. With the exclusion of interjected remarks chronicled there, it runs as follows:

> 'The sequence of the Prophets is Joshua, Judges, Samuel, Kings, Jeremiah, Ezekiel, Isaiah, the 12 [minor] prophets; that of the Hagiographa is Ruth, Psalms, Job, Proverbs, Ecclesiastes, Song of Solomon, Lamentations, Daniel, Esther, Ezra, Chronicles. Who wrote the books? Moses wrote his book, the section of Balaam and Job; Joshua wrote his book, and the last eight verses of the Torah; Samuel wrote his book, Judges, and Ruth; David wrote the Psalms, by the hand of the ten Ancients; namely, through Adam (Psalm cxxxix. 16, perhaps also xcii.), through Melchizedek, Ps. cx.: through Abraham, Ps. lxxxix. (אֵיתָן הָאֶזְרָחִי explained to = Abraham); through Moses, Ps. xc.-c.; through Heman, Ps. lxxxviii.; through Jeduthun, Ps. lxii.; perhaps lxxvii.; through Asaph, Ps. l., lxxiii.-lxxxiii.; and through the three sons

of Korah, Ps. xlii. xlix., lxxviii., lxxxiv., lxxxv., lxxxviii. [The question whether Solomon should be included among the Psalmists is discussed in Tosafot 15a.] Jeremiah wrote his book, the Book of Kings, and Lamentations; King Hezekiah, and his council that survived him, wrote Isaiah, Proverbs, Song of Solomon, and Ecclesiastes; the men of the Great Synagogues wrote Ezekiel, the Twelve Prophets, Daniel, and Esther, Ezra wrote his book and the genealogy of Chronicles down to himself.'

The Septuagint texts used a different sequence for the books of the Bible.

Some believe that the original and proper sequence of the books of the Hebrew Bible should be, **with the speculated dates** of the writing shown: Genesis c. 1430, Exodus c. 1420, Leviticus c. 1415, Numbers c. 1410, Deuteronomy c. 1406, Joshua c. 1370 (or c. 1100 if Samuel was the author), Judges c. 1100-1050, I & 2 Samuel & 1 &2 Kings c. 756-695 (if Isaiah was the author or around 550 if Ezra was the author), Isaiah c. 700, Jeremiah c. 600, Ezekiel c. 570, Hosea c. 720, Joel c. 580 (Ryrie c. 835), Amos c. 795, Obadiah c. 589, Jonah c. 797, Micah c. 720, Nahum c. 710, Habakkuk c. 620, Zephaniah c. 625, Haggai c. 519, Zechariah c. 518, Malachi c. 400, Psalms c. 1050-971, Proverbs c. 1010-695, Job c. 1700, Song of Songs c. 1000, Ruth c. 1110 (if Ruth is the author), Lamentations c. 585, Ecclesiastes c. 1000, Esther c. 455, Daniel c. 540, Ezra c. 470, Nehemiah c. 450, I Chronicles c. 530, and II Chronicles c. 515 (Coulter F. The Holy Bible in its Original Order. York Publishing, 2011, pp. 6-7; dates derived mainly from Coulter and Ryrie Study Bible, Moody Bible Institute, 1985).

This seems fairly correct, though it is possible that Daniel should be in a different location. And there were definitely later edits to books like Deuteronomy.

It should be pointed out that secularists do not believe that Daniel and Isaiah, to cite two examples, could have been written when those men were alive. Why? Because the FACT that their books have some predictions that secularists acknowledge have come to pass, makes their prior writing impossible according to the sensibilities of some of those who refuse to accept the Divine origin of scripture. The Apostle

Paul was inspired to warn of those "Professing to be wise" (Romans 1:22) "who exchanged the truth of God for the lie" (Romans 1:25).

Complete or Incomplete?

As far as the Old Testament being complete, the *Jewish Encyclopedia* claims that all evidence supports that the following from a writer named

Zunc is correct:

> ... long before the destruction of the Temple, and not long after Sirach was translated, the Holy Writings comprised their present cycle. (Jewish Encyclopedia of 1906, Bible Canon, Chapter 8)

The *Jewish Encyclopedia* also teaches in the Tosefta (considered a supplement to the Mishnah, official oral traditions of the Jews), that, 'Neither the Ben Sira nor any of the books written thereafter' are canonical (Ibid, Chapter 10).

Ben Sira Sirach is also known as the Book of Ecclesiasticus (not to be confused with the canonical book Ecclesiastes), and it is one of the so-called deuterocanonical books.

It should be added that there was something called the Council of Jamnia, which may have taken place around 90 A.D., which discussed the appropriate books of the Hebrew scriptures. This Jewish council allegedly confirmed the canon authoritatively for nearly all Jews (some scholars have questioned the council's authenticity). It, if held, really made no changes, and it basically only discussed a few books. But the books that are attributed to this possible council are the same books now used by Protestants and the *Continuing* Church of God (which is not Protestant).

As far as Jamnia goes, here is a report from a Catholic source:

> *The Council or School of Jamnia*

Following the destruction of the Second Temple in 70 AD, Rabbi Yohanan ben Zakkai relocated to the city of Jamnia (also known as Yavne) and founded a school of Jewish law there. ...

However, regardless of whether or not there was even a Council of Jamnia, the outcomes attributed to the Council of Jamnia certainly did occur; ...

A rejection of the Septuagint or Koine Greek Old Testament widely then in use among the Hellenized diaspora along with its additional books not part of the text now known as the Tanakh and which eventually became the Masoretic text. (Septuagint, Jamnia, the Masoretic Text and the Qumran discoveries. St. Michael's Media, Inc., © 2010, pp. 2-3)

Whether or not there was a Council of Jamnia, the Septuagint, and the additional books were rejected by the orthodox Jews as well as the true Church of God.

Melito's List

While it is true that it was the Jews that originally were to maintain what is now called the Old Testament canon, there was one early Church leader who essentially listed it. And that was Melito of Sardis.

It appears that even though those of Asia Minor knew the correct books from the time of the Apostle John and Church of God leader Polycarp of Smyrna, that some questions arose that Melito of Sardis decided would be best to investigate himself.

After doing so, Melito wrote:

Melito to his brother Onesimus, greeting:--

As you have often, prompted by your regard for the word of God, expressed a wish to have some extracts made from the Law and the Prophets concerning the Saviour, and concerning our faith in general, and have desired, moreover, **to obtain an accurate account of the Ancient Books, as regards their number and their arrangement**, I have striven to the best of my

34

ability to perform this task: well knowing your zeal for the faith, and your eagerness to become acquainted with the Word, and especially because I am assured that, through your yearning after God, you esteem these things beyond all things else, engaged as you are in a struggle for eternal salvation.

I accordingly proceeded to the East, and went to the very spot where the things in question were preached and took place; and, having made myself accurately acquainted with the books of the Old Testament, I have set them down below, and herewith send you the list. Their names are as follows:--

The five books of Moses--Genesis, Exodus, Leviticus, Numbers, Deuteronomy; Joshua, Judges, Ruth, the four books of Kings, the two of Chronicles, the book of the Psalms of David, the Proverbs of Solomon, also called the Book of Wisdom, Ecclesiastes, the Song of Songs, Job, the books of the prophets Isaiah, Jeremiah, of the twelve contained in a single book, Daniel, Ezekiel, Esdras. From these I have made my extracts, dividing them into six books. (Melito. From the Book of Extracts. Cited in Eusebius. The History of the Church, Book IV, Chapter XXVI. Digireads.com Publishing, Stilwell (KS), 2005 edition. p. 90)

(The above is the *Roberts and Donaldson* translation. While some translators believe that the 'Wisdom' is a separate book, even *The Catholic Encyclopedia* concluded that only the 'protocanonicals' are in Melito's list—thus Melito's list did not contain any of the books Protestants and the *Continuing* Church of God would consider to be apocryphal.)

The books listed by Melito are the books in the Old Testament used by most Jews, Protestants, and those in the COGs (Esther is believed by *The Catholic Encyclopedia* to have been left out for political reasons as it shows the Jews killing many of their enemies--but to this author, and some other researchers, Esther looks to have been combined with others in that list).

It should also be noted that since the Jews sometimes combined Nehemiah with Ezra, that perhaps Melito actually listed all the Old

Testament books. If punctuation, which was not in extensive use when this letter was written, is added differently than some translators have come up with on their own, look at what the last paragraph from Melito above shows (with numbers being added here in **bold**):

> The five books of Moses--Genesis, Exodus, Leviticus, Numbers, Deuteronomy **{5}**, Joshua **{1}**, Judges **{1}**, Ruth **{1}**, the four books of Kings **{4}**, the two of Chronicles **{2}**, the book of the Psalms of David **{1}**, the Proverbs of Solomon, also called the Book of Wisdom **{1}**. Ecclesiastes **{1}**, the Song of Songs **{1}**, Job **{1}**, the books of the prophets Isaiah **{1}**, Jeremiah **{1}**, of the twelve contained in a single book **{12}**. Daniel, Ezekiel, Esdras, from these I have made my extracts, dividing them into six books **{6}**.

If one adds up 5 + 1 + 1 +1 + 4 +2 + 1 + 1 +1 + 1 +1 + 1 + 1 + 12 + 6, one ends up with 39 books. *The Catholic Encyclopedia* concludes Melito's list is only 38, by not using the six as possibly being related to Daniel, Ezekiel, Esdras, while presuming Jeremiah includes Lamentations and Esdras includes Nehemiah, but not Esther. Presuming that understanding is mostly correct, I believe Esther can be implied as being in the Ezra-Nehemiah category because it is within the Ezra-Nehemiah time period. 39 is the number of books that are in modern Old Testaments (other than those with the later additions, also called the Apocrypha—which the Septuagint has, that Melito did not accept).

It should be noted that Melito claims his was an accurate list. ***The fact that Melito calls these the books of "the Old Testament" demonstrates the deuterocanonical books were not accepted by the Church of God in Asia Minor and presupposes that the Church had to have had a New Testament***. Melito's writing seems to be the first time in the preserved literature we see the term 'Old Testament.' That strongly implies that the term 'New Testament' was also in use then by Christians.

Even *The Catholic Encyclopedia* notes this about Melito's list:

> St. Melito, Bishop of Sardis (c. 170), first drew up a list of the canonical books of the Old Testament. While maintaining the familiar arrangement of the Septuagint, he says that he verified his catalogue by inquiry among Jews; **Jewry by that time had**

everywhere discarded the Alexandrian books, and Melito's Canon consists exclusively of the protocanonicals *minus* Esther. It should be noticed, however, that the document to which this catalogue was prefixed is capable of being understood as having an anti-Jewish polemical purpose, in which case Melito's restricted canon is explicable on another ground. (Reid G. Canon of the Old Testament)

Amazingly then, even though *The Catholic Encyclopedia* calls Melito a saint (as do the Eastern Orthodox) and admits that he verified his list with the Jews, the Roman Catholic and Orthodox Bibles, include at least 7 additional books (plus parts of other books) in the Old Testament that Melito did not list. As far as Esther goes, this author believes it was at least indirectly referred to as seemingly do some other scholars (Wendland, p. 37). It should be noted that while Melito used the Greek names of most of the books he listed, he did NOT have them arranged in the same sequence that the Septuagint did.

The Catholic Encyclopedia also notes:

> St. Jerome, speaking of the canon of Melito, quotes Tertullian's statement that he was esteemed a prophet by many of the faithful. (Hudleston G.R. St. Melito. The Catholic Encyclopedia, Volume X Copyright © 1911 by Robert Appleton Company, NY. Nihil Obstat, October 1, 1911. Remy Lafort, S.T.D., Censor. Imprimatur. +John Cardinal Farley, Archbishop of New York, pp. 166-167)

Melito held what we consider to be Church of God doctrines.

According to Polycrates of Ephesus, Melito was a Bishop/Pastor of Smyrna between the time of Bishops/Pastors Polycarp and Polycrates and, like them, Melito kept the Passover on Nisan 14 in accordance with the Gospel, and in contrast to what was then being done in Rome (see Eusebius. Church History. Book V, Chapter 24). He and they held to what should be considered to be Church of God doctrines on many matters that differ from the Greco-Roman-Protestant churches.

Although the Church of Rome considers him to be a saint, Melito did not accept the so-called deuterocanonical books. Plus, Melito held other views that the Church of Rome strongly condemns, like millenarianism (Danielou, Cardinal Jean-Guenole-Marie. The Theology of Jewish Christianity. Translated by John A. Baker. The Westminister Press, 1964, p. 389; also check out our free booklet *Continuing History of the Church of God*, available at www.ccog.org).

The Hebrew scriptures were known to Jesus, they were known to the Jews in Palestine, they were known to the apostles, they were known to early Christians in Asia Minor, and Melito verified them.

They are the 39 books which are currently accepted by the Greco-Roman-Protestants and the Church of God.

4. The Septuagint and the Eastern Orthodox

Now, what about the Greek Old Testament known as the Septuagint?

The term 'Septuagint' (LXX) is from the Latin *septuaginta*, 'seventy.' This term *septuaginta* seems to have been first used by Augustine in his *City of God* (Sundberg AC, Jr. The Septuagint: The Bible of Hellenistic Judaism. In: The Canon Debate. Baker Academic, 2002) which was published in 426.

The Septuagint is a translation of Hebrew writings, which now includes ones known as the Old Testament as well as those often referred to as the Old Testament Apocrypha.

According to legend, seventy-two Jewish scholars were asked by the Greek King of Egypt Ptolemy II Philadelphus to translate the Torah (the first five books of the Bible) from biblical Hebrew into Greek. This was to be done on a scroll to be included in the famous Library of Alexandria shortly before it ended up burning down (Dines JM. The Septuagint. Michael A. Knibb, Ed., London: T&T Clark, 2004).

The legend claims that the translators each came up with identical translations of the Torah — Irenaeus of Lyon also pushed this story (Adversus Heresies, III, Chapter, 21, verse 2). That legend came from a falsified work. Here is some information about it:

> **Letter of Aristeas**, pseudepigraphal work of pseudo-history produced in Alexandria ... The author assumed the name of a 2nd-century-bc writer and purported to give a contemporary account of the translation of the Hebrew Pentateuch, the first five books of the Bible, into Greek. He presented himself as a pagan admirer of Judaism who held a high position in the court of Ptolemy II Philadelphus (285–246 bc) in Alexandria. The writer used current Hellenistic literary conventions and the technical language of the Alexandrian court, but his Greek style and several historical inaccuracies indicate that he was a deliberate archaist. (Letter of Aristeas. Encyclopædia Britannica --- accessed 04/17/20)

The initial 'Septuagint' translation was believed to have been done in the 2nd and/or 3rd century B.C. The Hellenistic Jews of Alexandria in Egypt ended up accepting and promoting this translation.

The Eastern Orthodox essentially believe that the Septuagint translators improved the Bible:

> The Orthodox Church has the same New Testament as the rest of Christendom. As its authoritative text for the Old Testament, it uses the ancient Greek Septuagint. When this differs from the original Hebrew (which happens quite often), Orthodox believe that the changes in the Septuagint were made under the inspiration of the Holy Spirit, and are to be accepted as part of God's continuing revelation. (Ware T. The Orthodox Church. Penguin Books, London, 1997, p.200)

Orthodox Metropolitan Hilarion Alfeyev notes:

> … though **the Greek text is not the original language of the Old Testament books**, the Septuagint does reflect the state of the original text as it would have been found in the third to second centuries BCE … St. Philaret of Moscow considers it possible to maintain that "in the Orthodox teaching of Holy Scripture it is necessary to attribute a dogmatic merit to the Translation of the Seventy, in some cases placing it on equal level with the original and even **elevating it above the Hebrew text**, as is generally accepted in the most recent editions." (Alfeyev H. Orthodox Christianity, Volume II: Doctrine and Teaching of the Orthodox Church, New York: St. Vladimir Seminary Press, 2012, p. 34)

Therefore, the Eastern Orthodox believe that the original inspiration of the Old Testament (which was mainly written in Hebrew) was improved by humans who translated it into Greek, in the version known as the Septuagint.

Jewish, as well as Church of God, scholars would consider that to effectively be a blasphemous position to take. Humans cannot improve the originally inspired word of God.

That being said, Greek Christians (like Theophilus of Antioch) who seemingly did not read Hebrew tended to read the Septuagint or similar translations of the Old Testament (not because they accepted the Apocrypha, but because it was available), but that does not mean they called it superior to the Hebrew text.

Notice also:

> In the 3rd century ce Origen attempted to clear up copyists' errors that had crept into the text of the Septuagint, which by then varied widely from copy to copy, and a number of other scholars consulted the Hebrew texts in order to make the Septuagint more accurate. (Septuagint. Encyclopædia Britannica --- accessed 04/17/20)

> Since the manuscripts of the Septuagint were copied by hand and by people of differing abilities, there were different versions of the Septuagint in existence. The translation of the book of Daniel was so poor that the second-century translation attributed to Theodotion replaced it.

> By the 3rd century, the textual problem had become so bad that Origen collected all the existing versions of the Septuagint and created a six-column work called the *Hexapla*. The *Hexapla* … was Origen's 'corrected' text of the Septuagint. (Carlson K. Hidden in Plain Sight, Part I: The Development of the Canon. Dormition Publishing, 2019, p. 47)

So, this demonstrates whatever version that exists now was not fully in place during the time of Jesus and His disciples.

Furthermore, it should also be pointed out that Lucian of Antioch (late 3rd and early 4th century) while opposing allegorical positions (such as held by Origen) tried to correct translation errors in the Septuagint by consulting with the Hebrew texts:

> Lucian was a Hebrew scholar, and his version was adopted by the greater number of the churches of Syria and in Asia Minor. (Duchesne L. Early History of the Christian Church: From Its Foundation to the End of the Third Century, Volume 1, 4th edition. Longmans, Green & Co., 1912, p. 362)

Lucian also rejected the Apocrypha (Wilkinson BG. Truth Triumphant, ca. 1890. Reprint: Teach Services, Brushton, NY, 1994, p. 51). Waldensian and pre-Waldensians later used information from Lucian (Wilkinson BG. Our Authorized Bible Vindicated. 1930, reprint TEACH Services, 2014, pp. 31, 40).

Augustine of Hippo thought the Hebrew (the Masoretic) and Septuagint were both authoritative, even where they contradicted each other (Augustine. City of God, Book 18, Chapter 44). But he also seemed to show a preference for the Masoretic as 'authoritative' (Wendland E. HOW WE GOT THE BIBLE: Overview of Aspects of the Scripture Transmission Process, Version 2.6. Lusaka Lutheran Seminary, August 29, 2017, p. 20).

Jesus declared, "Scripture cannot be broken" (John 10:35), hence to suggest that scripture was broken and then declare it was later improved/fixed is theologically unsound. Changing/improving scripture is also in violation of numerous scriptures (e.g. Deuteronomy 4:2, 12:32; Proverbs 30:5; Psalm 12:6-7, 33:4, 119:160, Revelation 22:18).

We in the *Continuing* Church of God believe that the Bible is infallible as originally written and do not believe that the Holy Spirit improved the word of God through human translators. We believe God gave the world the Bible, through His chosen human instruments (2 Timothy 3:16-17; 2 Peter 1:19-21), and it was infallible when given.

Some scholars have claimed that the term 'Septuagint' was developed from Exodus 24:1,9 where seventy elders were referred to, and that Moses and Aaron were added to come up with 72 translators (Sundberg AC, Jr. The Septuagint: The Bible of Hellenistic Judaism. In: The Canon Debate. Baker Academic, 2002). However, irrespective of where the term Septuagint may have come from, Moses did not write the Torah in Greek.

Chronology Errors

The Septuagint has errors in chronology related to Genesis 5 and 11.

Even according to defenders of the Septuagint, this results in adding 1386 additional years as compared to the Masoretic text (e.g. Smith, HB, Jr. 2018. The case for the Septuagint's chronology in Genesis 5 and 11.

In Proceedings of the Eighth International Conference on Creationism, ed. J.H. Whitmore, pp. 117–132. Pittsburgh, Pennsylvania: Creation Science Fellowship).

Notice what a translation of the Septuagint teaches:

> [25] And Mathusala lived an hundred and sixty and seven years, and begot Lamech. [26] And Mathusala lived after his begetting Lamech eight hundred and two years, and begot sons and daughters. [27] And all the days of Mathusala which he lived, were nine hundred and sixty and nine years, and he died. [28] And Lamech lived an hundred and eighty and eight years, and begot a son. (Genesis 5:25-28, Elpenor's Bilingual (Greek / English) Old Testament. English translation by L.C.L. Brenton)

> [21] And there died all flesh that moved upon the earth, of flying creatures and cattle, and of wild beasts, and every reptile moving upon the earth, and every man. [22] And all things which have the breath of life, and whatever was on the dry land, died. [23] And [God] blotted out every offspring which was upon the face of the earth, both man and beast, and reptiles, and birds of the sky, and they were blotted out from the earth, and Noe was left alone, and those with him in the ark. (Genesis 7:21-23, Ibid)

The Septuagint has Methuselah living 802 years after Lamech was born and Lamech having a son Noah at age 188. This means that Methuselah lived 614 years after Noah was born. Yet, the Great Flood came in the 600th year of Noah's life per Genesis 7:10-12.

This is a major problem for the Septuagint. Since all humans died from the Flood except those with Noah (Genesis 7:23), and Mathusula/Methuselah was not among them, because "Scripture cannot be broken" (John 10:35), the Bible itself proves that the Septuagint was wrong and the translation was NOT inspired by God. (Note: The Roman Catholic *Douay Old Testament of 1609* does not agree with the Septuagint on Genesis 5:25-26, but with the chronology of the Masoretic text.)

According to the Masoretic text, Methuselah lived 782 years after Lamech was born and 600 years after Noah was born (Genesis 5:26-29).

That means either Methuselah died right before the flood or, probably more likely, in the Flood. Methuselah did not live past the Flood.

There is another chronological item to consider with the Septuagint. "Figures from the LXX place creation at ca. 5554 BC" (Smith, p. 117).

This creates a problem for the Eastern Orthodox because several of their early saints taught that a millennial reign of 1,000 years would begin at the end of the 6,000 years (e.g. Irenaeus. Adversus haereses, Book V, Chapter 28:2-3; 29:2 and Methodius. Banquet of the Ten Virgins, Discourse 9, Chapter 1). Since the Septuagint's 6,000 years would have been up in the 5th century A.D., and the millennium then did not happen, this demonstrates that either Greco-Roman saints were in error and/or the Septuagint's chronology was off.

Since the Masoretic text, in this author's view, points to the creation being c. 3959-3971 B.C., we have not yet come to the end of the 6,000 years, though we are getting close.

Superiority?

Many, particularly among the Eastern Orthodox, believe that the Septuagint is superior to the original Hebrew. Notice the following summary of claimed reasons from Alexandru Mihaila from the University of Bucharest Orthodox Theology Department:

> I summarize the principal arguments in favor of the exclusiveness of the Septuagint:
>
> - the Septuagint is older than the Masoretic Text;
>
> - the Septuagint is inspired (a conception that started with Philo of Alexandria);
>
> - the Holy Apostles and New Testament authors used the Septuagint;
>
> - the Fathers of the Church quoted the Septuagint;
>
> - the rabbis modified the Masoretic Text in order to eliminate the Messianic prophecies concerning Jesus Christ;

- the Septuagint is the official version of the Orthodox Church. (Mihăilă A. The Septuagint and the Masoretic Text in the Orthodox Church(es) Download Date | 9/18/19.

https://docplayer.net/156142221-The-septuagint-and-the-masoretic-text-in-the-orthodox-church-es-alexandru-mihaila-recent-positions-of-romanian-theologians.html --- accessed 03/24/20)

Let's look at each of those.

First, it is true that several of the Septuagint documents are older than the Masoretic texts, but it is not in the original language of the Old Testament. It should be noted that the 'Silver Scrolls' provide evidence of the accuracy of the Masoretic text as far back as the 6th and/or 7th centuries B.C.—and they are older than the earliest Septuagint texts that have been found (c. 2nd century B.C.). Additional reasons to accept the Masoretic text are found later in this book.

Second, claims of inspiration of translators have no basis in scripture and are mainly speculation. Because of errors in the Septuagint, any claims of Divine inspiration can be fully discounted. Furthermore, Philo of Alexandria believed that the world existed eternally in contradiction to the account in the Book of Genesis — he also held many other non-biblical positions.

Third, Jesus, at least sometimes, quoted from the Hebrew. And while New Testament authors and others writing in Greek sometimes quoted in ways consistent with the Septuagint, they never indicated that the Septuagint was in any way superior to the Hebrew originals or they would ALWAYS quote it precisely. The fact that a Greek translation of the Hebrew was sometimes correct, does not prove that God inspired the entire translation. Plus the fact that the Septuagint was changed after the original apostles died should show all that it was NOT directly inspired.

Fourth, the fact that some early Greek writers sometimes used a Greek translation of Hebrew does not mean that it was superior. Melito's not listing the books in the order found in the Septuagint is, in essence, additional concurrence of that point.

Fifth, there is no proof that rabbis (or Levites) specifically altered the Masoretic text in order to eliminate prophecies associated with Jesus. Actually, the *Great Isaiah Scroll* found in Qumran, demonstrates that the Jews did not alter Isaiah.

Portion of the Great Isaiah Scroll

Furthermore, there are hundreds of prophecies from the Masoretic text that Jesus fulfilled—so obviously the Jews had not intentionally removed those. Those prophetic verses can be found in the free book, online at ccog.org, *Proof Jesus is the Messiah*.

Sixth, the fact that the *Orthodox Catholic Church* (as it is officially called) has adopted the Septuagint is true, but those in the COG and most other faiths do not consider their determination as authoritative (see also the free book, online at ccog.org, titled *Beliefs of the Original Catholic Church*).

Seventh, the modern Septuagint contains books that neither Jesus nor the apostles accepted as valid.

Additional Books

After the Greek version of the Torah was completed, more books were later translated — but the original Septuagint did NOT include the Apocryphal books — they were added later.

Apocrypha comes from the Greek ἀπόκρυφος meaning 'hidden' or 'secret wisdom.' The apocryphal books, in other words, had a hidden beginning, a secret origin — not openly given to the community at first.

The Catholic Encyclopedia claims that the expanded list of Septuagint books (the Apocryphal ones), and not just the books that Jesus and others in Palestine used, is more complete and should be considered as sacred scripture:

> ... that there is a smaller, or incomplete, and larger, or complete, Old Testament. Both of these were handed down by the Jews; the former by the Palestinian, the latter by the Alexandrian, Hellenist, Jews. ...

> The most striking difference between the Catholic and Protestant Bibles is the presence in the former of a number of writings which are wanting in the latter and also in the Hebrew Bible, which became the Old Testament of Protestantism. These number seven books: Tobias (Tobit), Judith, Wisdom, Ecclesiasticus, Baruch, I and II Machabees, and three documents added to protocanonical books, viz., the supplement to Esther, from x, 4, to the end, the Canticle of the Three Youths (Song of the Three Children) in Daniel 3, and the stories of Susanna and the Elders and Bel and the Dragon, forming the closing chapters of the Catholic version of that book. Of these works, Tobias and Judith were written originally in Aramaic, perhaps in Hebrew; Baruch and I Machabees in Hebrew, while Wisdom and II Machabees were certainly composed in Greek. The probabilities favour Hebrew as the original language of the addition to Esther, and Greek for the enlargements of Daniel.

> The ancient Greek Old Testament known as the Septuagint was the vehicle which conveyed these additional Scriptures into the Catholic Church. (Reid G. Canon of the Old Testament)

Sadly, improper books have been used as the vehicle to provide support for various non-scriptural positions related to the dead and improper worship.

Like the Catholics of Rome, the Eastern Orthodox believe it took many centuries to determine the books of the Bible that they accepted:

> The Hebrew version of the Old Testament contains thirty-nine books. The Septuagint contains in addition ten further books not present in the Hebrew, which are known in the Orthodox Church as the 'Deutero-Canonical Books'. These were declared by the Councils of Jassy (1641) and Jerusalem (1672) to be 'genuine parts of Scripture'; (Ware, p. 200)

The late Septuagint included the Apocrypha, the so-called Deutero-Canonical Books, which means it had extra-books. These extra books are not inspired by God.

It may be of interest to note that those apocryphal books were not found in the *Dead Sea Scrolls* at Qumran.

> "Based on the findings at Qumran, the Apocrypha was not viewed as canonical by the Qumran community. It was only during and after the time of Augustine (AD 354-430), when he, along with the local councils he influenced, declared the books of the Apocrypha inspired." (Holden, p. 90)

Notice the following admission from an Eastern Orthodox source:

> [M]ost Orthodox scholars ... consider that the Deutero-Canonical Books, although part of the Bible, stand at a lower footing than the rest of scripture. (Ware, p.200)

So, while the Old Testament Apocrypha is accepted as scripture by the Eastern Orthodox, their scholars believe it is of lower footing than the actual biblical books.

This seems to be confusing for the Orthodox: it either is scripture or it is not! Of course, "God is not the author of confusion" (1 Corinthians 14:33).

The extra books were not divinely inspired. Though they can have some interesting historical information, they should not be considered part of the biblical canon.

Notice the following observation:

> Numerous spurious books were gradually introduced into the inspired Canon. No two copies of the earliest Catholic Bibles agree as to which apocryphal books were to be added. It was not until 397 A.D., at the Council of Carthage, that Augustine, the Canaanite Bishop from Hippo in North Africa, led the Council of Carthage to generally approve seven Apocryphal books. As late as 363 A.D., at the Council of Laodicea the Greek Church rejected the Apocryphal books as a whole. … At the Council of Trent on April 8, 1546, those who rejected the Apocrypha were declared to be 'anathema of Christ'! Here was the authority of men determining what others must believe. This was not the authority of God. (Do We Have The COMPLETE BIBLE? Ambassador College Publications, 1974)

Before going further, it may be of interest to note that the Church of Rome and the Eastern Orthodox do not accept ALL the extra books that are part of the Septuagint. Though, the Eastern Orthodox claim:

> The official version of the Old Testament authorized by the Orthodox Church for use in worship and reading is that of the Septuagint. The number of books in the Septuagint Old Testament edition of the Bible are forty-nine books, twenty-seven in the New Testament. (Holy Scripture In The Orthodox Church. 'The Bible.' Compiled by Father Demetrios Serfes, Boise, Idaho, USA. August 20 2000)

Essentially, the Roman and Orthodox Catholics do not consider 2 Esdras, to be canonical (though it is in an appendix to the Slavonic Bible) nor 4 Maccabees (though it is in an appendix to the Greek Bible). 1 & 2 Esdras were part of the Latin Vulgate that Jerome originally prepared (though he endorsed neither one).

2 Esdras was possibly rejected by the Catholics of Rome and most of the Eastern Orthodox because it teaches that one should not pray for the dead as that will not affect their "punishment or reward" (2 Esdras

7:105; cf. 7:88). This is in contradiction to the Septuagint text of 2 Maccabees 12:45-46, which improperly endorses prayer for the dead.

The following additional Septuagint books are accepted by the Eastern Orthodox, but not the Roman Catholics:

- 1 Esdras
- Prayer of Manasseh
- 3 Maccabees
- 4 Maccabees
- Psalm 151 (in the Septuagint)
- Odes

Thus, neither the Church of Rome nor the Eastern Orthodox seemingly accept *all* the Septuagint books, and they also do not accept all of the same books. Note that the Eastern Orthodox say they have 79 books and the Church of Rome 73.

This would seem to be problematic in their talks about ecumenical unity. However, some of the text is the same in both Bibles, but categorized differently.

Some Quotes from the Apocrypha

Beyond the Jews and history, one can determine that the Apocrypha should not be considered as scripture as it contains doctrinal contradictions to the Bible.

For example, notice something from the fifth chapter of the Apocryphal Book of Tobit:

> [4] Tobiah went out to look for someone who would travel with him to Media, someone who knew the way. He went out and found the angel Raphael standing before him (though he did not know that this was an angel of God).
>
> [5] Tobiah said to him, "Where do you come from, young man?" He replied, "I am an Israelite, one of your kindred. I have come here to work." ...

¹¹ Tobit asked him, "Brother, tell me, please, from what family and tribe are you?"

¹² He replied, "Why? What need do you have for a tribe? Aren't you looking for a hired man?" Tobit replied, "I only want to know, brother, whose son you truly are and what your name is."

¹³ He answered, "I am Azariah, son of the great Hananiah, one of your own kindred."

An angel of God would not lie about his ancestry. But that is what is happening in this book.

In chapter 6, this lying angel later told Tobit to get fish entrails:

⁷ Then the young man asked the angel this question: "Brother Azariah, what medicine is in the fish's heart, liver, and gall?"

⁸ He answered: "As for the fish's heart and liver, if you burn them to make smoke in the presence of a man or a woman who is afflicted by a demon or evil spirit, any affliction will flee and never return. ⁹ As for the gall, if you apply it to the eyes of one who has white scales, blowing right into them, sight will be restored."

The Bible does not enjoin anything like burning fish entrails for removing demons. This is not something that Jesus did (Matthew 5:8; 17:18), nor the Apostle Paul (Acts 16:18). Jesus also did not apply gall to eyes for healing (cf. Matthew 20:34; John 9:6-7).

Another false book of the Apocrypha is called *Wisdom* (or the Wisdom of Solomon). Its third chapter teaches:

¹⁶ But the children of adulterers will not reach maturity, the offspring of an unlawful bed will disappear.

¹⁷ Even if they live long, they will count for nothing, their old age will go unhonoured at the last; ¹⁸ while if they die early, they have neither hope nor comfort on the day of judgement, ¹⁹ for the end of a race of evil-doers is harsh.

So, in other words, *Wisdom* is teaching that if you are born outside of proper wedlock, you will likely not reach maturity. That is simply false.

Furthermore, *Wisdom* is teaching that a child of adultery will perish and there's nothing anyone can do about it! This is against scriptures in the New Testament such as Mark 3:28, 1 Corinthians 6:9-11, and John 3:16-17 — as well as some in the Old Testament like Ezekiel 18:19-20.

The sixth chapter of the *Book of Wisdom* contains the following lie:

> [24] In the greatest number of the wise lies the world's salvation, in a sagacious king the stability of a people.

The wisdom of the world IS NOT salvation (cf. 1 Corinthians 1:19-29) — salvation only comes through Jesus (1 Corinthians 1:30; Acts 4:10-12).

Here are some passages from the third chapter of the book of *Sirach* also called *Ecclesiasticus*:

> [3] Those who honor their father atone for sins;

> [14] Kindness to a father will not be forgotten; it will serve as a sin offering — it will take lasting root. [15] In time of trouble it will be recalled to your advantage, like warmth upon frost it will melt away your sins.

> [30] As water quenches a flaming fire, so almsgiving atones for sins.

While we are to honor our father (cf. Exodus 20:12) and give to the poor (cf. 2 Corinthians 9:9), these are not offerings that atone for sins. *Sirach* is clearly in conflict with New Testament scriptures such as Ephesians 2:8-10, Titus 3:3-7, Hebrews 10:4-10, and 1 John 2:2.

Notice the first several verses of the 12th chapter of Sirach:

> [1] If you do good, know for whom you are doing it, and your kindness will have its effect.

> [2] Do good to the righteous and reward will be yours, if not from them, from the LORD.

³ No good comes to those who give comfort to the wicked, nor is it an act of mercy that they do. ⁴ Give to the good but refuse the sinner; ⁵ refresh the downtrodden but give nothing to the proud. No arms for combat should you give them, lest they use these against you; Twofold evil you will obtain for every good deed you do for them.

These passages clearly go against the teachings of Jesus in passages such as Matthew 5:43-48, 6:3, and Luke 6:27-36.

Sirach takes a negative stance against women (cf. Sirach 22:3). It also has the following statement which conflicts with scripture:

²⁴ With a woman sin had a beginning, and because of her we all die. (Sirach 25:24)

On this, let us look at some of what the New Testament teaches:

²¹ For since by man came death, by Man also came the resurrection of the dead. ²² For as in Adam all die, even so in Christ all shall be made alive. (1 Corinthians 15:21-22)

The New Testament is blaming Adam, not Eve (cf. Romans 5:12-14; 1 Timothy 2:14) for death.

Sirach is obviously opposed to the Bible and no one should consider it as part of the Old Testament Canon.

There are many other passages from the Apocrypha that could be cited here to show that they should not be scripture. Hopefully, enough are cited here to provide you sufficient proof of that.

Note: The version of the Apocrypha shown in this section is that used at the website of the United States Conference of Catholic Bishops in 2017 (www.usccb.org) — lest any feel that a translation bias distorted their meaning.

The *Jewish Encyclopedia of 1906* notes, "no controversy arose concerning the Apocrypha: all were agreed that they were non-canonical."

Justin and Other Books?

Is there justification for other books in the Old Testament?

In what looks like a rather weak attempt to try to justify its use of the additional books, *The Catholic Encyclopedia* states:

> St. Justin Martyr is the first to note that the Church has a set of Old Testament Scriptures different from the Jews', and also the earliest to intimate the principle proclaimed by later writers, namely, the self-sufficiency of the Church in establishing the Canon; its independence of the Synagogue in this respect. (Reid, Old Testament Canon)

Specifically, Justin claimed, that the Jews ('they') removed scriptures:

> And I wish you to observe, that they have altogether taken away many Scriptures from the translations effected by those seventy elders who were with Ptolemy ...
>
> Trypho remarked, "Whether [or not] the rulers of the people have erased any portion of the Scriptures, as you affirm, God knows; but it seems incredible."
>
> "Assuredly," said I, "it does seem incredible". (Justin Martyr. Dialogue with Trypho, Chapters 71,73)

Justin seemed to teach that Jewish leaders removed passages from the Bible — he did not clearly teach that books were missing (Ibid. Chapters 71-73). Scholar F.F. Bruce indicated that Justin erroneously thought that words which were later added to the Septuagint by 'Christians' had been removed by the Jews in their scriptures (Bruce, The Canon of Scripture, p. 66).

Justin also stated that the Jews did NOT trust the Septuagint as they asserted the Septuagint translators improperly changed passages, but he wanted Trypho to trust it anyway (Justin Martyr. Dialogue with Trypho, Chapter 68).

Furthermore, Justin Martyr, in this author's view, was an apostate and not a faithful Christian. While in Ephesus, Justin admitted that he did not live differently than the Gentiles (in violation of Paul's admonition in Ephesians 4:17), taught God's law was not in force, and did not observe the Sabbaths or the other Holy Days that the early Church did (Dialogue. Chapter 18). And, apparently, he did not accept the same content of the books that the disciples did for the Old Testament. Justin seemed to teach that the Jews eliminated parts by not accepting everything from the Septuagint translators. It may be important to note that Justin wrote decades BEFORE Melito, and Melito did not include any of the deuterocanonical books in his list.

After Justin Martyr left Ephesus he became influential in Rome. Eusebius noted:

> And in Rome ... Anicetus assumed the leadership of the Christians there ... But Justin was especially prominent in those days. (Eusebius Church History. Book IV, Chapter 11)

Justin became so prominent that his influence was later being used as justification that ultimately led to the adoption of extra books in the Old Testament (Reid, Old Testament Canon) that were not in those scriptures used by Christ and the original apostles! He influenced Rome's preference for the Septuagint.

Apocrypha Not Accepted by Certain Famous Greco-Roman Saints

As mentioned earlier, the books that the Roman Catholics and Eastern Orthodox tend to call the deuterocanonical books, are normally called the Apocrypha or the apocryphal books associated with the Old Testament. (There are also ones associated with the New Testament and they are specifically rejected by Roman Catholics, Eastern Orthodox, Protestants, and those in the Churches of God.)

These books were not included in Melito's list of the 2nd century. They were also rejected in the third and fourth centuries by Greco-Roman scholars such as Origen, Athanasius, and Jerome (who was named Eusebius Hieronymus Sophronius), essentially because they understood that the books were not properly accepted by the Jews and did not agree with certain church teachings.

Origen of Alexandria (c. 200 A.D.), taught:

> "It should be stated that the canonical books, as the Hebrews have handed them down, are twenty-two; corresponding with the number of their letters". (Eusebius. Church History, Book VI, Chapter 25, verse 1)

He then listed the books as we know them from the Hebrew Bible. He did not list the Apocrypha as canonical and put Maccabees in a different category than canonical scripture (Ibid, verse 2).

Athanasius of Alexandria (c. 330 A.D.) taught:

> The books of the Old Testament are twenty-two, which is the number of the letters among the Hebrews. Genesis, Exodus, Leviticus, Numbers, Deuteronomy, Joshua, Judges, Ruth, of Kings four, two books; of Paralipomenon (Chronicles) two, one book; Esdras two, one book; Psalms, Proverbs; twelve prophets, one book; then Isaiah, Jeremiah with Baruch, Lamentations, and epistles; Ezekiel and Daniel. Then there are books uncanonical, but readable, the Wisdom of Solomon, Sirach, Esther, Judith, Tobit. (As cited in Stowe CE. Apocryphal Books of the Old Testament. Bibliotheca sacra: a theological quarterly, Volume 11. Dallas Theological Seminary and Graduate School of Theology, April 1854, p. 298)

Notice, that although he was wrong about Esther and Baruch, Athanasius basically did not consider that the Apocrypha was part of the canon. He also stated:

> Since some persons have attempted to set in order the books that are called apocryphal, and to mix them with the divinely inspired Scriptures, of which we have been fully certified, as those who saw them from the beginning, and who, being ministers of that word, handed them down from our fathers, it seemed fitting to me, being exhorted thereto by the orthodox brethren, and having learned the truth, to set in order the canonical Scriptures, which have been handed down, and are believed to be from God; that every one who has been

deceived, may convict those who led him astray. (ibid, pp. 298-299)

So, Athanasius said that people had been deceived by non-canonical books and that the Apocrypha was not canonical. He also claimed that the true books had been handed down from the beginning: and even though he himself did not know the precise list well, he was right about the correct books being handed down to the faithful (he also did list the 27 books of the New Testament in a letter in 367: Athanasius. 39th Letter. Nicene and Post-Nicene Fathers, Second Series, Vol. 4. Edited by Philip Schaff and Henry Wace).

It should be noted that Athanasius is considered to be a major saint by the Greco-Romans as he was the biggest advocate of the trinity at the Council of Nicea and was outnumbered by non-trinitarians by about 8:1. Clearly, he did not accept the 'deuterocanonical' books.

Notice something from a Roman Catholic author:

> The Septuagint tradition, which included not only the protocanonicals but also seven additional books ... this tradition also had fuzzy boundaries. Some editions of the Septuagint included additional books such as *1-2 Esdras*, *3-4 Maccabees*, and the *Prayer of Manasseh*. (Akin J. The Bible is a Catholic Book. Catholic Answers Press, 2019, p. 41)

'Fuzzy boundaries' means that scholars realize that the Septuagint's traditional inclusion of various books cannot be trusted and some versions of the Septuagint have even more improper books.

"God is not the author of confusion but of peace, as in all the churches of the saints" (1 Corinthians 14:33).

Jerome and the Deuterocanonical Books

The Catholic Encyclopedia notes:

> St. Jerome cast his weighty suffrage on the side unfavourable to the disputed books ... Jerome lived long in Palestine, in an environment where everything outside the Jewish Canon was

suspect, and that, moreover, he had an excessive veneration for the Hebrew text, the *Hebraica veritas* as he called it. ... the inferior rank to which the deuteros were relegated by authorities like Origen, Athanasius, and Jerome, was due to too rigid a conception of canonicity, one demanding that a book, to be entitled to this supreme dignity, must be received by all, must have the sanction of Jewish antiquity, and must moreover be adapted not only to edification, but also to the 'confirmation of the doctrine of the Church', to borrow Jerome's phrase. (Reid, Old Testament Canon)

But Jerome did not simply consider these additions were inferior.

Notice here where he calls *Judith* a historical book (as opposed to divinely inspired), but says he was forced to include it:

> Among the Jews, the book of Judith is considered among the apocrypha; its warrant for affirming those [apocryphal texts] which have come into dispute is deemed less than sufficient. Moreover, since it was written in the Chaldean language, it is counted among the historical books. But since the Nicene Council is considered to have counted this book among the number of sacred Scriptures, I have acquiesced to your request (or should I say demand!): and, my other work set aside, from which I was forcibly restrained, I have given a single night's work, translating according to sense rather than verbatim. (Jerome. Jerome, The Preface on the Book of Judith: English translation by Andrew S. Jacobs)

Notice that Jerome called it apocrypha and that he did not consider that it actually was considered sacred at the time of Nicea (325 A.D.). Notice also the following he wrote about Tobias:

> I do not cease to wonder at the constancy of your demanding. For you demand that I bring a book written in Chaldean words into Latin writing, indeed the book of Tobias, which the Hebrews exclude from the catalogue of Divine Scriptures, being mindful of those things which they have titled Hagiographa. I have done enough for your desire, yet not by my study. For the studies of the Hebrews rebuke us and find fault with us, to translate this for

the ears of Latins contrary to their canon. (Jerome, Prologue to Tobit. Translated by Kevin P. Edgecomb, 2006)

Notice also that Jerome specifically stated that the churches condemned the Septuagint additions to the Book of Daniel:

> In reference to Daniel ... I also told the reader that the version read in the Christian churches was not that of the Septuagint translators but that of Theodotion. It is true, I said that the Septuagint version was in this book very different from the original, and that it was condemned by the right judgment of the churches of Christ ... I repeat what the Jews say against the Story of Susanna and the Hymn of the Three Children, and the fables of Bel and the Dragon, which are not contained in the Hebrew Bible. (Jerome. Apology Against Rufinus, Book II, Chapter 33)

The Septuagint version includes a section called Bel and the Dragon and the Susanna story — which were originally written in Greek (Bruce, The Canon of Scripture, p. 76) — these are two sections that the original Hebrew does not have, but they have been accepted by the Roman Catholic and Eastern Orthodox churches as part of their Bible.

Here is a Roman Catholic claim:

> Saint Jerome ... used the Septuagint Greek version and retained all forty-six Old Testament books with the twenty-seven New Testament books to formulate the first single-volume edition of the Christian Bible, totaling seventy-three books. Things didn't change for fifteen centuries until the Protestant Reformation. (Brighenti KK, Trijilio J Jr. The Catholicism Answer Book: The 300 Most Frequently Asked Questions. Sourcebooks, Inc, 2007, p. 23)

Yet that certainly gives the wrong impression. Jerome was opposed to the Apocrypha and other Roman leaders were uncertain about them. Nor was it 15 centuries to the Protestant Reformation — it was just over 11. Plus, Jerome used the Hebrew text for the Old Testament when he could (Francis, Pope. APOSTOLIC LETTER SCRIPTURAE SACRAE AFFECTUS OF THE HOLY FATHER FRANCIS ON THE SIXTEEN HUNDREDTH ANNIVERSARY OF THE DEATH OF SAINT JEROME. Copyright - Libreria Editrice Vaticana, September 30, 2020)—he used comparatively little of the Septuagint itself as he preferred the Hebrew first and the Greek text by Theodotion and others secondarily (Worth Jr, RH. Bible Translations: A History Through Source Documents. McFarland Publishing, 1992, pp. 19–30).

Regarding Jerome and his involvement with scripture, Pope Francis went so far as to declare:

> Jerome can serve as our guide because, like Philip (cf. *Acts 8:35*), he leads every reader to the mystery of Jesus, while responsibly and systematically providing the exegetical and cultural information needed for a correct and fruitful reading of the Scriptures. (Francis, APOSTOLIC LETTER SCRIPTURAE SACRAE AFFECTUS)

Yet, if Jerome is the guide for Roman Catholics, they would have to admit that he did not want people to value the Apocrypha of the Septuagint.

Consider that Jerome accepted the 22 books as the Hebrews numbered them as inspired and not the Apocrypha:

> Jerome, writing about A.D. 400, has left two lists of OT books. Both agree with the Protestant OT canon, though the order varies and the two lists differ in order. He lists the books of the OT in his *Prologus Galeatus* (written in 388) and numbers them twenty-two according to the letters of the Hebrew alphabet. Others he says are among the Apocrypha and names Wisdom of Solomon, Ecclesiasticus, Judith, Tobit, the post-Christian Shepherd of Hermas (or as some think 4 Esdras), and the books of Maccabees. It has always been regarded as curious that the man who translated the VULGATE Bible used by Roman Catholics with its Apocrypha is a most explicit witness against the Apocrypha. (Tenney MC. The Zondervan Encyclopedia of the Bible, Volume 1: Revised Full-Color Edition -- Kindle. Zondervan Academic, 2010)

Furthermore, Jerome specifically challenges the validity of the Septuagint and states that the Hebrew Bible was used by Jesus and the Apostles:

The Hebrew Scriptures are used by apostolic men; they are used, as is evident, by the apostles and evangelists. Our Lord and Saviour himself whenever he refers to the Scriptures, takes his quotations from the Hebrew; as in the instance of the words "He that believes in me, as the Scripture has said, out of his belly shall flow rivers of living water," and in the words used on the cross itself, "Eli, Eli, lama sabachthani," which is by interpretation "My God, my God, why have you forsaken me?" not, as it is given by the Septuagint, "My God, my God, look upon me, why have you forsaken me?" and many similar cases. I do not say this in order to aim a blow at the seventy translators; but I assert that the Apostles of Christ have an authority superior to theirs. Wherever the Seventy agree with the Hebrew, the apostles took their quotations from that translation; but, where they disagree, they set down in Greek what they had found in the Hebrew. (Jerome. Apology Against Rufinus, Book II, Chapter 34)

Jerome, the person who, in a sense, gave the Church of Rome the Bible, was opposed to books that he was required to include. He also correctly believed that the translation of the Septuagint was inferior to the Apostles' writings.

While Jerome was apparently pressured to state otherwise later in his life, his writings clearly show he had serious misgivings about the Apocrypha and realized those books were not originally part of the Bible.

Historical Catholic Concerns

Origen, Jerome, and Athanasius were not the only Roman or Eastern Orthodox leaders with concerns about the extra books.

Cyril of Jerusalem (4th century) also indicated that the Apocryphal books were considered to be of lesser reliability as he wrote:

We speak not from apocryphal books, but from Daniel; for he says, *And they shall be given into his hand until a time and times and half a time. A time* is the one year in which his coming shall for a while have increase; and *the times* are the remaining two years of iniquity, making up the sum of the three years; and *the half a time* is the six months. (Cyril of Jerusalem. Catechetical Lecture 15 On the Clause, And Shall Come in Glory to Judge the Quick and the Dead; Of Whose Kingdom There Shall Be No End, Chapter 16. From Nicene and Post-Nicene Fathers, Second Series, Vol. 7. Edited by Philip Schaff and Henry Wace. Buffalo, NY: Christian Literature Publishing Co., 1894)

The Roman Catholic Church recognizes its leaders had concerns about these additional Old Testament books for centuries. *The Catholic Encyclopedia* notes:

THE CANON OF THE OLD TESTAMENT DURING THE FOURTH, AND FIRST HALF OF THE FIFTH, CENTURY

In this period the position of the deuterocanonical literature is no longer as secure ... Alexandria, with its elastic Scriptures, had from the beginning been a congenial field for apocryphal literature, and St. Athanasius, the vigilant pastor of that flock, to protect it against the pernicious influence, drew up a catalogue of books with the values to be attached to each. First, the strict canon and authoritative source of truth is the Jewish Old Testament, Esther excepted ... Following the precedent of Origen and the Alexandrian tradition, the saintly doctor recognized no other formal canon of the Old Testament than the Hebrew one; but also, faithful to the same tradition, he practically admitted the deutero books to a Scriptural dignity, as is evident from his general usage ...

THE CANON OF THE OLD TESTAMENT FROM THE MIDDLE OF THE FIFTH TO THE CLOSE OF THE SEVENTH CENTURY

This period exhibits a curious exchange of opinions between the West and the East, while ecclesiastical usage remained unchanged, at least in the Latin Church. During this intermediate age the use of St. Jerome's new version of the Old Testament (the Vulgate) became widespread in the Occident. With its text went Jerome's prefaces disparaging the deuterocanonicals, and under the influence of his authority the

West began to distrust these and to show the first symptoms of a current hostile to their canonicity ...

The Latin Church

In the Latin Church, all through the Middle Ages we find evidence of hesitation about the character of the deuterocanonicals. (Reid, Canon of the Old Testament. The Catholic Encyclopedia)

Even into the Middle Ages, the Roman Catholic Church was not sure if the deuterocanonical books were on a par with scripture!

Either they always were inspired by God or always were not.

Thus, while many of the Greco-Roman churches knew which were and were not the true books at least as early as the fourth and fifth centuries, there still was contention. Additional books came to be accepted by them that were NOT part of the original faith, which true Christians are to earnestly contend for (Jude 3).

Catholic theologians, like 11th century Saxony priest Hugh of St. Victor, taught that the additional books were not scripture (Hugh. On the Sacraments, I, Prologue. As cited in Bruce, The Canon of Scripture, p. 99).

Notice something from ArmenianBible.org (accessed 04/16/20):

Not till the 8th century was the Apocrypha rendered into Armenian: it was not read in Armenian churches until the 12th.

Furthermore, these additional books were not once and for all officially adopted by Rome until 1546. The use of the term 'deuterocanonical' seems to have first been used in the 16th century (Bruce, The Canon of Scripture, p. 105) and is essentially an admission that they were not original.

The Catholic Encyclopedia also states:

The protocanonical books of the Old Testament correspond with those of the Bible of the Hebrews, and the Old Testament as received by Protestants. The deuterocanonical (*deuteros*, 'second') are those whose Scriptural character was contested in some quarters, but which long ago gained a secure footing in the Bible of the Catholic Church, though those of the Old Testament are classed by Protestants as the 'Apocrypha'. ... The Septuagint version was the Bible of the Greek-speaking, or Hellenist, Jews, whose intellectual and literary centre was Alexandria (see SEPTUAGINT). The oldest extant copies date from the fourth and fifth centuries of our era ... The most explicit definition of the Catholic Canon is that given by the Council of Trent, Session IV, 1546 ... The order of books copies that of the Council of Florence, 1442, and in its general plan is that of the Septuagint. (Reid, Old Testament Canon)

Why were they adopted in the 16th century?

Here is the view of a Protestant writer:

There is a mistaken belief among some that the Apocrypha books were part of the Bible, and that these were rejected by the Protestant Reformers. On the contrary, the Apocrypha books were never a part of the Old Testament Canon. Thus there is no question of the Reformers dropping out some books from the Canon. Rather, it is the Roman Catholic Church which ADDED these books to the Canon by a proclamation made at the Council of Trent...

With the Protestant Reformation, many of the Reformers challenged the Catholic church to prove their doctrine by supporting these from the Canon. To their dismay the Roman Catholics discovered that many of their doctrines are not derived from the Canon. At the same time they realized that at least some of these erroneous doctrines are supported by the Apocrypha. Thus for their survival it became necessary to add the Apocrypha to the Canon.

In 1545 the Roman Catholic Church convened what is called the Council Of Trent. Here they passed numerous resolutions, including many curses against the Protestant Believers. In April 1545 the Council declared that the Apocrypha are also part of the Bible. Thus for the first time in history the Apocrypha books were ADDED by the Roman Catholic church to the Bible. This was done in order to justify their doctrinal errors (for which support was available only in the Apocrypha), and also to oppose the Protestant believers. The first Vatican Council held 1869-70 reaffirmed the decision of the Roman Catholic Church to add the Apocrypha to the Canon.

Historically and theologically the Apocrypha was never part of the Canon. (Philip JC. Reliability of The Canon. Indus School of Apologetics and Theology Textbook No -004A1, version used in 2006)

The Roman Catholics were not the only ones to adopt those so-called deuterocanonical books. The Eastern Orthodox Church did as well.

It should also be noted, further, that John Wycliffe included them in his 1384 and 1395 translations (Bruce, The Canon of Scripture, p. 100). Also, in the original of the King James Version of the Bible in 1611, Protestants did also include the Old Testament Apocrypha, but later they were dropped from it (for the last time around 1666).

An Anglican canon, with the Apocrypha declared not to be of 'divine origin,' appeared in 1644 (Bruce, The Canon of Scripture, p. 109). In 1826, after the Protestant National Bible Society of Scotland petitioned the British and Foreign Bible Society not to print the Apocrypha, they ceased to be in most Protestant Bibles.

Protestants have claimed the Apocrypha were originally included in their Bibles for historical, not scriptural, value.

The following is from the *Statement of Beliefs of the Continuing Church of God*:

THE HOLY BIBLE

The Holy Bible is the inspired Word of God and was finalized by the Apostle John (see also *Who Gave the World the Bible?*). As commonly divided, it is a collection of 66 books, with 39 from the Hebrew scriptures (The Old Testament Canon) and 27 from the Greek Scriptures (The New Testament Canon). Scripture is inspired in thought and word and contains knowledge of what is needed for salvation (2 Timothy 3:15-17; Matthew 4:4; 2 Peter 1:20-21). Scripture is truth (John 17:17) and is infallible and inerrant in its original manuscripts (John 10:35).

We in the *Continuing* Church of God are following the Apostle Jude's admonition "to contend earnestly for the faith which was once for all delivered to the saints" (Jude 3). The Roman and Eastern Orthodox churches clearly are NOT doing this as they adopted books that early leaders knew were not part of the true canon.

The 39 books that are in the Old Testaments that those in the COGs and Protestant Churches use are the correct books of the Old Testament.

Even the Roman Catholic supporting Jerome recognized some of the flaws of the deuterocanonical books. His original research made him only accept the 39 Old Testament books as truly valid and seemingly he partially consulted with those who held Church of God doctrines when he put his books together.

The true Old Testament canon is based on the biblical criteria and this canon essentially was affirmed during the 2nd century by one considered to have been faithful (Melito).

While it is true, in a sense, that 'the Church gave the world the Bible' — it was the church established by Christ through the apostles Peter, Paul, and John and their successors as inspired by the Holy Spirit that did so. This was the Church of God which Polycarp and other early saints became part of.

Consider that:

> just because a book is found in the Septuagint, doesn't automatically mean that it is canonical. Do you believe the Prayer of Manasseh is canonical? The Vulgate's 3 Esdras, or Maccabees 3 and 4? How about Psalm 151 or the Psalms of Solomon? No, I don't think you would believe that, yet these

books are in some of the Septuagint manuscripts. So, don't try to say that the deuterocanonicals are equal in inspiration to the protocanonical books just because they are found in the Septuagint. (http://answeringcatholicclaims.blogspot.com/2012/02/did-catholic-church-give-us-bible.html)

The Catholic Encyclopedia refers to the "admitted absence of any explicit citation of the deutero writings … the non-citation of the deuterocanonicals in the New Testament" (Reid, George. Canon of the Old Testament. The Catholic Encyclopedia. Vol. 3., 1908), while also admitting that most of the other books of the Old Testament are cited in the New.

Jesus and His apostles DID NOT consider that the extra books that the Church of Rome accepts were valid or that they were validated by events recorded in the New Testament.

Quotes in the New Testament from the Greek

Does the Greek New Testament ever quote the Septuagint?

Here is what the Greco-Roman Catholic priest Jerome wrote about the Book of Matthew and its use of the Old Testament:

> Matthew, also called Levi, apostle and aforetimes publican, composed a gospel of Christ at first published in Judea in Hebrew for the sake of those of the circumcision who believed, but this was afterwards translated into Greek though by what author is uncertain. The Hebrew itself has been preserved until the present day in the library at Caesarea which Pamphilus so diligently gathered. I have also had the opportunity of having the volume described to me by the Nazarenes of Beroea, a city of Syria, who use it. In this it is to be noted that wherever the Evangelist, **whether on his own account or in the person of our Lord the Saviour quotes the testimony of the Old Testament he does not follow the authority of the translators of the Septuagint but the Hebrew**. Wherefore these two forms exist "Out of Egypt have I called my son," and "for he shall be called a Nazarene". (Jerome. De Viris Illustribus [On Illustrious Men]. Excerpted from Nicene and Post-Nicene Fathers, Second Series,

Volume 3. Edited by Philip Schaff and Henry Wace. American Edition, 1892)

This was cited to show that the Hebrew scriptures were what were normally used for scripture in Palestine/Judea.

But, since nearly all of the New Testament was written in Greek, it is logical that Greek translations were sometimes quoted.

John Ogwyn noted:

> Should we be concerned that some New Testament quotations from the Old Testament {seemingly} were taken from a Greek translation—the Septuagint—rather than from the Hebrew Masoretic Text? Greek was the most universal language at the time when the New Testament was being written.
>
> Gentile converts were unfamiliar with the Hebrew language and even most Jews outside of Palestine no longer had a good reading knowledge of Hebrew.
>
> The Septuagint was a Greek translation of the Old Testament that had been made in Egypt.
>
> But it was not the only Greek translation of the Old Testament available in the time when the New Testament was written. There was at least one Greek translation that differed significantly from the Septuagint.
>
> It was used by Theodotion in the second century ad for his revised Greek text of the Old Testament.
>
> The book of Daniel, as preserved in Greek translation by Theodotion, matches far more closely the quotations from Daniel in the New Testament than does the Septuagint, for instance. Though none of the Greek translations of the Old Testament were totally accurate, most of their deviations from the Hebrew text were in areas that did not affect the overall sense of the message ...

Gleason Archer and G. C. Chirichigno in their comprehensive work, Old Testament Quotations in the New Testament: A Complete Survey, make the following points about New Testament quotations: 1) in 268 New Testament citations both the Septuagint and Masoretic Text are in complete harmony; 2) in 50 citations the New Testament agrees with the Septuagint, even though it differs slightly from the Masoretic Text (although not seriously enough to distort the meaning); 3) in 33 citations the New Testament adheres more closely to the Masoretic Text than to the Septuagint; 4) in 22 citations the New Testament adheres closely to the Septuagint even when it deviates somewhat from the Masoretic Text.

The New Testament writers only made use of Septuagint quotations if those passages properly conveyed the inspired meaning of the Hebrew text. (Ogwyn J. How Did We Get The Bible? Tomorrow's World, January-February 2002)

Essentially, John Ogwyn was saying that New Testament writers did not rely on translated passages of the Old Testament into Greek that differed materially from the original Hebrew. Therefore, one should not conclude that the entire, flawed, Septuagint was acceptable to them (though where it was not flawed and a proper translation, they could have used it or something similar).

Others have claimed that:

TWO OUT OF EVERY THREE QUOTATIONS from the OLD TESTAMENT FOUND IN THE NEW DO NOT AGREE VERBALLY WITH THE READING OF THE SEPTUAGINT translation of the Old Testament. (Do We Have The COMPLETE BIBLE? Ambassador College Publications, 1974)

Now, the Eastern Orthodox believe that the majority of Old Testament quotes are *based* on the Septuagint, but that is mainly an assumption since most are not direct quotes, which one would logically conclude they would have to be if the Septuagint was the preferred and divinely inspired source.

While the Eastern Orthodox generally claim that the Masoretic Text (Hebrew Bible with vowels and limited punctuation) is flawed and has been changed, their proof is lacking (more on the Masoretic Text is in the next chapter).

This author states that the type of 'proof' that the Septuagint was inspired is reminiscent of the same type of 'proof' that people bring out when they claim that the New Testament was written in Aramaic and not Greek (for specific details, check out the following link: www.cogwriter.com/greek-aramaic-hebrew-new-testament.htm).

Furthermore, unlike the Septuagint, the Masoretic text does not include the Old Testament Apocrypha.

5. Masoretic Text

It is widely understood that the original written language in most of the Old Testament was a form of Hebrew that did not use vowels (though some insist otherwise). And this was fine when the Jews spoke that same dialect of Hebrew.

Due to exile and other reasons, many of the Jews switched from speaking Hebrew to speaking Aramaic. Because of that, many had difficulty reading the original biblical texts. (It should be added that a small amount of the Old Testament was written in Aramaic.)

Over time, vowels and some punctuation were added to the Hebrew text. This resulted in what is called the Masoretic Text. It is called 'Masoretic' because it was put together by Jewish scholars and scribes called Masoretes between the 6th and 10th centuries A.D. (Wegner, Paul. The Journey From Texts to Translations. Baker Academic, 1999, p. 172). What was called the "proto-Masoretic Text" reportedly became the standard text of the rabbis by around 100 A.D. (Ibid, p. 170), with spellings standardized between then and 500 A.D (Ibid, p. 171). A version called the Aleppo Codex c. 930 A.D. has been called "the most authoritative copy of the Hebrew Bible. The Aleppo Codex is not complete, however, as almost 200 pages went missing between 1947 and 1957" (Drummond J. What Is the Oldest Hebrew Bible? Biblical Archeaology Society, January 10, 2021). While the Aleppo Codex is considered the "oldest Hebrew Bible," the Leningrad Codex (c. 1008) is now generally considered "the oldest complete Hebrew Bible" (Ibid).

How can we know that the text of the Old Testament has been accurately preserved in what is called the Masoretic Text? How was this done?

Note the explanation from Appendix 30 of *The Companion Bible of 1922*:

> The text itself had been fixed before the Masorites were put in charge of it ... the Masorites were authorized custodians of it. Their work was to preserve it. The Masorah is called 'A Fence to the Scriptures,' because it locked all words and letters in their places. ... It records the number of times the several letters occur in the various books of the Bible; the number of words,

and the middle word; the number of verses, and the middle verse ... for the set purpose of safeguarding the Sacred Text, and preventing the loss or misplacement of a single letter or word.

The simple fact was that in Jesus' day, there still were scribes (e.g. Matthew 17:10,12, Matthew 23:13-15,23,25,27,29). And these scribes not only copied (transcribed) scripture, they counted each character and cross-checked it to ensure that it was as error free as they basically could. The meticulous attention to detail by the Jewish scribes provides a background for understanding the literal truth of Jesus' statement in Matthew 5:18 that not "one jot or one tittle will by no means pass from the law." Presuming Jesus spoke this originally in Aramaic, the jot refers to the smallest letter in the Aramaic alphabet (✻) *yodh* (which can be a vowel or consonant), and the tittle seemingly describes the second smallest letter (✻) *waw*. No book of the Hebrew Bible was lost nor was Jesus confused about what they were.

As far as the Masoretic text itself goes, notice the following:

> For years the critics claimed the Hebrew Bible was of no authority. 'A late and altered form of earlier Hebrew writings,' they claimed!

> Then came the year 1947.

> In the summer of '47 a sheer coincidence led to the discovery of the oldest manuscripts of the Bible so far known. Among a collection of literary works found in a cave in Wadi Qumran on the north side of the Dead Sea, a 23-foot leather scroll was found to contain the complete text of the book of Isaiah in Hebrew! Expert examination of the document revealed beyond doubt that this Isaiah text dated from about 100 B.C.

> This copy of Isaiah, now about 2000 years old, is unique proof of the reliability of the text of the Holy Scriptures that have been handed down to us. The text in all fundamentals agrees with what we have in our present-day Bibles! The only differences are minor spelling changes and misplaced words, changes that represent the carelessness of unofficial sectarian scribes who copied that text of the book of Isaiah.

In other words, the present Masoretic Hebrew text, which is a continuation of the official Old Testament Hebrew, is far superior in preservation to the unofficial copy of Isaiah made 2000 years ago. Furthermore, the ancient scroll of Isaiah, just like the printed copies of Isaiah in any modern-day Bible, whether Hebrew, Greek, English or German, has the same 66 chapters of our present-day text.

Until this find, the oldest and fullest Manuscript in Hebrew was the Codex Petropolitanus, dating from about 916 A.D. This proves how accurate the Jews have been in copying, generation after generation, the books of the Old Testament. How can anyone deny that God is giving divine protection to the Book which contains His commands and revelations to man! (Hoeh H. The Bible Myth Or Authority. Plain Truth, January 1966)

The Isaiah *Dead Sea Scroll* is factual evidence that the Jews did NOT alter the Hebrew when they produced the Masoretic text (which certain supporters of the Septuagint have claimed).

While some have wondered if the discovery of the *Dead Sea Scrolls* cast doubts on the Bible, F. F. Bruce (then of the University of Manchester) echoed the conclusions of many that "in general the new discoveries have increased our respect for the Masoretic Hebrew text" (Second Thoughts on the Dead Sea Scrolls. Reprint, 2006, p. 69).

Reliability and Age

Notice what some scholars have reported:

The Masoretes had as their primary concern the preservation of the sacred Hebrew Bible. Their attention to detail was remarkably evident within their work. They went to great lengths to develop the system of marginal notes with pronunciation marks and various instructions to make sure that the smallest detail of the text would not go unnoticed by the copying scribe. Every biblical book contained a "colophon" (that is, a scribe's notation of the details of his work, usually attached at the end of his manuscript) and a count of the total number of consonants. Moreover, scribal notes were taken identifying the

73

middle letter of the book by location and stating the exact number of characters that preceded the letter and followed after it. (Holden JM, Geisler N. The Popular Handbook of Archaeology and the Bible. Harvest House, 2013, p. 24)

Although the oldest Masoretic texts we now have seem to date from a little more than a thousand years ago (Ibid, p. 24), the *Dead Sea Scrolls* (believed to have been produced during the 3rd century B.C. through the 1st century A.D.) affirm their accuracy (Ibid, pp. 26,40):

> Qumran, however, has provided remains of an early Masoretic edition predating the Christian era on which the traditional MT is based. A comparison of the MT to this earlier text revealed the remarkable accuracy with which scribes copied the sacred texts. Accordingly, the integrity of the Hebrew Bible was confirmed, which generally has heightened its respect among scholars and drastically reduced textual alteration.
>
> Most of the biblical manuscripts found at Qumran belong to the MT tradition or family. This is especially true of the Pentateuch and some of the Prophets. The well-preserved Isaiah scroll from Cave 1 illustrates the tender care with which these sacred texts were copied. Since about 1700 years separated Isaiah in the MT from its original source, textual critics assumed that centuries of copying and recopying this book must have introduced scribal errors into the document that obscured the original message of the author.
>
> The Isaiah scrolls found at Qumran closed that gap to within 500 years of the original manuscript. Interestingly, when scholars compared the MT of Isaiah to the Isaiah scroll of Qumran, the correspondence was astounding. The texts from Qumran proved to be word-for-word identical to our standard Hebrew Bible in more than 95 percent of the text. The 5 percent of variation consisted primarily of obvious slips of the pen and spelling alterations (Archer, 1974, p. 25). (Brantley GK. The Dead Sea Scrolls and Biblical Integrity. Copyright © 1995 Apologetics Press)

As far as age of the proto-Masoretic texts go (the Hebrew scriptures that became the Masoretic text), there is also something called the Ketef Hinnom, also known as the *Silver Scrolls,* that pre-date the *Dead Sea Scrolls* by about 400 years.

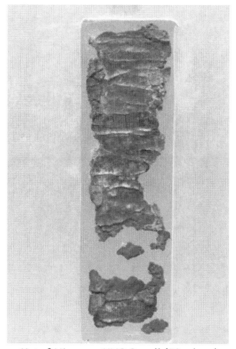

Ketef Hinnom KH2 Scroll (Pixabay)

They have biblical texts written in the 6th and/or 7th centuries B.C. (Barkay G, et al. The Amulets from Ketef Hinnom: A New Edition and Evaluation. Bulletin of the American Schools of Oriental Research. No. 334, May, 2004, pp. 41-71). It has been claimed that, "they are currently the oldest copies of biblical passages in the world" (Holden, p.48).

Notice also:

> The text, inscribed on a silver scroll in the old Hebrew script dating to the 7th Century B.C., is the Aaronic blessing (Numbers 6:24-26), which begins, "yeverekh'kha YHWH Vayishmarekha" (May Yahweh bless you and keep you). (Benner JA. Extant Manuscripts of the Hebrew Bible. Ancient Hebrew Research Center, Ancient-Hebrew.Org --- accessed 03/24/20)

The existence of the *Silver Scrolls* not only support the Masoretic text, they also help dispel the assertion by some that the Old Testament was not written until the 3rd or 4th century B.C. (Holden, p. 48).

There is also a document from the 2nd or 3rd century A.D. called the En-Gedi text which has a portion of the Book of Leviticus (Segal M., et al. "An Early Leviticus Scroll from En Gedi: Preliminary Publication," Textus 26, 2016).

Fragment of En-Gedi scroll (Israel Antiquities Authority שי הלוי)

So, there are several ancient items that provide support for the Masoretic text.

As far as the reliability of the Masoretic texts go, consider the following:

> In 1970 Israeli archaeologists digging at the ancient site of En-Gedi near the Dead Sea discovered a charred lump of what was a leather scroll in the remains of an ancient synagogue ... The oldest complete Hebrew Bible (Old Testament) in the Masoretic form is the Leningrad Codex from AD 1008 and other copies with only portions of the text survive from a couple centuries earlier ... the En-Gedi Leviticus scroll demonstrates the Masoretic tradition nearly 1000 years before Leningrad Codex, yet perfectly matching it.
>
> Dr. Emanuel Tov from Hebrew University in Jerusalem is a linguist, biblical scholar and leading authority on the Dead Sea scrolls that participated in the study. He stated that the charred

En-Gedi scroll is "100 percent identical" to the version of the Book of Leviticus that has been in use for centuries. "This is quite amazing for us. In 2,000 years, this text has not changed."

"The En-Gedi scroll even duplicates the exact paragraph breaks seen later in the medieval Hebrew. The only difference between the two is that ancient Hebrew had no vowels, so these were added in the Middle Ages." ...

The style of the writing on the scroll has also caused a revision of the date for its origin to between 50 and 100 AD. "We may safely date this scroll to about the second half of the 1st century and at latest, the beginning of the 2nd century CE" wrote Ada Yardeni, an expert on Hebrew paleography ... (Law S. STATE-OF-THE-ART TECHNOLOGY PROVES THE PURITY OF BIBLICAL TEXT. Patterns of Evidence, October 7, 2016)

The Old Testament that the *Continuing* Church of God uses is based upon the Masoretic Hebrew text. It is reliable and extremely accurate. "The Old Testament is the most accurately documented book from before the time of Christ" (Ibid, p. 51).

If you already believe that the Bible is true and what books are inspired, why should this matter?

There are several reasons.

One is to be able to share the truth with others:

[15] But sanctify the Lord God in your hearts: and be ready always to give an answer to every man that asketh you a reason of the hope that is in you with meekness and fear: (1 Peter 3:15, KJV)

Because of the decline of basic biblical knowledge in Western society, combined with items that have been popular in society (the best selling book *The DaVinci Code* comes to mind) and explanations from scholars that do not truly believe the Bible, many really are confused about the veracity and accuracy of the inspired books.

Consider also that both the KJV and DRB translation of 1 Thessalonians 5:21 say to "prove all things." Proving which books of the Bible are inspired, as well as the best available early manuscripts, would seem to be a foundational matter.

> [3] If the foundations fall to ruin, what can the upright do? (Psalm 11:3, NJB)

Another reason this is important is that intense persecutions are prophesied (Daniel 7:25; 11:30-35; Revelation 12:17, 13:7, 15-17), and Christians need to be totally sure of their foundation.

Consider something that Jesus taught:

> [47] Whoever comes to Me, and hears My sayings and does them, I will show you whom he is like: [48] He is like a man building a house, who dug deep and laid the foundation on the rock. And when the flood arose, the stream beat vehemently against that house, and could not shake it, for it was founded on the rock. [49] But he who heard and did nothing is like a man who built a house on the earth without a foundation, against which the stream beat vehemently; and immediately it fell. And the ruin of that house was great. (Luke 6:47-49)

Notice the following from Isaiah:

> [4] Trust ye in Jehovah for ever, For in Jah Jehovah [is] a rock of ages, (Isaiah 26:4, Young's Literal Translation)

If people cannot totally trust God's word, they will not totally trust Him.

The word of God, including the Hebrew scriptures, is trustworthy.

Key Points on the Old Testament Canon

- The Jews in Palestine were tasked with preserving the books of the Old Testament, which were almost exclusively written in Hebrew and naturally contained no Greek.
- The originally accepted Old Testament contained 39 books as we now tend to count them.

- The oldest text fragments known are Hebrew ones dating from c. 7th century B.C., with parts of the Greek (Septuagint) text from the 2nd century B.C.
- Jesus and His disciples knew the true Old Testament books, which were those preserved by the Jews in Palestine/Judea.
- In the second century A.D., Polycarp told the Philippians that they were "well versed in the Sacred Scriptures" which points to the fact that in order to do so, they had to know what they were.
- In the 2nd century A.D., Melito, Bishop of the Church of God in Sardis (and a saint even according to Roman Catholic sources), verified that list (the so-called protocanonical books) and did not include one book from the additional ones that the Hellenists preserved (sometimes called deuterocanonical books).
- In the late 2nd century, Polycrates of Ephesus said he and others had "gone through every Holy scripture."
- In the early 3rd century, Serapion of Antioch stated that the books of the Bible had been handed down.
- In the 3rd and 4th century, Lucian of Antioch made translations of the Hebrew text and improved the Greek translation of it.
- In the 4th and 5th century, the Roman Catholic saint and doctor of that church, Jerome, put together the Latin Vulgate after consulting with Jews and Christians in Palestine.
- Jerome finished the translation in 405 A.D. and stated that he was essentially forced to include the so-called deuterocanonical books and said that they were not appropriate to be considered as scripture.
- Nazarene Christians said that God had given them the Bible.
- Proto-Waldenses and Waldenses preserved scripture during the Middle Ages.
- It took the Church of Rome until 1546 to finalize their canon.
- The Eastern Orthodox believe that the translation from the Hebrew to Greek resulted in a superior Old Testament than the original that God inspired Moses and others to write.
- It took the Eastern Orthodox until 1672 to essentially finalize their canon — which includes books that the Protestant and Roman Catholics do not accept as canonical.
- It was not until 1826 that many of the Protestants stopped including the deuterocanonical books in their Bibles.

- The true Church of God never considered that the deuterocanonical books were inspired scripture.
- Because of various scriptures, it is theologically improper to believe that God would allow His true Church to not know which books of the Old Testament He inspired until centuries after Jesus died (cf. Acts 17:11; 2 Timothy 3:16-17).

6. Lost Books of the Bible?

Book, first published in 1926, claiming that
other writings were lost/missing from the Bible

Are there lost books of the Bible? Why did the Greco-Roman-Protestants take so long to finalize their canons?

Part of the reason for the delays by the Greco-Roman-Protestants is that they considered some people to be true Christians who cited books as scripture that were not part of the true canon.

In addition to the Old Testament Apocrypha (the so-called deuterocanonical books), there were other books that some early Greco-Roman writers cited.

For example, Origen and Clement of Alexandria frequently cited the Jewish pseudepigrapha. They wrote of these books assisting with mysteries or "deeper principles" (Adler W. The Pseudepigrapha in the Early Church. In: The Canon Debate. Baker Academic, 2002).

Various Gnostics also cited those books. While the Greco-Romans have tended to distance themselves from many of the early Gnostics, it is widely admitted (including in *The Catholic Encyclopedia* article about him) that Clement of Alexandria often blended Gnosticism with his version of Christianity. And his influence, as well as Origen's, affected the churches in Rome and Egypt.

Pseudepigrapha?

What are pseudepigrapha?

The pseudepigrapha are books that attempt to imitate scripture that were written under false authorship. The term *pseudepigrapha* comes from the Greek *pseudo*, meaning 'false,' and *epigraphein*, meaning 'to inscribe.' Basically, a pseudonymous writing is one where an author is falsely claimed to have written it, when in truth someone else wrote it and, thus, tries to deceive by putting a (normally) famous person's name on it.

For example, the biblical Barnabas of the Book of Acts did not write the so-called *Epistle of Barnabas*.

There are many ancient books that fall under the category of pseudepigrapha. Those books some have tried to associate with the Old Testament/Hebrew scripture include the *Testament of Adam, Book-of Enoch, Secrets of Enoch, Book of Noah, Testament of Abraham, Testament of Job, Prayer of Joseph, Testaments of the Twelve Patriarchs, Apocalypse of Moses* (also called the *Book of the Jubilees), Assumption of Moses, 6th and 7th Books of Moses (first appeared in the 18th century), Psalter of Solomon, Odes of Solomon, Testament of Hezekiah, Vision of Isaiah, Apocalypse of Baruch (Baruch was Jeremiah's scribe according to Jeremiah 36:4), Rest of the Words of Baruch, Book of Jasher, Apocalypse of Ezra, Elijah the Prophet, Urantia,* and *Zechariah the Prophet.*

Yet all these books were written with the intent to deceive. Now with deception, normally you need to include some truth. Generally speaking, the pseudepigrapha and other improperly claimed 'scriptures' contain both truth and error.

Because there is some truth in them, some claim that they are inspired.

Consider, for example, that Satan has been shown to both quote scripture and mislead at the same time (cf. Luke 4:3-11), as well as use truth and error to tempt Eve (cf. Genesis 3:1-13).

Between 200 B.C. and 100 A.D. numerous pseudepigraphal works appeared also among the Essene Jews.

So did ones alleging to be Christian. Church of God Overseer/Bishop Serapion of Antioch used the actual Greek word, pseudepigrapha (ψευδεπιγραφα), when he denounced the false *Gospel of Peter* (Eusebius. Church History, Book 6, Chapter 12).

Although there have been many claimed to be 'lost books,' no book of the Bible has been lost. Those improperly claimed are fraudulent.

Urantia Book

The Urantia Book disagrees with the Bible in many ways. Its understanding of the Godhead is severely flawed. It claims that Michael is either Jesus or a title of Jesus. *The Urantia Book* disagrees with the accounts of Adam and Eve's creation and claims that the story of the Great Flood was made up over 1700 years after it happened.

Here is an example of its wrong teachings:

> ADAM AND EVE arrived on Urantia, from the year A.D. 1934, 37,848 years ago. It was in midseason when the Garden was in the height of bloom that they arrived. At high noon and unannounced, the two seraphic transports, accompanied by the Jerusem personnel intrusted with the transportation of the biologic uplifters to Urantia, settled slowly to the surface of the revolving planet in the vicinity of the temple of the Universal Father. All the work of rematerializing the bodies of Adam and Eve was carried on within the precincts of this newly created shrine. And from the time of their arrival ten days passed before

they were re-created in dual human form for presentation as the world's new rulers. They regained consciousness simultaneously. (The Urantia Book, Paper 74)

Adam and Eve did not arrive over 37,000 years ago, etc. So, no *The Urantia Book* is not scripture nor should it be part of the Bible.

Book of Jasher

Some writings, like *The Book of Jasher,* popped up much later. Sometimes that book has been claimed to be the *Book of Jasher* referred to in Joshua 10:13 and 2 Samuel 1:18. It is not.

"Books of Jasher. There are several (as many as five) separate works by this title, all composed much later than Biblical times" (The Book of Jasher: Referred to in Joshua and Second Samuel. J.H. PARRY & COMPANY, Salt Lake City, 1887—SacredTexts.com). Another source claimed there have been at least a dozen versions. Some assert what now exists was written before the rest of scripture, but even if that were true, that would not make *The Book of Jasher* scripture.

Here is information about it from the old Radio Church of God:

> In the <u>Schaff-Herzog Encyclopaedia of Religious Knowledge</u>, volume II, in the article "Jasher," we read: "The [original] volume itself has perished.... There have also been several books written which pretended to be the <u>Book of Jasher</u>, or, at all events, bore this title. Three of these are of Jewish origin. One is a moral treatise, written in A.D. 1394 by Rabbi Shabbatai Carmuz Levita, and exists in manuscript in the Vatican Library. Another, by Rabbi Tham (died 1171), is a treatise on the Jewish ritual. It was published in Hebrew in Italy (1544) ... The third, which is a fabulous history or the events of the Hexateuch, was probably written by a Spanish Jew of the thirteenth century, and has been published at Venice (1625) ... A fourth Book of Jasher was a palpable and malicious fraud, perpetrated by Jacob Ilive, an infidel printer and type-founder of Bristol, and published at London, in 1751, [as] <u>The Book of Jasher, translated into English from the Hebrew by Alcuin of Britain</u>, who went on a Pilgrimage into the Holy Land.

Notice that all these volumes are recent and spurious!

Now let us examine another work which speaks authoritatively on this same subject. In the Davis Dictionary of the Bible, in the article, "Jasher, in A. V. Jasher," we read: "In 1751 there appeared a volume which professed to be an English translation of The Book or Jashar (Jasher), alleged to have been found, but the production was an impudent forgery." (emphasis ours).

Other authorities have equally proved the fraudulent qualities of these books. In the Encyclopaedia Biblica, volume II, in the article, "Jasher," we also read: "In later Christian times the Book of Jasher' is the title of a ritualistic treatise by Jacob B. Meir (died 1171), and of one or two forgeries which are only remarkable for the undeserved success they obtained...."

The fraudulent volumes deceptively labeled "The Book of Jasher" contain error and contradict Scripture. They were written one or two thousand years after the authentic "Book of Jasher" had become lost. In order to cloak their fraudulent works with respectability and make them look innocent — so that readers would trust the lies and hypocrisy contained in those books — the authors of these forgeries gave them a respected Biblical name. ...

The Book of Jasher referred to in the Bible was never destined to be Scripture. Any book claiming that title today is a deliberate fraud! (L920, 1960)

Although some have claimed that the *Book of Jasher* does not contradict the Bible, that is not so. Notice a partial list of contradictions:

In Jasher 42:30-41, Rachel talks to Joseph from the grave. This is of course necromancy and is an abomination unto the Lord (Deuteronomy 18:11-12). ...

Jasher 81:40-41 says that all but Pharaoh perished in the Red Sea. Pharaoh thanks the Lord and the Lord sends an angel who casts him upon the land of Ninevah where Pharaoh reigned for a long time. ...

Jasher 32:1-40 -- Esau comes to harm Jacob but angels of the Lord scare Esau, v.55 Esau fears Jacob. Genesis 33:3 Jacob bows seven times to Esau.

Jasher 43:35 -- Isaac went from Hebron to comfort Jacob, his son, because Joseph is dead (sold). Gen. 35:27-29 Isaac died before Joseph even dreamed his dreams.

Jasher 81:38 -- "And the Waters of the sea were divided into twelve parts." Exodus 14:22 "And the children of Israel went into the midst of the sea upon the dry ground and the waters were a wall unto them on their right hand and on their left." (Schaub D. AN OVERVIEW OF THE BOOK OF JASHER (CALLED THE UPRIGHT BOOK) COMPARED TO THE AUTHORIZED KING JAMES BIBLE. Logos Research. © 2012 - 2015)

So, no, the mainly claimed version *Book of Jasher* was not inspired by God. Again, it is not that it might not have some interesting historical details that may be true, but it is not sacred scripture.

Book of Enoch

Having read the *Book of Enoch*, this author will attest that it is not scriptural nor could Enoch of the 4th and 5th chapters of the Book of Genesis possibly have written more than part of the first chapter (nor is it likely Enoch actually wrote any of it).

Beyond that, the *Book of Enoch* contains a variety of falsehoods.

For example, here is some of what the *Book of Enoch* claims:

Chapter VI

1. And it came to pass when the children of men had multiplied that in those days were born unto them beautiful and comely daughters. 2. And the angels, the children of the heaven, saw and lusted after them, and said to one another: 'Come, let us choose us wives from among the children of men and beget us children.' 3. And Semjâzâ, who was their leader, said unto them: 'I fear ye will not indeed agree to do this deed, and I alone shall

have to pay the penalty of a great sin.' 4. And they all answered him and said: 'Let us all swear an oath, and all bind ourselves by mutual imprecations not to abandon this plan but to do this thing.'

Chapter VII

1. And all the others together with them took unto themselves wives, and each chose for himself one, and they began to go in unto them and to defile themselves with them, and they taught them charms and enchantments, and the cutting of roots, and made them acquainted with plants. 2. And they became pregnant, and they bare great giants, whose height was three thousand ells: 3. Who consumed all the acquisitions of men. And when men could no longer sustain them, 4. the giants turned against them and devoured mankind. 5. And they began to sin against birds, and beasts, and reptiles, and fish, and to devour one another's flesh, and drink the blood. 6. Then the earth laid accusation against the lawless ones. (The Book of Enoch, by R.H. Charles, 1917)

Now an 'ell' is a length of 45 inches or 1.14 meters. So, according to the *Book of Enoch*, these giants were about 11,000 feet tall or a little over 3 kilometers. This is absurd.

Here is another translation of the height of the giants (which numbers the verses differently) that supposedly came from angels breeding with human females:

7:12 Whose stature was each three hundred cubits. These devoured all which the labor of men produced; until it became impossible to feed them. (The Book of Enoch the Prophet, tr. by Richard Laurence, 1883)

With a cubit about 1.5 feet, this would make those giants 450 feet tall. This is also absurd.

Let me state that Enoch was NOT on the earth by the time of the flood according to the Bible (Genesis 5:24) and did NOT state or write (there does not seem to have been writing in his day) much of what is attributed to him. While there can be value in ancient non-biblical writings, doctrine should NOT be based on them when they are in conflict with the Bible.

Notice something else from the *Book of Enoch* which conflicts with scripture:

> Chapter XL
>
> 9. And he said to me: 'This first is Michael, the merciful and long-suffering: and the second, who is set over all the diseases and all the wounds of the children of men, is Raphael: and the third, who is set over all the powers, is Gabriel: and the fourth, who is set over the repentance unto hope of those who inherit eternal life, is named Phanuel.' And these are the four angels of the Lord of Spirits and the four voices I heard in those days.

While the Bible does mention Michael and Gabriel, it does NOT mention Raphael (though the Apocrypha does, where he is a lying angel) nor does it teach that there is an angel named Phanuel over repentance. The alleged Book of Enoch also has other odd assertions.

Some claim the following proves that the *Book of Enoch* should be considered as scripture:

> [14] Now Enoch, the seventh from Adam, prophesied about these men also, saying, "Behold, the Lord comes with ten thousands of His saints, [15] to execute judgment on all, to convict all who are ungodly among them of all their ungodly deeds which they have committed in an ungodly way, and of all the harsh things which ungodly sinners have spoken against Him." (Jude 14-15)

But, the reality is that statement was from an ancient Hebrew tradition and/or God in some other way (perhaps through James' half-brother Jesus) conveyed this to James. James did not get it from the false *Book of Enoch*.

> Some have made claims that the Book of Enoch should be a part of the Bible. But the so-called 'Book of Enoch' was not written by the Patriarch Enoch who lived before the Noachian Flood.

The book was the product of first — or second-century B.C. mystical writers, thousands of years after Enoch had died.

But still some assert that Jude quoted from the apocryphal writing. Granted, there are a few passages in Jude, especially verses 15-16, which resemble sections of this uninspired Book of Enoch. But the passages are not exactly the same as the Book of Enoch -

Jude did not quote from it. Jude obtained his information directly from Jewish tradition, which this Book of Enoch also drew on. Obviously, all such tradition is not correct. But the information Jude used is accurate because God had it incorporated into inspired Scripture. The Book of Enoch, on the other hand, contains such unbiblical myths as angels marrying women, and the 'fall' of Adam. The spurious Book of Enoch was definitely not regarded as inspired by New Testament writers. (Do We Have The COMPLETE BIBLE? Ambassador College Publications, 1974)

The *Book of Enoch* is not sacred/canonical scripture.

Book of Jubilees (also called the Apocalypse of Moses)

A book that many, sadly, have been intrigued by is called the *Book of the Jubilees*. It seems to have been written in the second century B.C. It essentially claims to have been written by ten or so authors, but is basically believed to have been written by a priest who was a Pharisee. (Charles RH. The Apocrypha and Pseudepigrapha of the Old Testament. Oxford, Clarendon Press, 1913).

Its many names also include *Little Genesis*, *The Testament of Moses*, *The Book of Adam's Daughters*, and *The Life of Adam*.

One of its problems is that it essentially claims to contain a supplement to the laws in the Bible:

The author represents his book to be as a whole a revelation of God to Moses, forming a supplement to and an interpretation of the Pentateuch, which he designates 'the first law' (vi. 22).

This revelation was in part a secret republication of the traditions handed down from father to son in antediluvian and subsequent times. From the time of Moses onwards it was preserved in the hands of the priesthood, till the time came for its being made known.

Our author's procedure is of course in direct antagonism with the presuppositions of the Priests' Code in Genesis, for according to this code 'Noah may build no altar, Abraham offer no sacrifice, Jacob erect no sacred pillar. No offering is recorded till Aaron and his sons are ready' (Carpenter, The Hexateuch, i. 124). This fact seems to emphasize in the strongest manner how freely our author reinterpreted his authorities for the past (Charles RH. The Apocrypha and Pseudepigrapha of the Old Testament. Oxford, Clarendon Press, 1913).

Anyway, the *Book of Jubilees* emphasizes adding extra 'rules' and 'laws' that seemed to be based upon traditions of the Pharisees. Jesus condemned the reliance on those traditions above the true word of God (Mark 7:9-13). The *Book of Jubilees* is not part of the true Bible.

One of the other things it attempts to do is to assign specific dates to various events in the Old Testament without biblical support. Furthermore, the author of the Book of Jubilees advocates a solar calendar based on days and months rather than on the biblical, lunar-based calendar. Some scholars have speculated that the book was written exactly for that purpose — to push its author's idea that the solar-based calendar more accurately represents the Jubilee and provides for a better understanding of prophecy. Those who rely on it will be misled prophetically also.

The *Book of Jubilees* is considered to be part of the pseudepigrapha by the *Continuing* Church of God as well as Protestant, Roman Catholic, and Eastern Orthodox Churches.

Yet, the Ethiopian Orthodox Church believes it is inspired scripture. But without going into all the details, that church does not "contend earnestly for the faith that was once for all delivered to the saints" (Jude 3). Furthermore, its canon consists of 81 books, including additional New Testament ones that are not accepted by the *Continuing* Church of

God as well as Protestant, Roman Catholic, and the other Eastern Orthodox Churches.

Lost Books of the New Testament?

Various books also make up the pseudepigrapha some have claimed should be part of the New Testament. These include *the Father of John, Gospel According to the Egyptians, Gospel of the Birth of Mary, Gospel of Mary Magdalene, The Acts of Peter, The Apocalypse of the Virgin, the Itinerary of Paul, the Acts of Paul, Apocalypse of Paul, Gospel of Peter, Itinerary of Peter, Itinerary of Thomas, Gospel According to Thomas, Gospel of Jesus' Wife, the History of James, the Apocalypse of Peter,* and the *Epistles of Barnabas*.

The best selling novel *The Da Vinci Code*, popularized a couple of those false 'gospels.' It basically, and falsely, claimed that the 4th century Emperor Constantine eliminated many in order to suppress women. The book also stated:

> More than *eighty* gospels were considered for the New Testament, and yet only a relative few were chosen for inclusion--Matthew, Mark, Luke, and John. (*The Da Vinci Code*, page 231)

But, of course, second century pseudepigraphal writings being referred to in a book of fiction, does not make the books canonical. Furthermore, the idea that there were four, and only four, gospel accounts was recorded by Irenaeus in the 2nd century (Irenaeus. Adversus Haereses, Book III, Chapter XI, verse 8).

Additionally, the true Christian church never considered the false gospels as canonical, nor did the faithful cite them as scripture. The Apostle John passed on to Overseer/Bishop/Pastor Polycarp the canon in the late 1st century, and that was before nearly all the false gospels were even written.

Let's look at some of the false books to show that their content also eliminated them.

False Gospel Accounts

The Apostle Paul warned about writings "as if from us" (2 Thessalonians 2:2), hence he knew that false writings were seemingly being produced and/or soon would be produced.

That happened.

Sometimes on purpose, sometimes through insinuation.

This author's reading of the so-called *Gospel of Philip* suggests it is simply called the *Gospel of Philip* because it allegedly quotes the Apostle Philip in ONE passage:

> Philip the apostle said, "Joseph the carpenter planted a garden because he needed wood for his trade. It was he who made the cross from the trees which he planted. His own offspring hung on that which he planted. His offspring was Jesus, and the planting was the cross."

There is nothing in the Bible to suggest, or even hint, that the above is true. Nor is there any indication in the Bible that Philip ever said anything about a cross.

Perhaps it should be mentioned that the word commonly mistranslated as "cross" in the New Testament is the koine Greek word σταυρός (stauros) which simply meant "a pole in the ground" (Bauer W, Danker FW. A Greek-English Lexicon of the New Testament, 3rd edition. University of Chicago, 2000, p. 941).

Notice something else from the *Gospel of Philip*:

> The world came about through a mistake. For he who created it wanted to create it imperishable and immortal. He fell short of attaining his desire.

This is blasphemous as God did not make the world through a mistake.

The fact is that the Bible records that there was an apostle named Philip (John 1:45-48). In the late 2nd century, Polycrates records that the

Apostle Philip kept the Passover on the 14th, and he and the other followers of Christ, did what the scriptures said (Eusebius. The History of the Church, Book V, Chapter XXIV, Verses 2-7). Those are the true facts about Philip.

Furthermore, the so-called *Gospel of Philip* has virtually nothing in common with the canononical gospels (Matthew, Mark, Luke, and John). The so-called *Gospel of Philip* simply does not read like a gospel account. It does not have the narrative of Jesus' death and resurrection, does not discuss miracles, nor does it even much discuss His teachings.

It reads like a Gnostic account of mystic knowledge. Here is one such passage:

> Light and Darkness, life and death, right and left, are brothers of one another. They are inseparable. Because of this neither are the good good, nor evil evil, nor is life life, nor death death. For this reason each one will dissolve into its earliest origin. But those who are exalted above the world are indissoluble, eternal.
>
> Names given to the worldly are very deceptive, for they divert our thoughts from what is correct to what is incorrect. Thus one who hears the word "God" does not perceive what is correct, but perceives what is incorrect. (The Gospel of Philip. THE GNOSTIC SOCIETY LIBRARY. James M. Robinson, ed., *The Nag Hammadi Library*, revised edition. HarperCollins, San Francisco, 1990)

Another problem with the so-called *Gospel of Philip* is that it clearly contradicts the biblical accounts in various areas. Here is one such contradictory passage:

> Some said, "Mary conceived by the Holy Spirit." They are in error. (ibid)

Yet, the Bible itself teaches that Mary conceived by the Holy Spirit in Luke 1:26-38. Therefore, it should be clear that no one who professes Christ and believes in the virgin birth, as taught in the Bible, could possibly accept the claims in the Philip 'gospel' account.

Perhaps it needs to be mentioned that the so-called gospels of Thomas, Mary Magdalene, Judas, James, Peter, Philip, and Barnabas were not written by the famous people in their titles — they are also pseudepigrapha. Nor were they accepted by faithful Christians as inspired by God (though some Greco-Roman types accepted some of them for a while).

The *Gospel of Thomas* is held by certain scholars to be the earliest of the "gnostic" gospels composed. Scholars generally date the Gnostic 'gospels' text to the early-late 2nd century (Ehrman B. Lost Christianities. New York: Oxford University Press, 2003, pp. xi–xii).

Most scholars do not believe that any of them were written until after John, the last of the original apostles, died (e.g. Ibid).

The *Gospel of Thomas* wrongly teaches the following:

> 49. Jesus said, "Congratulations to those who are alone and chosen, for you will find the kingdom. For you have come from it, and you will return there again."
>
> 50. Jesus said, "If they say to you, 'Where have you come from?' say to them, 'We have come from the light, from the place where the light came into being by itself, established [itself], and appeared in their image.'
>
> 114. Simon Peter said to them, "Make Mary leave us, for females don't deserve life."
>
> Jesus said, "Look, I will guide her to make her male, so that she too may become a living spirit resembling you males. For every female who makes herself male will enter the kingdom of Heaven."

Jesus did not say that people came from the Kingdom or the light, but that He came from above (John 8:23) and that God will give His flock the Kingdom (Luke 12:32) — not that they once had it to receive again. And statements that females don't deserve life and must become males is blasphemous, as well as in conflict with scripture (e.g. Galatians 3:28, Mark 12:23-25).

The so-called *Gospel of Jesus' Wife* has been recognized as a forgery (Kruger, p. 16).

The so-called *Gospel of Mary Magdalene* is so unlike the rest of the Bible, that even within it, it states that one of the apostles did not believe that Jesus had spoken various things to Mary Magdalene:

> Chapter 9
>
> 1) When Mary had said this, she fell silent, since it was to this point that the Savior had spoken with her.
>
> 2) But Andrew answered and said to the brethren, Say what you wish to say about what she has said. I at least do not believe that the Savior said this. For certainly these teachings are strange ideas. (The Gospel According to Mary Magdalene. THE GNOSTIC SOCIETY LIBRARY, Gnostic Scriptures and Fragments)

In other words, even within the so-called 'Gospel of Mary Magdalene' an original apostle allegedly states that it contains strange teachings.

Greco-Roman Confusion

There were also problems that the Greco-Romans had with books like the false *Apocalypse of Peter, the Epistle of Barnabas, the Shepherd of Hermas, the Gospel of Thomas, 1 Clement, the Didache, Acts of Paul, Acts of Andrew, Acts of John,* and the *Gospel of Peter*. These books were not accepted by the true Church of God in Asia Minor or Antioch as inspired, but were accepted for a time by various Greco-Roman churches in Rome and in Alexandria. (Akin, pp. 136-138). Canon 85 of the *Apostolic Constitutions*, c. 380, includes the "two Epistles of Clement" among its "sacred books" (Apostolic Constitutions. From Ante-Nicene Fathers, Vol. 7. Edited by Alexander Roberts, James Donaldson, and A. Cleveland Coxe. 1886).

The *Apocalypse of Peter* claims that Jesus did not really die, in conflict with New Testament scriptures (e.g. John 19:30, Romans 6:10, 2 Corinthians 5:15), but instead laughed as His physical body was killed (Bock, p. 107).

Justin, who moved to Rome, looks to have cited the *Gospel of Peter* (First Apology Chapter 6) just like he cited canonical books (Bruce, The Canon of Scripture, pp. 200-201). He also taught such false doctrines as that fasting brings the remission of past sins (The First Apology. Chapter 61), Jesus was born in a cave like the sun-god Mithras (Trypho, Chapters 70,78), Satan did not blaspheme God until after Jesus came (Irenaeus. Against Heresies. Book 5, Chapter 26), and more.

Later, Roman Bishop and saint Hippolytus looks to have cited the *Gospel of Thomas* (Hippolytus. Refutation of Heresies, Book 5) just like he cited canonical books (Bruce, The Canon of Scripture, p. 201).

The Gnostic Valentinus wrote in the mid-2nd century something falsely called the *Gospel of Truth*. It appears to be the earliest record of something that resembles the Greco-Roman trinity. Valentinus was denounced by Polycarp of Smyrna, and decades later by the Church of Rome, as a heretic. There is also something called the *Letter to Rheginos*, that Valentinus influenced, that claimed that the resurrection of 1 Corinthians 15:51-54 had taken place for Rheginos (Bock, p. 103) — that is in conflict with scripture.

Origen of Alexandria called what should be considered to be the 'demonically-influenced' *Shepherd of Hermas* as "divinely inspired" (Cited in Metzger, Bruce M. The Canon of the New Testament: Its Origin, Development, and Significance. Clarendon Press. Oxford. 1987, p.140). While accepting Revelation, in his *Homologoumena*, he mentioned Hebrews, 2 Peter, 1 and 2 John, James, and Jude as "contested writings," while (c. 250) "St. Cyprian, whose Scriptural Canon certainly reflects the contents of the first Latin Bible, received all the books of the New Testament except Hebrews, II Peter, James, and Jude" (Reid, Canon of the New Testament).

Origen seems to also have possibly accepted the falsely titled *Gospel of Peter* (see Commentary on Matthew, Book X, Verse 17. In Roberts and Donaldson).

Perhaps it should be mentioned that while Origen was from Alexandria, he did visit Rome and spent time with a Bishop of Rome named Zephyrinus. It is believed that in the second century the apostate, Justin (who went to Rome from Asia Minor) cited the false *Gospel of Peter* in one of his writings (First Apology, Chapter 36, verse 6; see also Bruce, The Canon of Scripture, pp. 200-201).

Perhaps it should be pointed out that this author does not believe that the faithful among the 4th century Nazarenes canonically used the Gospel of Peter. We agree with various ones that Theodoret (who made a Gospel of Peter connection) misidentified them with the Ebionites (e.g. Krauss S. Nazarenes. Jewish Encyclopedia, 1906).

One way to prove that the *Gospel of Peter* is false is to consider the following quote from it:

> [55] And having gone off, they found the sepulcher opened. And having come forward, they bent down there and saw there a certain young man seated in the middle of the sepulcher, comely and clothed with a splendid robe, who said to them: [56] 'Why have you come? Whom do you seek? Not that one who was crucified? He is risen and gone away. But if you do not believe, bend down and see the place where he lay, because he is not here. For he is risen and gone away to there whence he was sent.' [57] Then the women fled frightened.
>
> [58] Now it was the final day of the Unleavened Bread; and many went out returning to their home since the feast was over.

Jesus was killed on Passover and put in the tomb just prior to the first Day of Unleavened Bread, which was a 'high day' (John 19:31). Since there are seven days of Unleavened Bread (Leviticus 23:6-8) and Jesus said He would be in the grave three days and three nights (Matthew 12:40), He would have been resurrected several days prior to the final day of Unleavened Bread. Hence, the *Gospel of Peter* is in conflict with the canonical gospels and is false.

Eusebius records that Serapion of Antioch went to see a group that he thought was Christian in the seaside port of Rhossus. When he got there, he was disappointed to learn that they were reading this *Gospel of Peter* and thus he realized that they were not all part of the 'true faith,' so Serapion stated:

For we, brethren, receive both Peter and the other apostles as Christ; but we reject intelligently the writings falsely inscribed with them, knowing that such were not handed down to. When I visited you I supposed that all of you held the true faith ... I had not read the Gospel which they put forth under the name of Peter ... we have been able to read it through and, and we find many things in accordance with the true doctrine of the Saviour, but some things added to that doctrine ... (Eusebius. The History of the Church, Book VI, Chapter XII, verses 3-4, p. 125-126)

Serapion is clearly denouncing the pseudepigrapha — even if it did contain some truth. This denouncement is believed to have happened in the late 2nd century (Bock DL. The Missing Gospels. Thomas Nelson, 2006, p. 78). Further notice that Serapion said he had NOT read it before (hence it was not being used in his church in Antioch) and he was teaching that the proper books were "handed down to us" (or "received" as it has alternatively been translated). The true books were known and accepted by the faithful long before any canonical Greco-Roman council.

Items such as the false *Gospel of Peter* show there was canonical confusion within the Greco-Roman churches — confusion that we did not see in the faithful churches in Asia Minor nor Antioch for that period.

This canonical confusion is probably because historical records show that Asia Minor and Antioch communicated with each other until at least the early third century, yet they did not seem to try to communicate much with Alexandria, Jerusalem, or Rome by then (they tried with Rome at least twice in the 2nd century — once when Polycarp tried to get the Roman Bishop Anicetus to change the date of Passover and second when Polycrates wrote the Roman Bishop Victor that he did not recognize Victor's authority over the word of God).

Also, the fact that the *Gospel of Peter*, Sections 12-14, suggests that the resurrection of Jesus was on the last day of unleavened bread — which is clearly in conflict with the canonical gospels — may have also been a major factor in Rome and Alexandria finally rejecting that book. But again, the faithful did not rely on it from the beginning.

All the New Testament books accepted by the *Continuing* Church of God and most other churches were written before the close of the first century.

So, where did the others come from and why?

Before going further, here is the position of Darrell Bock, a research professor at Dallas Theological Seminary and the author of the book *The Missing Gospels*:

> We have 52 books that are not in our Bible from the second and third centuries that give evidence of a kind of Christianity that is an attempt to meld Greco-Roman philosophy and Christianity – and to make Christianity more palatable to a Greco-Roman world. That is really what those texts are about. (Carpenter C. The Missing Gospels: Unearthing the Truth Behind Alternative Christianities. CBN, 2016)

While that is somewhat correct, it is only partially so. Some of the non-canonical books were produced by Gnostics and others who wanted to have 'proof' for non-biblical doctrines. History also shows that the Greco-Roman churches themselves intentionally partially melded Greco-Roman philosophy with their practice of Christianity (e.g. Catechism of the Catholic Church. Imprimatur Potest + Joseph Cardinal Ratzinger. Doubleday, NY 1995, p. 74).

Greco-Roman canonical confusion was a factor in certain improper doctrines being adopted. These later became entrenched traditions, before those groups adopted the proper New Testament canon. Consider that the false Apocalypse of Peter pushed wrong views of heaven and punishment in Hades. The improperly named Epistle of Barnabas endorsed allegory and unclean meat consumption. The falsely named Gospel of Peter looks to be the oldest document that wrongly identified Sunday as the Lord's Day. The Shepherd of Hermas pushed the idea of penance, that Bishop Callistus later endorsed. And allegedly Hermas, claimed to have an angelic vision changing Passover to Sunday. Sadly those, and many other improper traditions exist in those churches to this day—they were not discarded when the books were later rejected as canonical. It is important to know which books were and were not inspired by God.

Origins of the False Gospels

As far as origins of other 'gospels' go, there is also a story, preserved by Arab sources, that apparently took place between 130-135 A.D. which gives another reason:

> (71a) ... (And the Romans) said: "Go, fetch your companions, and bring your Book (*kitab*)." (The Christians) went to their companions, informed them of (what had taken place) between them and the Romans and said to them: "Bring the Gospel (*al-injil*), and stand up so that we should go to them."

> But these (companions) said to them: "You have done ill. We are not permitted (to let) the Romans pollute the Gospel. In giving a favourable answer to the Romans, you have accordingly departed from the religion. We are (therefore) no longer permitted to associate with you; on the contrary, we are obliged to declare that there is nothing in common between us and you;" and they prevented their (taking possession of) the Gospel or gaining access to it. In consequence a violent quarrel (broke out) between (the two groups). Those (mentioned in the first place) went back to the Romans and said to them: "Help us against these companions of ours before (helping us) against the Jews, and take away from them on our behalf our Book (*kitab*)." Thereupon (the companions of whom they had spoken) fled the country. And the Romans wrote concerning them to their governors in the districts of Mosul and in the Jazirat al-'Arab. Accordingly, a search was made for them; some (*qawm*) were caught and burned, others (*qawm*) were killed. (As for) those who had given a favorable answer to the Romans they came together and took counsel as to how to replace the Gospel, seeing it was lost to them. (Thus) the opinion that a Gospel should be composed (*yunshi`u*) was established among them...a certain number of Gospels were written. (Pines S. The Jewish Christians of the Early Centuries of Christianity according to a New Source. Proceedings of the Israel Academy of Sciences and Humanities, Volume II, No.13; 1966. Jerusalem, pp. 14-15)

Now this account is important for many reasons. One is that it shows that the companions (those who distanced themselves from the

Romans/Latins) had the Gospels and likely all the other books of the New Testament. Another, is that it shows that those who were inclined to compromise with the Romans did not have the biblical books—it was the true COG, and not the group that became Eastern Orthodox, that maintained the chain of custody of scriptures.

Additionally, it shows that those associated with the Romans developed false gospels, which is probably why it took a while for the Greco-Romans to get their New Testament straightened out.

Furthermore, history records that there were positive communications between those faithful Christians in Asia Minor, Judea, and Antioch during the 2nd and early 3rd centuries (Eusebius. The History of the Church, Book IV, Chapter XXVI and Book V, Chapters 18-19), not really with Rome. This indicates that it was the faithful in Asia Minor and Antioch, as well as those that did not wish to compromise with the Romans in Judea, that had the canon in the second century.

Essentially, the Arab-preserved account shows that those who were willing to compromise with the Romans did not have the four gospels. So, some made 'gospels' up—apparently through their own imaginations as well as using memories, stories, and/or rumors that circulated at that time.

Other false gospels came from Gnostic and pagan sources, essentially to teach whatever the false teachers wanted to teach.

Doctrine of the Perpetual Virginity of Mary

Various ones have pointed to non-canonical books as proof that Jesus' mother Mary was a "perpetual virgin."

While the claimed "perpetual virginity" of Mary is now a Roman Catholic dogma, it was not until the 6th century, that the Greco-Roman "Fifth General Council (553) gives Mary the title of honour 'perpetual virgin' " (Ott L. Fundamentals of Catholic Dogma, 4th ed. Imprimatur: + Cornelius, 7 October 1954, Printed 1974, TAN Books, p. 206).

Origen of Alexandria basically stated that this 'doctrine' was based upon two false gospels:

> And they spoke, wondering, (not knowing that He was the son of a virgin, or not believing it even if it was told to them, but supposing that He was the son of Joseph the carpenter,) "is not this the carpenter's son?" And depreciating the whole of what appeared to be His nearest kindred, they said, "Is not His mother called Mary? And His brethren, James and Joseph and Simon and Judas? And His sisters, are they not all with us?" They thought, then, that He was the son of Joseph and Mary. But some say, basing it on a tradition in the Gospel according to Peter, as it is entitled, or "The Book of James," that the brethren of Jesus were sons of Joseph by a former wife, whom he married before Mary. Now those who say so wish to preserve the honour of Mary in virginity to the end. (Origen. Commentary on Matthew, Book X, 17)

The Book of James in this case, is not the epistle found in the New Testament, but instead the book known as the *Protoevangelium of James*. It is one of the pseudepigraphal books. Yet, supporters of the 'perpetual virginity of Mary' have often cited it as proof.

And, as mentioned before, the book(s) called the *Gospel of Peter* was (were) not written by Peter.

Relying on false books leads to false teachings. Despite this, notice something from the 19th century Protestant historian Philip Schaff:

> Origen was the greatest scholar of his age, and the most gifted, most industrious, and most cultivated of all the ante-Nicene fathers. … His great defect is the neglect of the grammatical and historical sense and his constant desire to find hidden meaning. (Schaff P. Ante-Nicene Christianity, A.D. 100-325, Volume 2. Wm. B. Eerdmans, 1910, pp. 790,792)

No, if being a real Christian matters, Origen was not the greatest scholar. Yet his 'scholarship' resulted in the greater acceptance of not relying on the truest manuscripts and the excessive acceptance of allegory (e.g. Origen. De Principiis, Book II, Chapter IV, Verse 4. Excerpted from Ante-Nicene Fathers, Volume 4. Edited by Alexander Roberts & James Donaldson. American Edition, 1885).

The Qur'an

After the rise of Muhammed in the 7th century, writings were put together in what is called the *Qur'an*. The *Qur'an* is the holy book of the Muslims. Though Muslims theoretically consider the Old and New Testaments are sacred, they believe that the Jews and Greco-Romans tampered with them to the point that they do not consider the Bible to be reliable.

The *Qur'an* itself denies Jesus being the Son of God, disputes various accounts in the New Testament, and teaches its own ideas about salvation.

(For a biblical approach to salvation, see the free online book: *Universal OFFER of Salvation, Apokatastasis: Can God save the lost in an age to come? Hundreds of scriptures reveal God's plan of salvation*.)

Christians did not accept the contents of the *Qur'an* as divine when written, nor do they today.

Book of Mormon

The Latter Day Saints (LDS) movement uses what is commonly called the *Book of Mormon*. It consists of 15 books which adherents believe contains writings of ancient prophets who lived on the American continent from approximately 2200 B.C. to A.D. 421. They were allegedly revealed to Joseph Smith in the 19th century and first published by him in 1830.

No early Christian saint is believed to have used or otherwise relied upon the *Book of Mormon*.

Without going into a lot of details about why this is not accepted as scripture, it is believed that a couple of quotes from the books should suffice.

Let's start with the following:

> [10] And behold, he shall be born of Mary, at Jerusalem which is the land of our forefathers, she being a virgin, a precious and

chosen vessel, who shall be overshadowed and conceive by the power of the Holy Ghost, and bring forth a son, yea, even the Son of God. (Alma 7:10)

The Bible teaches that Jesus would be born in Bethlehem (Micah 5:2) and that He was born there (Matthew 2:1). Hence, Alma 7:10 is in error.

Here is another:

[20] But behold, as I said unto you concerning another sign, a sign of his death, behold, in that day that he shall suffer death the sun shall be darkened and refuse to give his light unto you; and also the moon and the stars; and there shall be no light upon the face of this land, even from the time that he shall suffer death, for the space of three days, to the time that he shall rise again from the dead. (Helaman 14:20)

But the Bible does not teach three days of darkness while Jesus was being executed on the stake, but three hours (Luke 23:44).

Perhaps it should also be mentioned that the account of the language situation with Jaredites in Ether 1:33-39 is in conflict with the account of the Tower of Babel in Genesis 11.

The *Book of Mormon* is in conflict with the Bible.

Neither the *Book of Mormon*, the 'lost books,' or the Apocrypha were part of the Hebrew or Greek scriptures. None of them are accepted by the *Continuing* Church of God as divinely inspired.

7. New Testament Predicted in the Old? To Be Published in the New?

It has been claimed that the New Testament "is the most magnificent book in the world — greater than the Old Testament because the New Testament interprets the Old" (Coulter, p.32).

Perhaps it should be added that there is a passage in the Old Testament that predicts a New Testament as it shows that the disciples would essentially finalize the Bible. Notice:

> [16] Bind up the testimony, Seal the law among my disciples. (Isaiah 8:16)

While other portions of this book have shown that various of Christ's disciples were involved, the above verse suggests that there would be no additions 'to the law and to the testimony' (an expression for the Bible, see Isaiah 8:20) after those disciples were gone. Isaiah is thus indicating that Jesus' original disciples would have finalized the New Testament — that would include people such as Peter, Paul, and John.

F.F. Bruce observed:

> The New Testament was complete, or substantially complete, about AD 100, the majority of the writings being in existence twenty to forty years before this. (Bruce FF. The New Testament Documents: Are They Reliable? 6th edition, pp. 6-7)

Before the Apostle John's death (c. A.D. 100), the New Testament for the church age was totally complete.

Early Documents

The cover of this book shows the reverse side of Rylands Library Papyrus P52, also known as the St. John's fragment. It is believed to date from around A.D. 100 (90-125 A.D.) and is the oldest confirmed fragment of the New Testament (there is a document from Qumran, 7Q5, once dated no later than A.D. 50 that was claimed by Priest José O'Callaghan, to be a Greek text from Mark's Gospel, but the fragment is so unreadable that most scholars are not yet convinced that it is a text from Mark — but it is possible that it could be. It may take better detection equipment to determine this for certainty. Another fragment from Mark, known as P137, has been dated to what seems to be the late 2nd century).

While only parts of the original Greek are shown in Rylands Library Papyrus P52, what is interesting is that it contains John 18:37-38. Here is the full statement of those verses:

> 37 Pilate therefore said to Him, "Are You a king then?"
>
> Jesus answered, "You say rightly that I am a king. For this cause I was born, and for this cause I have come into the world, that I should bear witness to the truth. Everyone who is of the truth hears My voice."
>
> 38 Pilate said to Him, "What is truth?" And when he had said this, he went out again to the Jews, and said to them, "I find no fault in Him at all. (John 18:37-38)

Pilate did not wait for the answer. He, like many, either did not recognize truth and/or did not believe that there was absolute truth. Jesus taught:

> 17 Sanctify them by Your truth. Your word is truth. (John 17:17)

Christians are to be set apart by believing and living the truth of the Bible.

The Book of Proverbs teaches:

> 19 So that your trust may be in the Lord; I have instructed you today, even you. 20 Have I not written to you excellent things Of counsels and knowledge, 21 That I may make you know the certainty of the words of truth, That you may answer words of truth To those who send to you? (Proverbs 22:19-21)

Christians should have absolute certainty of the words of truth (cf. Luke 1:1-4).

Perhaps it should be pointed out that one of the reasons we do not have certain early manuscripts is that in the early 4th century, Emperor Diocletian "compelled Christians to turn over their sacred writings to the authorities to be burned" and many, though not all, did comply instead of facing punishment (McDonald LM, Sanders JA. The Canon Debate. Baker Academic, 2002, p. 417).

Was Publishing Predicted?

Was publishing the gospel in written form predicted by Jesus?

One of the more recent Bible translations, called *A Faithful Version*, has the following:

> 10 And the gospel must first be published among all nations. (Mark 13:10, AFV)

Notice something else from that translator:

> 14 And this gospel of the kingdom shall be proclaimed in all the world for a witness to all nations; and then shall the end come. (Matthew 24:14, AFV)

Although the *Strong's Exhaustive Concordance* number is the same for the words 'published' and 'proclaimed' in Mark 13:10 and Matthew 24:14 respectively (Strong's #2784), the actual Greek is not identical in those texts.

There are minor differences in the verb tenses of the Greek terms translated as published and proclaimed in Mark 13:10 and Matthew 24:14 respectively. The Greek term transliterated by BibleSoft as *keeruchtheénai* in Mark 13:10 differs from the term transliterated as *keeruchtheésetai* in Matthew 24:14.

In Mark 13:10 the verb is in the infinitive form, whereas in Matthew 24:14 it is in the third person singular future passive indicative form. According to the AFV translator (telecom between Fred Coulter and Bob Thiel, August 24, 2017), what is more important was not the minor differences of the verb, but other Greek words in Mark 13:10 that were not in Matthew 24:14. Those other words in Mark 13:10 are transliterated by BibleSoft as *proóton deí* and mean *first must*. The translator stated that the Greek is showing that Jesus was saying that the gospel MUST be in written form to be published (Mark 13:10), so then it could be preached to the world as a witness (Matthew 24:14). Therefore, he stated that is why he translated the Greek terms differently.

Perhaps it should be mentioned that the translation in the AFV is consistent with that of the original King James:

> [10] And the gospel must first be published among all nations. (Mark 13:10, KJV)

> [14] And this gospel of the kingdom will be preached in all the world as a witness to all the nations, and then the end will come. (Matthew 24:14, KJV)

(This is also consistent with *Thayer's Greek English-Lexicon*.) Thus, we see that the actual Greek supports that there was a plan to get the written word to the world as a witness from the time of Jesus. Jesus further confirmed this when He told John to write the Book of Revelation (Revelation 1:1,11). (Note: This is not clear from the English NKJV which uses "preached" in the accounts in Mark 13:10 & Matthew 24:14.)

This plan is one of many reason why there are so many ancient copies of portions of the New Testament—over 5,800 (Holden, p. 103). So, despite Imperial burnings etc., there are still more copies of parts of the New Testament than any other comparable ancient document.

8. The New Testament

What about the canon of the New Testament?

The same 27 books are agreed to by the Church of God, Church of Rome, Eastern Orthodox, Jehovah's Witnesses, and traditional Protestant faiths (though many rely on less accurate manuscripts).

The Bible does not in one place lay out all the steps of how the New Testament canon was finalized. Yet by relying on the scriptural position that all scripture is profitable for doctrine (2 Timothy 3:15-16) and that 'precept must be upon precept, precept upon precept, Line upon line, line upon line, Here a little, there a little' (Isaiah 28:10), it becomes clearer how the NT canon came about by the time of the Apostle John's death.

Yet, *The Catholic Encyclopedia* asserts the following:

> The idea of a complete and clear-cut canon of the New Testament existing from the beginning, that is from Apostolic times, has no foundation in history. (Reid G. Canon of the New Testament. The Catholic Encyclopedia. Vol. 3., 1908)

The above is only true if one considers that the Vatican has always represented the true Christian church.

If, however, one believes the Bible and considers the fact that the Church of Rome was not dominating all of Christendom in the first and second centuries—which their own scholars recognize (Duffy E. Saints & Sinners: A History of the Popes. Yale University Press, New Haven, CT, 2002, pp.2,6; Sullivan F.A. From Apostles to Bishops: the development of the episcopacy in the early church. Newman Press, Mahwah, NJ, 2001, pp. 13-15,147)— then the idea that the true Christian Church knew the books from the beginning does have a foundation.

Yet, contemporary Protestant scholars often take the Roman Catholic view:

> The canon of the NT, as commonly received at present, was ratified by the third council of Carthage (A.D. 397.) (Unger M. The New Unger's Bible Dictionary. Moody Press, 2009, p. 204)

But the view of early Christians, including Greco-Roman Catholic ones, was that the New Testament canon was known at the time of the apostles.

Consider this from Augustine of Hippo:

> In order to leave room for such profitable discussions of difficult questions, there is a distinct boundary line separating all productions subsequent to apostolic times from the authoritative canonical books of the Old and New Testaments. The authority of these books has come down to us from the apostles through the successions of bishops and the extension of the Church. (Augustine. Contra Faustum, Book XI, chapter 5)

Augustine is acknowledging that the canon came from the apostles, that bishops/overseers confirmed this, and thus what he considered to be the church accepted it. He did not indicate that the books were unknown and that a council was needed to determine the books.

Bishops, like Polycarp of Smyrna and Serapion of Antioch, who had succession from the apostles, confirmed that they knew the writings handed down from the apostles.

The late Dr. Ernest Martin wrote:

> Some historians would have people believe that the church of the early 2nd century (or even the 3rd or 4th century) probably formulated the final New Testament. There has always been a problem with this appraisal because there is not a sliver of evidence that such a thing took place. The truth is, when the early church fathers began to talk about the canon of the New Testament near the end of the 2nd century, it is assumed that it was already in their midst. The first recorded discussion among Catholic scholars about the books of the New Testament only concerned whether certain books in the canon were of lesser rank, not which books were needed to form the official canon. (Eusebius, Ecclesiastical History III.25). (Martin E. Restoring the Original Bible. A.S.K. 1994, p 295)

If you read Dr. Martin's reference to Eusebius, you will see that Eusebius did not refer to the Church of Rome in that chapter, but that some people had doubts about the Book of Revelation as well as other books.

Biblical Foundation of the Canon of the New Testament

Jesus is identified as "the Word" four times in the first chapter of John's Gospel (1:1,14). This fact alone should give us pause to consider that the word of God is something that God wanted all to highly value.

Between them, the Apostles Peter, John, and Paul wrote 21 of the 27 books of the NT (plus, between them, they personally knew all the other NT writers). The Bible also suggests that Peter, John, and Paul all had roles in the process of finalizing the NT canon. Even though many Roman Catholics believe that their church 'gave the Bible to the world,' the Church of Rome admits that it wrote none of the books of the NT (though as it includes all the writers as theirs, they would in that sense).

Peter wrote:

> [15] Moreover I will be careful to ensure that you always have a reminder of these things after my decease...[19] And so we have the prophetic word confirmed, which you do well to heed as a light that shines in a dark place, until the day dawns and the morning star rises in your hearts; [20] knowing this first, that no prophecy of Scripture is of any private interpretation, [21] for prophecy never came by the will of man, but holy men of God spoke as they were moved by the Holy Spirit. (2 Peter 1:15, 19-21)

Thus, the Bible teaches that God gave scripture to humans. 2 Peter 1:15 demonstrates that Peter intended for God's teachings to be remembered — and since he was writing at the time, this (as well as common sense) suggests that properly preserving canonical writings would be the way to accomplish this.

Since the Bible, in 1 Peter 1:25, teaches, "But the word of the LORD endures forever," it would not seem to be biblically correct to believe that portions of it were lost for centuries — which is the prevailing view that the world's scholars hold to!

The Bible is not any church's book in the sense that any church has authority to change it, add to it or subtract from it (cf. John 10:35; 2 Peter 3:16-17; Revelation 22:18-19). On the contrary, God gave the Book to the Church so that its members should accept it, submit to it and live by every word of it (Matthew 4:4), and proclaim it (cf. Matthew 28:19-20).

The Apostle Paul wrote:

> [16] Let the word of Christ dwell in you richly in all wisdom, (Colossians 3:12)

When Paul wrote that, the words of Jesus had already been recorded in the Gospels. Early Christian leaders must have known what they were.

Paul also wrote:

> [16] All Scripture is given by inspiration of God, and is profitable for doctrine, for reproof, for correction, for instruction in righteousness, [17] That the man of God may be complete, thoroughly equipped for every good work. (2 Timothy 3:16-17)

These verses show that it was necessary to know what ALL SCRIPTURE was. Otherwise, the man of God could never be complete, etc. Thus, the New Testament canon must have been finalized by the end of the first century A.D., before the last Apostle (John) died.

Paul basically makes a supporting point in Ephesians 6:13-17:

> [13] Therefore take up the whole armor of God, that you may be able to withstand in the evil day, and having done all, to stand. [14] Stand therefore, having girded your waist with truth, having put on the breastplate of righteousness, [15] and having shod your feet with the preparation of the gospel of peace; [16] above all, taking the shield of faith with which, you will be able to quench all the fiery darts of the wicked one. [17] And take the helmet of salvation, and the sword of the Spirit, which is the word of God;

If the proper New Testament canon would not be known for 300 or more years, then this would result in a massively incomplete word of God, which would represent a broken sword of the Spirit. Since a broken sword is of little value 'and the Scripture cannot be broken' (John 10:35), it makes no sense that there would not have been a reliable New Testament canon that the true Church of God recognized by the end of the first century.

Furthermore, the Bible clearly teaches that the faithful, at least in Thessalonica, understood that Paul's teachings were scripture (1 Thessalonians 2:13). Plus, Paul instructed them to be read in church (e.g. Colossians 4:16; 1 Thessalonians 5:27), and they were (cf. 2 Corinthians 10:9).

It should also be noted that the Bible teaches:

> [12] For the word of God is living and powerful, and sharper than any two-edged sword, piercing even to the division of soul and spirit, and of joints and marrow, and is a discerner of the thoughts and intents of the heart. (Hebrews 4:12)

It would not be possible for the word of God to be sharper than any two-edged sword if it was dulled because the true Church did not know what it was! The word of God could also not be much of a discerner of thoughts if the word of God itself had not been properly discerned.

The Bible clearly shows that there were false teachers in New Testament times that should not be relied upon (e.g. 2 Peter 2:1, 1 John 4:1, 2 Corinthians 11:12-13), including some with false writings (2 Thessalonians 2:2).

The Book of Revelation states:

> [3] Blessed is he who reads and those who hear the words of this prophecy, and keep those things which are written in it; (Revelation 1:3a,b)

As far as the Greek Orthodox go, their Council of Laodicea did not include Revelation in its c. 363 canon (Bruce, The Canon of Scripture, p. 210). Despite what Revelation states, the Orthodox Catholics do not read the Book of Revelation as part of their lectionary (Bruce, The Canon of Scripture, p. 215).

The fact that Greco-Roman Catholics and certain heretics held differing views of which books were in the New Testament canon until around the 5th century has no effect on what the COG knew and taught.

When Were the New Testament Books Written?

Many secular scholars assert that the Gospels and certain other books of the New Testament were written so far away from the events they refer to that the books are unreliable.

If, however, we look into the Bible and some records of history, we can get a better and more accurate idea.

Notice something from a first century document:

> The apostles have preached the gospel to us from the Lord Jesus Christ; Jesus Christ [has done so] from God. Christ therefore was sent forth by God, and the apostles by Christ. Both these appointments, then, were made in an orderly way, according to the will of God. Having therefore received their orders, and being fully assured by the resurrection of our Lord Jesus Christ, and established in the word of God, with full assurance of the Holy Ghost, they went forth proclaiming that the kingdom of God was at hand. ... Look carefully into the Scriptures, which are the true utterances of the Holy Spirit. (Letter from the Romans to the Corinthians, also known as 1 Clement, Chapters 42,45)

The certainty of the teaching and the resurrection were known and established as part of the word of God. And the scriptures were understood to be from the Holy Spirit, not from councils of men.

Notice also the following:

> [2] the twelve... said, "It is not desirable that we should leave the word of God and serve tables...[4] but we will give ourselves continually to prayer and to the ministry of the word." (Acts 6:2-4)

Beyond looking at just the Old Testament, part of being devoted to the 'ministry of the word,' was to compile some of what became the Gospels. It is logical to conclude that the original twelve apostles passed on their remembrances (and perhaps even some notes) to those that wrote the Gospels known as Matthew, Mark, Luke, and John (as even Matthew and John may have consulted with some of the other ten apostles).

Irenaeus wrote that Matthew's Gospel was written while Peter and Paul were still alive (Against Heresies, Book III, I, I). That would seem to put it in the early 60's A.D. He indicated that Mark wrote down Peter's account after he and Paul died (Ibid), which would seem to point to a c. 62-70 A.D. date. Irenaeus claimed Luke then wrote (Ibid), which would be c. 63-75 A.D. He then claimed John wrote last (Ibid). Some have speculated Matthew was written in Greek around 41 A.D. (e.g. Schultz J. The Gospel of Matthew. Lulu, 2013, p.1), perhaps from notes from the late 30's A.D.

Some believe that, instead, Mark was written first and perhaps as early as the 40's (Hiebert DE. An Introduction to the New Testament, Volume 1: The Gospels and Acts. Wipf and Stock Publishers, 2002, p. 92) or 50's A.D. (McDowell J, McDowell S. Evidence That Demands a Verdict. Josh McDowell Ministries, 2017, pp. 43-44; Akin, p. 103).

Acts looks to have been finished while Paul was still alive, and may have been completed in 61 A.D. (Ryrie C. The Ryrie Study Bible, New King James Version. Moody Press, 1985, p. 1695). Though some feel that "The best estimate for the dating of the Acts places the work between AD 62 and 64" (McDowell, p. 45). Luke's Gospel was written before he wrote Acts (cf. Luke 1:1-4, Acts 1:1).

As far as the epistles of Peter and Paul, obviously they would have been written while both were alive. Peter refers to Paul's epistles as scripture (2 Peter 3:15-16), hence they were considered to be part of the canon prior to Paul's execution.

Dr. Charles Ryrie (Ryrie, p. 1472) published the following "order of the writing of the books ... was approximately":

	A.D.		A.D.
James	45-50	Acts	61
Galatians	49	1 Timothy	63
1 and 2 Thessalonians	51	1 Peter	63

Mark	50's	Titus	65
1 Corinthians	56	2 Timothy	66
2 Corinthians	57	2 Peter	66
Romans	58	Hebrews	64-68
Luke	60	Jude	74-80
Matthew	60's	John	85-90
Colossians and Ephesians	61	1,2,3 John	90
Philippians and Philemon	61	Revelation	90's

As far as John's writings go, Irenaeus wrote that John lived until after the start of the reign of Emperor Trajan (Adversus Haereses. Book III, Chapter 3, Verse 4). Trajan reigned from 98-117. It is generally felt that John did not live too many years into the reign of Trajan. Hence, the Book of Revelation was most likely written in the 90's A.D.

In Revelation, John wrote the following:

> [9] I, John, both your brother and companion in the tribulation and kingdom and patience of Jesus Christ, was on the island that is called Patmos for the word of God and for the testimony of Jesus Christ. (Revelation 1:9)

Now, Patmos was not an island that Christian leaders went to just to live. Notice that John wrote he was there 'for the word of God and for the testimony of Jesus Christ.' It seems, he was imprisoned because he was a Christian leader and/or because God wanted him there to receive the Revelation.

When was John imprisoned there? According to Eusebius' church history John's imprisonment was during reign of Emperor Domitian (Eusebius. Church History. Book III, Chapter 23), which was 81-96 A.D.

Therefore since Domitian died in 96 A.D., we can conclude that since Revelation was the last of the books to be written while he was alive, all the New Testament books were written in the first century.

Bringing the Books Together

As Peter, Paul, John and others finally realized that Christ would probably not return in their lifetimes, they took steps to make sure that all the information needed by Christians would be written down. It is possible that Paul may have also encouraged Luke, his traveling companion (Colossians 4:14; 2 Timothy 4:11; Philemon 24), to write both the Book of Acts and the Gospel According to Luke. This way whatever teachings had not been written down, that were necessary, finally did get preserved through writing.

Notice what Luke was inspired to write:

> [1] Inasmuch as many have taken in hand to set in order a narrative of those things which have been fulfilled among us, [2] just as those who from the beginning were eyewitnesses and ministers of the word delivered them to us, [3] it seemed good to me also, having had perfect understanding of all things from the very first, to write to you an orderly account, most excellent Theophilus, [4] that you may know the certainty of those things in which you were instructed. (Luke 1:1-4)

Luke is making it clear that this writing is to set down in order the narrative (scripturally approved oral tradition) for the purpose of making what should be **known as a certainty**. Eyewitness testimony about Jesus was a significant constituent of the true Gospels.

Regarding keeping and collecting some of the books of the New Testament, the Apostle Paul wrote:

> [11] Only Luke is with me. Get Mark and bring him with you, for he is useful to me for ministry. [12] And Tychicus I have sent to Ephesus. [13] Bring the cloak that I left with Carpus at Troas when you come — and the books, especially the parchments. (2 Timothy 4:11-13).

Mark, scripture reveals (1 Peter 5:13), spent time with Peter and would have been a logical one to supply the parchments to Peter. The parchments, plural in 2 Timothy, implies numerous writings and perhaps also multiple copies. Peter basically put the initial New Testament canon together (consistent with Isaiah 8:16; Matthew 16:18-19); and we see some of the chain of custody from the Apostle Paul (also consistent with Ephesians 2:19-22).

Various theologians believe that Mark brought those books and parchments to Paul, who, presumably with consultations with Peter and probably John, made the final canonization decisions on all that was written until that time.

In his second epistle, Peter refers to Paul's writings as scripture (2 Peter 3:15-16), this provides even more of a scriptural basis for this position—Peter would not have called Paul's epistles scripture if he was not sure that they were. Scripture frequently shows that John and Peter were together (Matthew 17:1; Mark 5:37; Luke 22:8; John 18:15, 20:2-9; Acts 4:3, 8:14; Galatians 2:9).

The late John Ogwyn wrote:

> Who, then, did put together our New Testament? The answer is found in 2 Peter 1:12–21. The Apostle Peter explained to his readers that his death was imminent, and that he wished to ensure that after he was gone there would be an authoritative record of Jesus' real teachings. There were already, in the late 60s ad, "cunningly devised fables" (v. 16) circulating. Peter explained that the young Christian community should look to him, and to his fellow Apostle, John, for the "sure word of prophecy."
>
> This becomes clear when we read Peter's words carefully. Beginning in verse 12, Peter writes in the first person singular about his approaching death, and his desire to leave a permanent record. In verse 16, he abruptly switches from "I" to "we." Who is the "we?" The answer becomes plain in verses 16 through 18. The "we" are those who accompanied Jesus to the mountain where they saw His transfiguration, and heard the voice from heaven (Matthew 17:1–6). These were Peter, John, and James the brother of John.
>
> By the time Peter was writing 1 Peter, James had died—the first of the Apostles to be martyred (Acts 12:1–2)—so Peter's "we" had to refer to him and to John. Before his death ... Peter put together the very first "canon" of the New Testament, consisting of 22 books. Near the end of the first century, John added the five books that he wrote, bringing to 27 the number of books in the New Testament that we have today.

Already in the second century, in the earliest writings of the "Church Fathers," we see that the New Testament canon existed, and was quoted from and referenced frequently. (Ogwyn J. Do You Know the Real Jesus? Tomorrow's World. September-October 2004)

After Peter died, John would have taken over the responsibility as he wrote the last books of the Bible and is believed to have outlived the other original apostles.

As far as knowing the books, consider that John wrote:

> 9 Whoever transgresses and does not abide in the doctrine of Christ does not have God. He who abides in the doctrine of Christ has both the Father and the Son. (2 John 9)

You cannot abide in the doctrines of Christ by having the true Church changing which books contain the true doctrines.

Revelation 22:18-19, itself, has suggested to some scholars to mean that God had John then finalize all that would be scripture.

While some critics have pointed out that the books of the New Testament were not written until after Jesus was resurrected, not only were those of the Apostle Paul, as well as the other epistles basically written contemporaneously, the original apostles such as Peter and John — as they were eye witnesses — would have been able to attest to the veracity of the books of the New Testament.

Consider that John wrote Jesus said the following:

> 12. I have yet many things to tell you, but you are not able to bear them now. 13. However, when that one has come, even the Spirit of the truth, it will lead you into all truth. (John 16:12-13, AFV)

John insists that the Holy Spirit will deliver 'all the truth,' that it will

come through divine inspiration, and that it would happen in the future. And at that time, the Bible still had more to be added. These two verses given by Jesus, as recorded by John, are a powerful vindication that the written Christian message would be completed soon after John wrote his Gospel.

For more on the Apostle John's role, John Ogwyn wrote:

> As for the real New Testament, it was preserved exactly where we would expect it to be. Historians are unanimous in noting that John, the last original Apostle, died in Asia Minor at Ephesus. The writings of Eusebius and others make plain that during the second and third centuries ad, the churches in Asia Minor, which had had John's direct guidance, preserved the practices of the original Jerusalem Church (such as observing Passover on Abib 14 rather than keeping the Roman Easter). It is from Asia Minor that the Byzantine family of New Testament texts originated — the text officially preserved in the Greek world. (Do You Know the Real Jesus? Tomorrow's World. September-October 2004)

From what we know, the original autographs of the New Testament are closest to what was later called the 'Traditional Text.' The Byzantine text "is also known as the *Traditional Text* because it was used and preserved by the Greek church from the time of the apostles" (Coulter, p. 103).

On earth physical items deteriorate as Jesus reminds us when He said that it is "in heaven, where neither moth nor rust destroys" (Matthew 6:20). God has preserved the original words perfectly in heaven (Psalm 119:89), but also allowed men in Asia Minor and Antioch to make early copies of them.

The 'Traditional Text' appears to have been the text of the historic church from Asia Minor and Antioch. From that, the versions of the *Textus Receptus* (Received Text) originated (despite some errors intentionally later entered into it).

The *Textus Receptus* constituted the translation-base for the original German Luther Bible, the translation of the New Testament into English by William Tyndale, the King James Version, the Spanish Reina-Valera translation, the Czech Bible of Kralice, and most Reformation-era New Testament translations throughout Western and Central Europe.

Now, it should be noted that there were some obvious flaws in the 'version' of the *Textus Receptus* Desiderius Erasmus of Rotterdam put together in 1516. For example, he left out some verses and also relied on some Latin phrases which were not in the original Greek (Maniscalco EF, "Rhyme and reason in Erasmus' 1516 Greek text of Revelation 22:16-21" 1996. Dissertations: 1962 - 2010). Hence, his *Textus Receptus* did not properly represent the true chain of custody.

Erasmus later made various improvements after consulting more Greek texts, and published his 5th edition in 1534 (though he bowed to pressure related to 1 John 5:7-8 starting with his 3rd edition).

Robert Estienne (Roberti Stephani), also known as Stephens (or Stephanus), used that 5th edition and after consulting additional ancient Greek manuscripts, published that in 1550. The most faithful *Textus Receptus* seems to be the one put out by Stephens and is also known as Stephens 1550 or *Textus Receptus* (Berry GR. Interlinear Greek-English New Testament. Hinds and Noble, 1897, p. ii). Some simply refer to it as the *Textus Receptus* (Schaff P. Theological Propaedeutic, A General Introduction to the Study of Theology. Wipf & Stock, 1892, p. 167), though it is not perfect. Some scholars have called the Stephens 1550 the "standard *Textus Receptus*" (Green JP. Interlinear Greek-English New Testament, 3rd edition. Baker Books, 2002 printing, p. xii). It is also extremely similar to F.H.A. Scrivener's 1894 text which can also be considered as a "Received Text" (ibid, p. xii).

Stephens 1550

Interestingly, when the Greco-Roman churches tended to move away from the biblically 'Semi-arian' view of the Godhead in the late 4th century, they started to rely less on the "Traditional Text" and more on the Alexandrian texts favored by Dr. Hort (Burgon JW. The Causes of the Corruption of the Traditional Text of the Holy Gospels. Original 1896; reprint Cosimo Classics, 2007, p. 2-3).

Byzantine texts also make up a lot of what is commonly called the Majority Text, which agree with the *Textus Receptus* over 99% of the time and, according to D. A. Carson, result in no significant doctrinal differences, though some others disagree (Wallace D. The Majority Text and the Original Text: Are They Identical? Bible.org, accessed 03/23/20). It has been claimed that 95-98% of the ancient manuscripts of the New Testament are from the Majority Text family (Kroll P. Is the Bible a Protestant Book? Good News magazine, April 1964, p. 21; Sightler JH. A Testimony Founded For Ever, 2nd ed. Sightler Pubs., 2001, p. 12).

It needs to be emphasized that there is no debate that there are significant differences between the Alexandrian and Byzantine texts. "The Critical Text is based upon Alexandrian manuscripts which constitute only about 10% of the manuscripts in existence. By contrast, the Majority Text, also known as the Byzantine Majority text, is supported by around 90% of the existing manuscripts" (Carlson, p. 49).

It should be pointed out that there were two directions, two paths if you will, regarding the New Testament texts. One in Alexandria, the seat of the allegorists, and the other (the Byzantine) in Asia Minor and Antioch, where those who pushed for a more literal understanding of scripture were based. We in the CCOG (*Continuing* Church of God) tend to rely on the Byzantine text when there is a significant difference.

Furthermore, Origen of Alexandria wrote:

> ... the differences among the manuscripts [of the Gospels] have become great, either through the negligence of some copyists or through the perverse audacity of others; they either neglect to check over what they have transcribed, or, in the process of checking, they lengthen or shorten, as they please. (Translation as shown in Metzger B. The Text of the New Testament: Its

Transmission, Corruption, and Restoration, 3rd ed. Oxford, 1991, pp. 151-152)

In his *Commentary on Matthew* (e.g. Book XII, Chapter 15) Origen refers to differences. Some believe that Origen himself changed scripture further and that the Alexandrian text we have, including the *Vaticanus*, is a result of his tampering (Daniels DW. Did the Catholic Church Give Us the Bible? Chick Publications, 2013, pp. 31-39). While the degree of that tampering can be debated, the reality is that Origen did make changes to the Septuagint (Septuagint, Encyclopædia Britannica), was not a faithful Christian, and was excessively into his opinion and allegory. But since Origen CHANGED the Septuagint, what we now have, such as in the Codex B, is not what was in existence during the time of the original disciples.

Codex B is also called the *Vaticanus*:

> Codex B comes to us without a history: without recommendation of any kind, except that of its antiquity. It bears traces of careless transcription in every page. The mistakes which the original transcriber made are of perpetual recurrence. (Burgon DJ. Unholy Hands on the Bible. Original, 1871. Sovereign Grace Publishers, Reprint 1990 c-42)

The three chief Alexandrian texts are Codex B (*Vaticanus*), *Sinaiticus*, and Codex D. *Vaticanus* reportedly differs from Codex D 1,944 times (Williams HD. The Received Text for the Whole World. Williams, 2007, p. 172). *Vaticanus* reportedly differs from *Sinaiticus* 3,000 places in the four Gospels alone (Ibid, p. 172).

While there is a certain historical value in the non-Byzantine texts, we in the *Continuing* Church of God do not consider that they are quite to the level of the *Textus Receptus*.

God's Word is Pure

Isaiah 40:8 states:

> [8] The grass withers, the flower fades, But the word of our God stands forever.

The word of God was the word of God once God inspired it to be written. It does not become inspired because of the decisions of men (or women). And it STANDS FOREVER, hence is extremely important.

Not too long before writing 2 Timothy, Paul also wrote:

> [1] Now, brethren, concerning the coming of our Lord Jesus Christ and our gathering together to Him, we ask you, [2] not to be soon shaken in mind or troubled, either by spirit or by word or by letter, as if from us, as though the day of Christ had come. (2 Thessalonians 2:1-2)

Paul warned that false writings might come. It is a fact that there must have been some confusion about the canon when Paul wrote 2 Thessalonians or people would not be shaken by words or letters that were purported to be from him. And while that could be dealt with through visits while he was alive, Paul must have known that what constituted scripture must be known prior to his death. This is what most likely led to his call for Timothy to send for Mark and to bring the books and the parchments (2 Timothy 4:11-13) — as this was a matter that needed to be resolved quickly.

Even the Greco-Roman Catholic sources accept that at least the Gospels were known in the first and second centuries:

> The Bodmer Papyrus XIV-XV, handwritten in Greek around the year 200, contains 'about half of each of the Gospels of Luke and John,' Cardinal Tauran explained.

> 'With this new precious papyrus, the library of the pope possesses the most ancient witness of the Gospel of Luke and among the most ancient of the Gospel of John,' he said...

> Before the Bodmer documents were discovered in Egypt in 1952, it said, biblical scholars relied on references to the Gospels in the writings of the early church theologians to assert that by the year 100 the Christian community had accepted only four Gospels as inspired texts.

The Bodmer Papyrus XIV-XV, containing the last two Gospels, the newspaper said, provides concrete evidence that the four Gospels were circulating among Christian communities as a complete set by the year 200, although the twin papyrus containing the Gospels of St. Matthew and St. Mark has not been found. (Wooden C. American's donation lets pope peruse oldest copy of St. Luke's Gospel. Catholic News Service. POPE-PAPYRUS Jan-23-2007)

It is illogical, historically, that the true Church of God could have existed for over 300 years without knowing what books were actually part of the New Testament canon or not — not knowing them would contradict 2 Timothy 3:16-17, which cannot happen since "Scripture cannot be broken" (John 10:35). Surely the leaders of the true Church, as well as their followers, had to know the true canon. For any to conclude that Peter and John had nothing to do with the canonization of the New Testament does not square with what the Bible seems to be teaching on this subject. Nor does it make much historical sense.

Perhaps it should be mentioned that this author has been criticized for writing the preceding paragraph, and so it seems wise to address the main objection here.

The main objection is if the original NT Church did not have the full NT until John finished it, how did it function?

Well, the truth is that the original NT Church had John and the original apostles who knew what the teachings of the true Church should be since they, plus Paul, were taught directly by Christ.

Furthermore, this also is consistent with the scriptural record that Peter, Paul, and John all had some role in the canonization before they died to insure that there would not be disputes over the books for true Christians.

For others that is another matter. As even the *Catholic Encyclopedia* admits the following:

> The most explicit definition of the Catholic Canon is that given by the Council of Trent, Session IV, 1546 ... Since the Council of

Trent it is not permitted for a Catholic to question the inspiration of these passages. (Reid G. Canon of the Old Testament)

This would seem to mean that the Roman Catholics did not really finalize their canon in an explicit and clear way (including the Old Testament) until 1546. Would God have wanted humankind to wait 14-15 centuries before knowing which books are from Him?

Consider that Paul's letter to Timothy (1 Timothy 5:18) cites Luke's Gospel (Luke 10:7) as scripture. Peter also referred to Paul's writings as scripture:

> [15] and consider that the longsuffering of our Lord is salvation — as also our beloved brother Paul, according to the wisdom given to him, has written to you, [16] as also in all his epistles, speaking in them of these things, in which are some things hard to understand, which untaught and unstable people twist to their own destruction, as they do also the rest of the Scriptures. (2 Peter 3:15-16)

But it is clear not only from the Bible, but from post-New Testament writings as well, that the books of the New Testament were clearly considered to be scripture.

As far as the New Testament being called scripture goes, notice the following:

> An Ancient Christian Sermon (2 Clement) ... is, in fact, a sermon ... The sermon appears to contain the earliest instance of the New Testament being referred to as "Scripture" (2.4). ... around 100 A.D. (Holmes M.W. The Apostolic Fathers: Greek Texts and English Translations, 2nd ed. Baker Books, Grand Rapids, 2004, p. 102)

It has the following:

> 2:4 Again **another scripture** says, "I came not to call the righteous, but sinners" (cf. Matthew 9:13).

3:2 Yes, He Himself says, "Whoso confesseth Me, Him will I confess before the Father" (cf. Matthew 10:32).

Furthermore, Polycarp of Smyrna's Letter to the Philippians (A.D. 110-140) states:

12:1 ... It is declared then **in these Scriptures**, "Be angry, and sin not," and, "Let not the sun go down upon your wrath" (cf. Ephesians 4:26).

The New Testament was considered scripture at an early date.

God Provides What We Need

The *a fortiori* principle also demonstrates that God provided copies of the Scriptures to the church. Since Jesus taught that God provides food for the birds and people are worth more than birds (Matthew 6:25-34), it is logical that God will provide proper (and complete) spiritual food for people. Why? Because Jesus also taught that the word of God was more important than food: But He answered and said, "It is written, 'Man shall not live by bread alone, but by every word that proceeds from the mouth of God.' " (Matthew 4:4).

Also notice Jesus' teaching,

[7] 'Ask, and it will be given to you; seek, and you will find; knock, and it will be opened to you. [8] For everyone who asks receives, and he who seeks finds, and to him who knocks it will be opened. [9] Or what man is there among you who, if his son asks for bread, will give him a stone? [10] Or if he asks for a fish, will he give him a serpent? [11] If you then, being evil, know how to give good gifts to your children, how much more will your Father who is in heaven give good things to those who ask Him! [12] Therefore, whatever you want men to do to you, do also to them, for this is the Law and the Prophets. (Matthew 7:7-12)

Jesus is showing that as decent parents know to not give their children rocks or unclean meats, God provides good things to his people, especially when they ask Him.

It is simply inconceivable that no one in the early Church asked Jesus' apostles what Scripture was legitimate to believe and that God left that to the Roman Catholic Church to decide 300 (or even almost 1500) years later.

Also, notice Paul's writing:

> [14] How then shall they call on Him in whom they have not believed? And how shall they believe in Him of whom they have not heard? And how shall they hear without a preacher? [15] And how shall they preach unless they are sent? As it is written:
>
> 'How beautiful are the feet of those who preach the gospel of peace, Who bring glad tidings of good things!'
>
> [16] But they have not all obeyed the gospel. For Isaiah says, 'Lord, who has believed our report?' [17] So then faith comes by hearing, and hearing by the word of God. (Romans 10:14-17)

Since God sent preachers throughout history, God demands faith (Hebrews 11:6), and hearing comes by the word of God (Romans 10:17), there must have been a reliable word of God all along. A reliable New Testament canon would have been part of it.

Paul's letters seem to have traveled together (cf. 2 Peter 3:15-16).

Why Was It John Who Finalized the Canon?

The Old Testament Book of Isaiah prophesied that the LORD's disciples would bind up and seal the Bible (Isaiah 8:16). The Apostle John was the last of the original disciples to be able to do so.

Furthermore, early Christians seemed to have taken this 'bind up' statement quite literally in their day. While the Jews tended to keep the Hebrew scriptures in scrolls for centuries after Jesus came, Christians put the New Testament in what are called codices, which were fairly new at that time (Kruger, p. 100).

"Early in the second century (and perhaps even at the close of the first century), the *codex*, or leaf form of book came into use in the Church"

(Metzger BM, Ehrman B. The Text of the New Testament, 4th ed. Oxford University Press, 2004, p. 12)

A codex was an early forerunner to our modern bound books — they essentially had pages. This made accessing scripture easier. For example, if Luke's Gospel were on an ancient scroll it would be about 30 feet long. Looking from one part to the other of a scroll is more difficult than turning pages. While Luke's Gospel may well have originally been written on a lengthy scroll, transferring to a codex made it easier to use and study.

Isaiah 8:16 suggests that there would be no additions 'to the law and to the testimony' (an expression for the Bible, see Isaiah 8:20), after the ones the Bible refers to as the disciples were gone. Isaiah is thus indicating that the original disciples would have finalized the New Testament for our age — that would include people such as Peter and John.

As the longest surviving of the original apostles, John would have seen more problems with false teachers professing Christianity than possibly all the other apostles. Since John wrote the last books of the New Testament and was the longest surviving disciple, the Old Testament clearly supports that he would be the final one to bind up the testimony and seal the law.

Dr. Ernest Martin believed that various scriptures essentially revealed that John was of Aaronic heritage and that was a reason John was chosen by God to finalize the New Testament (Martin, pp 313-315). Whether one accepts the Aaronic connection from scripture or not, it should be pointed out that Polycrates of Ephesus wrote that John was of Aaronic heritage (Eusebius. The History of the Church, Book V, Chapter XXIV, Verse 3). Dr. Martin and various others have asserted that the Apostle John was the final 'editor' of the New Testament text. As such, John was possibly responsible for such parenthetical statements such as "let the reader understand" in Matthew 24:15 and Mark 13:14 (Coulter, pp. 72-73).

The New Testament also suggests that the disciple John finalized the Bible through his writing of the Book of Revelation:

¹⁸ For I testify to everyone who hears the words of the prophecy of this book: If anyone adds to these things, God will add to him the plagues that are written in this book; ¹⁹ And if anyone takes away from the words of the book of this prophecy, God shall take away his part from the Book of Life, from the holy city, and from the things which are written in this book. (Revelation 22:18-19)

While it is possible that he is only referring to the Book of Revelation when he penned the above, as the last New Testament writer, it would seem that God had him put in the above statement to show that the Bible, and not just Revelation, was finalized. Since 'the testimony of Jesus is the spirit of prophecy' (Revelation 19:10) and Jesus is the Word (John 1:1, 14), it makes sense that Revelation 22:18-19 is, at least in a sense, referring to the fact that none were to add to the word of God (and that is consistent with other scriptures, such as Deuteronomy 4:2; 12:32, Proverbs 30:6). And that this was the last intended book of the canon for the Church age.

Even some Protestant theologians understand that Revelation 22:18-19 supports the concept that the canon was then finalized. Notice what is stated in *Matthew Henry's Commentary*:

Rev 22:6-19

It is confirmed by a most solemn sanction, condemning and cursing all who should dare to corrupt or change the word of God, either by adding to it or taking from it, v. 18, 19. He that adds to the word of God draws down upon himself all the plagues written in this book; and he who takes any thing away from it cuts himself off from all the promises and privileges of it. This sanction is like a flaming sword, to guard the canon of the scripture from profane hands. Such a fence as this God set about the law (Deut 4:2), and the whole Old Testament (Mal 4:4), and now in the most solemn manner about the whole Bible, assuring us that it is a book of the most sacred nature, divine authority, and of the last importance, and therefore the peculiar care of the great God. (from *Matthew Henry's Commentary* on the Whole Bible: New Modern Edition,

Electronic Database. Copyright (c) 1991 by Hendrickson Publishers, Inc.)

Interestingly, in all of his epistles John repeatedly warns about false ones who try to influence Christians (1 John 2:4; 2:18-19; 3:10; 4:1; 2 John 7; 3 John 9-10). Hence, this may be part of why God had John write the passage in Revelation 22.

John also wrote:

> [25] And there are also many other things that Jesus did, which if they were written one by one, I suppose that even the world itself could not contain the books that would be written ... [31] but these are written that you may believe that Jesus is the Christ, the Son of God, and that believing you may have life in His name. (John 21:25, 20:31)

This statement, combined with his writings in Revelation 22:18-19, show that only certain things needed to be written and only certain writings accepted as scripture. Thus, it is logical to conclude that he, the last of the original apostles, finalized the NT canon (cf. Isaiah 8:16). Furthermore, this passage from John demonstrates that what is written is sufficient for life in Jesus, hence no non-biblical tradition is needed.

But why else would John have been the one to finalize the canon?

John was the last of the original apostles to die, that Jesus, prior to His resurrection, personally selected. And although the first proper baptisms in Ephesus were apparently done by Paul (Acts 19:1-6), it is John who was there later. Even the *Catholic Encyclopedia* admits that John was in charge of the church at Ephesus:

> ...the Apostle and Evangelist John lived in Asia Minor in the last decades of the first century and from Ephesus had guided the Churches of that province. (Fonck L. St. John the Evangelist, 1910)

It is important to note that the Church of Ephesus is the first of the seven churches mentioned in Revelation 1:11 as well as the first of the seven in Revelation to receive an individual letter that ends with 'He who has an ear, let him hear what the Spirit says to the churches' (see Revelation chapters 2 & 3).

Since these Churches are shown to those whom Christ walks in the midst of (2:1), it is logical that the first one would have received the entire, properly canonized, NT. The one that John personally oversaw. The same John who wrote that nothing should be added or taken away from the word of prophecy. The same John whose disciple Polycarp became in charge of the Church at Smyrna (the second of the seven churches of Revelation).

John knew Peter, wrote the last books of the New Testament, and hence would be the first with the final and complete canon of scripture.

Doesn't it make sense that before John died that he would pass on his knowledge of which books should be part of the New Testament canon? And does it not make sense that this would be to Polycarp, the one who appeared to be his most faithful disciple? John had the chain of custody and passed at least the knowledge of books (probably along with all the actual books of the New Testament) to Polycarp.

Furthermore, like Moses recorded God told him to write in a book (Exodus 17:14), John records that Jesus told him to write Revelation as a book and send it to the Churches in Asia Minor. Look what Jesus said:

> [11] "I am the Alpha and the Omega, the First and the Last," and, "What you see, write in a book and send it to the seven churches which are in Asia: to Ephesus, to Smyrna, to Pergamos, to Thyatira, to Sardis, to Philadelphia, and to Laodicea." (Revelation 1:11)

Thus, it is clear that the last book of the New Testament was to be published and sent to the seven churches in Asia Minor, including Smyrna!

The simple truth is that the Church in Asia Minor, where the seven churches of Revelation were located, did have the canon of both the Old and the New Testaments.

9. The Church of God Had the Full Canon from the Beginning

While some believe that because the Church of Rome, along with the Eastern Orthodox, held meetings to determine the canon for itself (and that to a major degree the Protestants followed many of the decisions), that they came up with the canon. Yet, the reality is that the Church of God had the books, and thus the canon, from the beginning (meaning once the Book of Revelation was finished). Early Christians would not have considered the canon to be fluid (Kruger, p. 31).

This is confirmed in many sources (some of which have already been cited).

Notice also the following related to the New Testament:

> To whom then was the New Testament given for preservation and transmission?
>
> **Greeks Preserve New Testament**
>
> Romans 1:16 reveals the answer. "For I am not ashamed of the gospel of Christ . . . *to the Jew first, and also to the Greek.*"
>
> God raised up the Apostle Paul to go to the Greeks. They received the New Testament oracles — and became responsible for their preservation and transmission.
>
> We saw the principle in Romans 1:16 that God was going to use the Greek-speaking world to *preserve and copy* the New Testament Canon. The leading Apostles and officials of His New Testament Church WROTE and under divine inspiration were led to COMPILE THE CANON. The Greeks had *nothing* to do with these two great functions. The *apostolic era of the Church of God* completed these two great acts.
>
> But the Greeks were given the responsibility to *copy and transmit* the New Testament Canon.

The truth of Romans 1:16 *dovetails* with many interesting historical developments that took place in the first century A.D.

Where was the Apostle John when he wrote the book of Revelation? He was on the island of Patmos (Rev. 1 :9). Where was this island? In the *Greek-speaking world!*

Where were the churches to which the Apostle Paul wrote most of his epistles? In Asia Minor-the *Greek-speaking world!* (I Pet. 1:1). ...

The point is that the *original copies* of the manuscripts were in the Greek-speaking world to begin with. They were NOT *in* Latin-speaking Italy! They were originally *written in Greek.* ... around 150 A.D. Polycarp of Greek Asia Minor was still preserving the Truth! He was a disciple of the Apostle John. (Kroll, p. 18)

We in the *Continuing* Church of God assert that the Apostle John, believed to have died in Asia Minor and to have lived past the deaths of the other original twelve apostles, had the entire canon from the time Jesus had him pen the last book of the Bible.

Another reason it is logical to conclude that the Church in Asia Minor would have the entire New Testament is because most of the New Testament was written to or from church leaders in Asia Minor (none were written to or from Alexandria, Egypt).

There are a total of 27 books in the New Testament. At least 9 books of the New Testament were directly written to the church leaders in Asia Minor. The ones clearly written to those in Asia Minor include Galatians, Ephesians, Colossians, 1 & 2 Timothy (Timothy was in Ephesus), Philemon, 1 Peter, 3 John, and Revelation. According to *The Ryrie Study Bible* John's Gospel, 1 Corinthians, 1 & 2 John, and possibly Philippians, were written from Ephesus. In addition to these, 2 Peter, and possibly Jude may have also been mainly directed to one or more of the churches in Asia Minor.

The Book of James was written to "the twelve tribes which are scattered abroad" (James 1:1). Some of them were in Asia Minor. Others according to the historian Josephus were "beyond Euphrates." It is also likely that some other books were written at least partially from Asia Minor. For example, the Book of Acts mentions "Ephesus" and "Ephesians" a dozen times and "Asia" 15 times (NKJV).

Plus, it has been *claimed* by one or more that all four gospel accounts were as well, though this is less certain (though one or more other than John may have been). So probably 14 to 22 New Testament books were written to or from Asia Minor.

There is only one book written to those in Rome (it never mentions any of the so-called Roman bishops), with 1 to Corinth, 2 to Thessalonica, and 1 to Crete (Titus), - a total of 5 letters neither sent from nor addressed to those in Asia Minor.

What this clearly shows, is that although there were Christians in various areas, the focus for the New Testament writers was the churches in Asia Minor. And interestingly, the last book of the Bible is specifically addressed to the churches of Asia Minor (Revelation 1:4,11). It was in Asia Minor that the NT canon was originally formed. There is no other place that could have had it earlier. And the Apostle John did have the full canon before his death.

Historical Confirmation from the Didache and Irenaeus

A writing from the late 1st or early 2nd century, called the *Didache,* contains the following:

> Forsake in no way the commandments of the Lord; but you shall keep what you have received, neither adding thereto nor taking away therefrom. (Didache, 4)

The above writing supports the view that by the end of the first century, some understood that Christians had a closed canon (cf. Kruger, p. 203)

Furthermore, Irenaeus, a Roman supporter, around 180, wrote:

> After this fashion also did a presbyter, a disciple of the apostles, reason with respect to the two testaments, proving that both were truly from one and the same God ...

For all the apostles taught that there were indeed two testaments among the two peoples; but that it was one and the same God who appointed both for the advantage of those men (for whose sakes the testaments were given) who were to believe in God. (Irenaeus. Adversus haereses, Book IV, Chapter 32, Verse 1,2. Excerpted from Ante-Nicene Fathers, Volume 1. Edited by Alexander Roberts & James Donaldson. American Edition, 1885)

Hence, Irenaeus is claiming that one or more of the apostles knew the books of the Old and New Testaments. Thus, he seemingly believed that the early church did have the entire canon of the Bible. It may be that the *presbyter, a disciple of the apostles,* Irenaeus is referring to was Polycarp of Smyrna (whom he claimed to have known) or Melito of Sardis. And if so, this is additional evidence that the church in Asia Minor had the complete biblical canon very early on. Furthermore, Irenaeus' strong insistence elsewhere that there were four and only four gospels (Irenaeus. Adversus Haereses, Book III, Chapter XI, verse 8) points to the view that at least their part of the canon was clearly known by Irenaeus. It should also be noted that in fragments ascribed to Polycarp or perhaps pseudo-Polycarp, each of the four Gospels are correctly named (Polycarp/pseudo-Polycarp. Fragments from Victor of Capua. Translated by Stephen C. Carlson. 2006).

An anonymous *Letter to the Corinthians* commonly called *1 Clement,* states:

For you know the Holy Scriptures right well, beloved, and you studied the words (logia) of God. (Chapter 53 as translated in Dehandschutter B. Polycarpiana, Selected Essays. Leuven University Press, 2007, p. 286)

So, the authors claimed that the Corinthians knew the Holy Scriptures.

Furthermore, its 36th chapter quotes Hebrews 1:3-4 whereas its 56th chapter quotes Hebrews 12:6, demonstrating it was written after the Book of Hebrews was. Research suggests that this letter was written in the late first century by the faithful in Rome shortly after the Apostle John was exiled from Rome to Patmos. These people perhaps had at least distant, temporal, contact with John, and thus, likely knew the proper books.

Furthermore, in his *Letter to the Philippians*, Polycarp quotes Hebrews 12:18; 1 Peter 1:8, 2:11,21,22,24, 3:9, 4:47; and 1 John 4:3. He also refers to 2 Peter 2:1-2, while alluding to passages in James 2:8-9, 5:10; 2 Peter 1:3, 3:15; 1 John 2:15, 4:9; 2 John 6, and 3 John 4 (Thiel, Trinity Journal).

One reason to mention this is, that about four to six decades later, some Latins came up with something called the *Muratorian Canon* (c. 175). It was "composed in the Roman Church in the last quarter of the second century" (Reid, Canon of the New Testament). It did NOT include the Book of Hebrews James, 1 Peter, or 2 Peter (plus it refers to two epistles of John, though John wrote three that are part of the canon), but did include the false *Apocalypse of Peter* (Bruce, The Canon of Scripture, pp. 164-165). This suggests that the dominant force then in the Church of Rome simply did not know what the New Testament canon was, despite Roman leaders presumably knowing they were inspired scriptures in the first century. It also shows that Asia Minor and Rome were not in agreement with the canon then.

Notice something from Eusebius (c. 320):

> It is not indeed right to overlook the fact that some have rejected the Epistle to the Hebrews, saying that it is disputed by the church of Rome. ...

> Among the disputed writings, which are nevertheless recognized by many, are extant the so-called epistle of James and that of Jude, also the second epistle of Peter, and those that are called the second and third of John, whether they belong to the evangelist or to another person of the same name.

> Among the rejected writings must be reckoned also the Acts of Paul, and the so-called Shepherd, and the Apocalypse of Peter, and in addition to these the extant epistle of Barnabas, and the so-called Teachings of the Apostles; and besides, as I said, the Apocalypse of John, if it seem proper, which some, as I said, reject, but which others class with the accepted books.

(Eusebius. The History of the Church. Book III, Chapter III verse 5 and Chapter XXV, verses 3-4, pp. 44, 59-60)

Clearly the Greco-Roman churches had canonical confusion.

Even as late as 405 A.D., Pope Innocent I left Hebrews out of his list of the New Testament canon he sent to Exsuperius, bishop of Toulouse (Bruce, The Canon of Scripture, p. 234). This is despite the claim that in "382 … The Damasan catalogue presents the complete and perfect Canon which has been that of the Church Universal ever since", while in 393 "St. Augustine … acknowledged that many contested this Epistle … Carthage in 419--found it necessary to formulate catalogues" (Reid, Canon of the New Testament).

This shows that the Church of Rome did NOT have the proper chain of custody of the New Testament. Unlike the Church of God which knew the books from the beginning (by the death of the Apostle John). It took the Church of Rome centuries to properly recognize the books of the New Testament.

Notice also:

> About 1450, Christ caused the art of printing by movable type to be developed in Germany. It was not accidental that the famous Gutenberg Bible was one of the first books to be printed. From there, printing spread to Holland, England and all over Europe, wherever God's people were found.
>
> The first edition of the Bible in the vernacular of the people was the German translation of 1466. Between this first edition and 1518 (the time of Luther) 14 editions of the Bible in German and 4 in Dutch were printed. Others appeared in England, Bohemia, Italy and other countries. One of these German Bibles printed in 1483 — a GENERATION before Luther — is in the Ambassador College Library.
>
> The New Testament of this first edition (1466) is demonstrably derived directly from the Waldensian version. Later, Baptists and Mennonites preferred the Waldensian version to the LUTHERAN for a century.

Clearly the impulse to spread the Word of God did not originate in Protestantism which began in 1517! (Lesson 52 - The Book And The Church They Couldn't Destroy. Ambassador College Bible Correspondence Course, 1968)

Perhaps, Martin Luther's and Huldrych/Ulrich Zwingli's position should also be mentioned.

> As for Protestantism, the Anglicans and Calvinists always kept the entire New Testament. But for over a century the followers of Luther excluded Hebrews, James, Jude, and Apocalypse. ... Zwingli could not see in Apocalypse a Biblical book. (Reid, Canon of the New Testament)

Martin Luther wrote about Hebrews and the books following it (his other prefaces confirm his opposition to James, Jude, and Revelation):

> Up to this point we have had the true and certain chief books of the New Testament. The four which follow have from ancient times had a different reputation. In the first place, the fact that Hebrews is not an epistle of St. Paul, or of any other apostle (Luther, M. Prefaces to the Epistle of the Hebrews, 1546)

Martin Luther really did not believe in *sola Scriptura* and he did not want taught certain matters in the above books (see also, the free book, online at ccog.org, *Hope of Salvation: How the Continuing Church of God Differs from Protestantism*).

Polycarp Was a Disciple of John and Originally Knew the Books

Historians understand that: "A direct link to the apostles themselves can be seen in the work of *Polycarp* from the early second century A.D. Polycarp was actually a disciple of the Apostle John. Significantly, he wrote his own 'Epistle to the Philippians,' where he referenced and cited Scriptures of the Old and New Testaments" (Holden, p. 125).

Furthermore, this author's published research pointed out that all the New Testament books are quoted from or alluded to in Polycarp's letter (Thiel B. Polycarp's Letter to the Philippians with New Testament

Scriptural Annotations. Trinity Journal of Apologetics and Theology, June 2008).

Polycarp of Smyrna, himself, made it clear that those he wrote to in Philippi had the correct canon, otherwise he would not have written:

> For I trust that ye are well versed in the Sacred Scriptures. (Polycarp. Letter to the Philippians. Ante-Nicene Fathers, *Volume 1*. Alexander Roberts & James Donaldson. American Edition, 1885)

One could not be 'well versed in the Sacred Scriptures' without knowing what they were. Notice this observation from The Catholic Encyclopedia:

> St. Ignatius, Bishop of Antioch, and St. Polycarp, of Smyrna, had been disciples of Apostles; they wrote their epistles in the first decade of the second century (100-110). They employ Matthew, Luke, and John. In St. Ignatius we find the first instance of the consecrated term "it is written" applied to a Gospel (Ad Philad., viii, 2). Both these Fathers show not only a personal acquaintance with "the Gospel" and the thirteen Pauline Epistles, but they suppose that their readers are so familiar with them that it would be superfluous to name them. (Reid, Canon of the New Testament).

Irenaeus of Lyon (c. 170) wrote in his letter to Florinus:

> **Polycarp related all things in harmony with the Scriptures**. (Eusebius. The History of the Church. Book V, Chapter XX, verses 5-8, p. 112)

It would be difficult to relate **all things in harmony with the Scriptures** if Polycarp did not know them.

This may be part of why Ignatius of Antioch wrote:

> Ignatius, who is also called Theophorus, to Polycarp, Bishop of the Church of the Smyrnæans ... For I trust that, through grace, you are prepared for every good work pertaining to God.

Knowing, therefore, your energetic love of the truth, I have exhorted you by this brief Epistle. (Letter to Polycarp, Chapters 0, 7)

Polycarp was energetic for the truth — God's word is truth (Psalm 119:160; John 17:17). Ignatius, himself, quoted sixteen or so New Testament scriptures in the letters we have from him in a manner that suggests that he and those in Asia Minor recognized their scriptural authority (cf. Kruger, pp. 189-193). That Polycarp was "prepared for every good work" also implies that he must have "known the Holy Scriptures" (cf. 2 Timothy 3:15-17).

Now, let's look at the following written about Polycarp:

And on the following sabbath he said; "Hear ye my exhortation, beloved children of God. I adjured you when the bishops were present, and now again I exhort you all to walk decorously and worthily in the way of the Lord ... *Watch ye,* and again *Be ye ready, Let not your hearts be weighed down,* the new commandment concerning love one towards another, His advent suddenly manifest as of rapid lightning, the great judgment by fire, the eternal life, His immortal kingdom. And all things whatsoever being taught of God ye know, when ye search the inspired Scriptures, engrave with the pen of the Holy Spirit on your hearts, that the commandments may abide in you indelible." (Life of Polycarp, Chapter 24. In: J. B. Lightfoot, The Apostolic Fathers, vol. 3.2, 1889, pp. 488-506)

Polycarp advanced greatly in the faith that is in Christ and that pursues a virtuous life. And in his untiring diligence, he from his Eastern stock bore (if one may so say) blossom as a token of good fruit hereafter to come. For the men who dwell in the East are distinguished before all others for their love of learning and their attachment to the divine Scriptures ... Thus reflecting on this with a godly delight he offered himself day and night wholly and entirely as a consecrated sacrifice to God, exercising himself in the oracles contained in the divine Scriptures and in continual services of prayer and in devotion to all those who needed either attention or relief and in contentment of living. (Ibid, Chapter 6)

Such was his behaviour towards those from whom no benefit could be got. But bad men he avoided as mad dogs or wild beasts or venomous serpents; for he remembered the Scripture. (Ibid, Chapter 7)

... proving this from all the Scriptures. (Ibid, Chapter 13)

For he would extend his discourse to great length on diverse subjects, and from the actual Scripture which was read he would furnish edification with all demonstration and conviction. (Ibid, Chapter 18)

So also he pursued the reading of the Scriptures from childhood to old age, himself reading in church; and he recommended it to others, saying that the reading of the law and the prophets was the forerunner of grace, preparing and making *straight the ways of the Lord,* that is the hearts, which are like tablets whereon certain harsh beliefs and conceptions that were written before perfect knowledge came, are through the inculcation of the Old Testament, and the correct interpretation following thereupon, first smoothed and levelled, that, when the Holy Spirit comes as a pen, the grace and joy of the voice of the Gospel and of the doctrine of the immortal and heavenly Christ may be inscribed on them. (Ibid, Chapter 19)

The wealth of the grace given by Christ to Polycarp has led us on, while recording his course of life, to explain in turn the character of his teaching likewise. How he used to interpret the Scriptures, we will defer relating till another time, setting it forth in order and showing our successors also how to minister correct instruction in the holy and inspired Scriptures. (Ibid, Chapter 19)

And all things whatsoever being taught of God ye know, when ye search the inspired Scriptures, engrave with the pen of the Holy Spirit on your hearts, that the commandments may abide in you indelible.' Thus speaking in this way from time to time, and being persistent in his teaching, he edified and *saved both himself and his hearers.* (Ibid, Chapters 24-25)

Polycarp is clearly communicating with people he felt were familiar with the true canon when he said they knew *all things* taught by God through searching the *inspired scriptures*. The original writer of the *Life of Polycarp* understood that Polycarp had all the scriptures.

Polycarp, himself, seems to quote directly from a Byzantium (like now part of the *Textus Receptus*) manuscript of the Bible, when, for example, he was quoting from Matthew's gospel.

Related to Matthew 26:41, he wrote (c. 135) in his *Letter to the Philippians* (7:2):

το μεν πνύεμα προθυμον η δε caρξ acθενης

The *Textus Receptus* has:

το μεν πνύεμα προθυμον η δε caρξ acθενης

Yet, the Alexandrian Codex Sinaiticus has:

το μεν πνα προθυμον η δε caρξ acθενης

While the meaning of all three is basically the same, the wording that Polycarp used was identical to the Byzantine text as Polycarp used the same Greek word for spirit (πνύεμα), which differed from the Alexandrian text (πνα) — which may have been an abbreviation.

Other quotations that Polycarp made, that this author checked, also were identical or essentially identical to the *Textus Receptus* (by 'essentially identical' meaning that the Greek words were the same, but that their endings may have varied for grammatical reasons — yet it should be pointed out that often the quote is also the same as in the *Codex Sinaiticus*).

Polycarp was quoting from a Greek source and not from a Hebrew version of Matthew (some have claimed that Matthew was originally written in Hebrew).

Also, a similar situation occurs with Ignatius of Antioch who knew Polycarp. When he quotes part of Matthew 19:31 in chapter 6 of his

Letter to the Smyrnaeans, the Greek he used is essentially identical to the *Textus Receptus*, but differs a bit from of the Alexandrian *Codex Sinaiticus*.

Polycarp received the texts from the apostles, like John. Consider the following from Irenaeus:

> But Polycarp also was not only instructed by apostles, and conversed with many who had seen Christ, but was also, by apostles in Asia, appointed bishop of the Church in Smyrna ... always taught the things which he had learned from the apostles, and which the Church has handed down, and which alone are true. To these things all the Asiatic Churches testify, as do also those men who have succeeded Polycarp down to the present time. (Adversus Haeres. Book III, Chapter 3, Verse 4)

Polycarp was appointed by the apostles and taught what was received ("handed down"). He respected and highly quoted scripture.

Furthermore, it also should be mentioned that there is an ancient historical document known as the *Harris Fragments* (ca. 2nd or 3rd century) that also discusses Polycarp. The University of Notre Dame Press states that it is "an important, if little known, text on Polycarp of Smyrna, Bishop and martyr, and his association with the apostle John."

Basically, the *Harris Fragments* stress Polycarp's connection with the Apostle John, teach he was appointed bishop of Smyrna by John, and that he died a martyr's death at age 104. Here are some translated quotes from the *Harris Fragments* ([ ] in source):

> There remained [---]ter him a disciple[e ---] name was Polycar[p and] he made him bishop over Smyrna ... He was ... old man, being one hundred and f[our] of age. He continued to walk [i]n the canons which he had learned from his youth from John the a[p]ostle. (Weidman, Frederick W. Polycarp and John: The Harris Fragments and Their Challenge to Literary Traditions. University of Notre Dame Press, Notre Dame (IL), 1999, pp. 43-44)

By mentioning the term "canons" the *Harris Fragments* could possibly be suggesting that John passed the knowledge of the proper books of the Bible to Polycarp — and that would seem to be the case. But even if canon(s) meant only the measure of the right way to be a Christian that early, that strongly supports the view that the Apostle John would have passed on his knowledge of the books of the Bible to Polycarp—plus he likely would have passed on the parchments of the actual New Testament books. The canon was known by the Church of God in Asia Minor in the 2nd century. All should realize that to be faithful to apostolic Christianity that one should imitate Polycarp and John as they themselves did Christ (cf. 1 Corinthians 11:1).

There was a chain of custody of the New Testament scriptures from the apostles to Polycarp and others in the 2nd century.

Irenaeus

Some scholars claim that Irenaeus either was the earliest developer, the 'principal architect,' of the New Testament canon or at least the developer of a proto-canon of the New Testament (Kruger, pp. 157-163).

This, however, seems to overlook that Irenaeus claimed to have 1) been in Asia Minor and 2) knew Polycarp. Hence, while Irenaeus may have written more than Polycarp (at least we have more writings from Irenaeus available than from Polycarp), since Irenaeus did not have a direct connection to the original apostles, it makes more sense to conclude that some of his writings were based upon what Polycarp and probably others in Asia Minor asserted.

Furthermore, Irenaeus himself wrote:

> ... those which have been handed down to us from the apostles ... the Scriptures themselves, that that which has been handed down from the apostles. (Against Heresies, Book III, Chapter 11, Verse 9)

Irenaeus was not saying he was an innovator here. But acknowledged that the Scriptures were handed down from the apostles, and the one apostolic connection he personally claimed was to Polycarp.

The canon was known to the faithful leaders in Asia Minor prior to the writings of Irenaeus. This view is also confirmed by scholars such as Dr. Michael J. Kruger (Kruger, pp. 169-197).

Papias and Polycrates

Papias was a Church of God leader in Hieropolis in Asia Minor. He was born in the 1st century, died in the 2nd century, and knew the Apostle John as well as Polycarp of Smyrna.

Notice the following:

> These things are attested by Papias, an ancient man who was a hearer of John and a companion of Polycarp ... there will be a period of some thousand years after the resurrection of the dead, and that the kingdom of Christ will be set up in material form on this very earth. (Eusebius. The History of the Church, Book 3, Chapter XXXIX, pp. 68-69)

This shows that Papias accepted the Book of Revelation as inspired as that teaching is from Revelation 5:10 and 20:4-6.

Here is some of what Papias wrote that John, called the 'presbyter,' told him:

> 14. Papias gives also in his own work other accounts of the words of the Lord on the authority of Aristion who was mentioned above, and traditions as handed down by the presbyter John; to which we refer those who are fond of learning. But now we must add to the words of his which we have already quoted the tradition which he gives in regard to Mark, the author of the Gospel.
>
> 15. This also the presbyter said: Mark, having become the interpreter of Peter, wrote down accurately, though not in order, whatsoever he remembered of the things said or done by Christ. For he neither heard the Lord nor followed him, but afterward, as I said, he followed Peter, who adapted his teaching to the needs of his hearers, but with no intention of giving a connected account of the Lord's discourses, so that

Mark committed no error while he thus wrote some things as he remembered them. For he was careful of one thing, not to omit any of the things which he had heard, and not to state any of them falsely. (Eusebius. The History of the Church, Book 3, Chapter XXXIX; Digireads, pp. 68-69)

So, Papias said that it was John who handed down what they needed (which would have included knowledge of the books) and it was John who told him that Mark wrote a gospel account, based upon information Mark got from Peter — and that the information Mark wrote was accurate. This further demonstrates that John and the faithful in Asia Minor knew the New Testament and believed it.

Irenaeus of Lyon wrote of the Gospel of Mark:

Mark, the disciple and interpreter of Peter, did also hand down to us in writing what had been preached by Peter. (Against Heresies, Book 3, Chapter 1).

So, the assertion was that this book was properly handed down—not that a council was needed to determine if it was a valid book.

A later leader in Asia Minor, Polycrates of Ephesus, claimed that he had the complete Bible (circa 193 A.D.):

For in Asia also great lights have fallen asleep ... Among these are Philip, one of the twelve apostles, ... John, who was both a witness and a teacher, who reclined upon the bosom of the Lord ... Polycarp in Smyrna, ... Melito, the Eunuch who lived altogether in the Holy Spirit, and who lies in Sardis ...

I ... **have gone through every Holy Scripture**. (Eusebius. The History of the Church, Book V, Chapter XXIV, Verses 2-7. Translated by A. Cushman McGiffert. Digireads.com Publishing, Stilwell (KS), 2005, p. 114)

And Polycrates would have agreed with the earlier list that Melito of Sardis put together as he also referred to Melito as being faithful. Polycrates could not have declared he went **"through every Holy Scripture"** if he did not know what the scriptures were.

The New Testament Canon Was Formed in Asia Minor

Some of the evidence from Papias, Polycarp, and Polycrates (all of whom were in Asia Minor) may have been part of why some scholars, such as the late James Moffatt, have understood that Asia Minor had the complete canon:

> Was not the Apostolic Canon of scripture first formed ... in Asia Minor? (Excerpt of James Moffatt's review, p.292. In: Bauer W. Orthodoxy and Heresy in Earliest Christianity, 2nd ed. Sigler Press Edition, Mifflintown, PA, 1996)

The true Church of God was predominant in Asia Minor until the early to mid-third century and it had the original and true canon. On the other hand, the fact is that the Church of Rome states it did not have the canon until centuries later.

Tertullian, the so-called 'father of Latin theology' taught:

> Come now, you who would indulge a better curiosity, if you would apply it to the business of your salvation, run over the apostolic churches, in which the very thrones of **the apostles are still pre-eminent in their places, in which their own authentic writings are read**, uttering the voice and representing the face of each of them severally ... Since you are able to cross to Asia, you get Ephesus. (Tertullian. Prescription Against Heretics, Chapter 36)

And while Tertullian had his own issues, he is correct that those who were truly apostolic churches at that time (like Ephesus/Smyrna in Asia Minor and Antioch) did know which books were valid.

Although apparently some had questions, Melito of Sardis confirmed the books of the Old Testament (Eusebius. The History of the Church, Book IV, Chapter XXVI, p. 90).

For another source, consider that in the early 3rd century, Serapion, Bishop of Antioch (an area on the outskirts of Asia Minor), and a supporter of Church of God doctrines, taught that the proper books were "handed down to us" (Eusebius. The History of the Church, Book

VI, Chapter XII, verses 3-4, p. 125-126), thus negating the idea of a late canonization for the faithful.

Also in Antioch, Church of God leader Theophilus wrote in the late 2nd century:

> Moreover, concerning the righteousness which the law enjoined, confirmatory utterances are found both with the prophets and in the Gospels, because they all spoke inspired by one Spirit of God. Isaiah accordingly spoke thus: … (Theophilus. To Autolycus, Book III, Chapter 12)

So, both the Old and New Testaments were considered as scripture.

Clearly those in Asia Minor and Antioch claimed to have and know the scriptures.

Nazarenes: Who Told Jerome the Canon?

Around the end of the 4th century, the 'Nazarenes' (people who held Church of God doctrines like the Sabbath) knew that they had the scriptures and that they came from God, not a Greco-Roman council. Jerome wrote that the Nazarenes stated:

> … God has given us the Law and the testimonies of scriptures. (Jerome, cited in Pritz R. Nazarene Jewish Christianity. Magnas, Jerusalem, 1988, p. 63)

The Greco-Roman Catholic Bishop and saint Epiphanius similarly taught about the Nazarenes:

> For they use not only the New Testament but also the Old. (cited in Pritz, p. 33)

So, the Nazarenes had the Old and New Testaments.

Now, while many believe that because of the *Latin Vulgate Bible* by Jerome, which he completed in 405 A.D. (Wegner PD. The Journey from Texts to Translations: The Origin and Development of the Bible. Baker Academic, 2004, p. 254), that the Greco-Roman Catholic Church gave the world the Bible, those who espouse that view tend to overlook the question of how Jerome got his information. Where did Jerome get the Bible canon, or at least information on which books were valid?

Based on records in Latin and other languages, Scholars Ray Pritz and the Roman Catholic Priest Bagatti both concluded that Jerome got some of his information on the Bible from the 'Nazarene' Christians and from various Jewish synagogues (Pritz, pp. 49-53; Bagatti, Bellarmino. Translated by Eugene Hoade. The Church from the Circumcision. Nihil obstat: Marcus Adinolfi, 13 Maii 1970. Imprimi potest: Herminius Roncari, 14 Junii 1970. Imprimatur: +Albertus Gori, die 26 Junii 1970. Franciscan Printing Press, Jerusalem, 1971, pp. 84-85; Jerome, De Viris Illustribus). Though he consulted with one or more Nazarenes about which books, Jerome did not use the best texts as he used essentially Alexandrian and Septuagint texts.

It is a fact that Jerome did deal with 'Nazarene Christians' who kept the Sabbath, taught the millennium, etc. (Jerome. Letter 112 to Augustine, Chapter 4).

Jerome also wrote that he was friendly with at least:

> "one of the Hebrews that believed." (Translation by Priest Bagatti of Jerome, Epistula CXXV, Chapter 12. Patrologia Latina (22, 1079). The edition by J. P. Migne, c. 1886, p. 1079)

Yes, Jerome got some of his information about the books of the New Testament from people who held what could be considered to be Church of God doctrines. He also looked to have consulted with some in Asia Minor and Antioch—and those there would have also assisted him in identifying the proper books since they knew the canon since the time of the apostles. Those in Asia Minor and Antioch would have included people with and without a Church of God background, as well as records from people such as Lucian and Serapion.

Therefore, realize that the claim that the Roman 'Church gave the world the Bible' neglects to mention that their church apparently got at least part of the Bible from those in the true Church of God, some also known as the Nazarenes in Asia Minor, Antioch, and in Jerusalem! Nor was the Church of Rome the source of the Masoretic or Byzantine texts!

As far as ancient literature goes, it points to the "original catholic church" being the Church of God in Smyrna of Asia Minor associated with Polycarp (for more details, check out the free book, online at ccog.org, *Beliefs of the Original Catholic Church*). Consider that since the Apostle John in Asia Minor passed the canons onto Polycarp of Smyrna, Polycarp was one who would have originally confirmed what the apostles had accepted—Polycarp received the correct and complete New Testament text. These were then passed on in Asia Minor (parts of which have been called Byzantium).

This seems to be, at least indirectly, acknowledged by some modern scholars. Notice a 21st century account by Gerd Theissen:

> Therefore we can advance the hypothesis that above all those writings entered the canon on which the Christian communities of Asia Minor and Rome could agree. (Theissen G. Fortress introduction to the New Testament. Fortress Press, 2003, p. 178)

Taking this a step further, even those who later compromised doctrinally in Asia Minor apparently recognized that they knew of the complete canon and thus they (and probably others) influenced the Church of Rome.

Of course, the Bible itself came from God via His Holy Spirit (2 Peter 1:21) as "All Scripture is given by inspiration of God" (2 Timothy 3:16).

Notice also something that happened around 650 A.D.:

> ... a reformer arose, esteemed by the *Paulicians* as the chosen messenger of truth. In his humble dwelling of Mananalis, Constantine entertained a deacon, who returned from Syrian captivity, and received the inestimable gift of the New Testament, (Gibbon E. The History of the Decline and Fall of the Roman Empire, Volume 7. London, 1809, p. 390)

So, from Greek speaking Syria, the New Testament was handed to one in Armenia, who is believed to have translated it. Though Gibbon thought that they rejected Peter's epistles, a later scholar found that they did accept them (Conybeare F.C. The Key of Truth: A Manual of the Paulician Church of Armenia. Clarendon Press, Oxford, 1898, p. xxxix).

The Bible also teaches:

> [89] Forever, O Lord, Your word is settled in heaven. (Psalm 119:89)

God gave the world the Bible and had that settled.

Jesus taught:

> [35] Heaven and earth will pass away, but My words will by no means pass away. (Matthew 24:35)

Note: That is a prophecy from Jesus that history shows has come to pass throughout the nearly 2,000 years since He stated that (for more prophecies related to Jesus, see also the free online book, available at ccog.org: *Proof Jesus is the Messiah: Biblical, Prophetic, and Historical Facts*).

Jesus' words were preserved in the Greek texts. This was understood by the true Church of God throughout history.

> The ... "received text" (also called "majority text, "textus receptus," or "Byzantine text"). This text was used by the Waldenses, and was preserved by the true church through the ages. (Webb R. Antioch Believer!, January 11, 2012)

> ... down through the centuries there were only two streams of manuscripts. The first stream which carried the Received Text in Hebrew and Greek, began with the Apostolic churches, and reappearing at intervals down the Christian Era ... by the Syrian Church of Antioch which produced eminent scholarship; by the Italic Church in northern Italy; and ... by the pre-Waldensian, the Waldensian. ... First of all, the Textus Receptus was the Bible of early Eastern Christianity. Later it was adopted as the official text of the Greek Catholic Church. (Wilkinson. Our Authorized Bible Vindicated, pp. 31, 40)

> The major labor of God's Church in the Thyatira Era was to translate, copy and make the Scriptures known. ... It is a little known fact that even most manuscripts which came to be stored away in Catholic monasteries and cathedrals are

ultimately traceable to the work of God's Church! You see, few scholars in the Middle Ages had ability to read or translate from the original Hebrew or Greek. So they used the Waldensian version ... as their main source! (LESSON 52, AMBASSADOR COLLEGE BIBLE CORRESPONDENCE COURSE Why Was Printing Invented? Ambassador College, 1969)

Peter ... Waldo had Bible translated into language of the laity. Led to catholic forbidding laity from reading the Bible {Council of Toulouse of 1229}. (Kelly R. Ambassador College Notes and Course Outlines Church History. Ambassador College, 1987, pp. 109-110)

Longing to be more knowledgeable in the Scriptures, Waldo conceived the idea of translating the Bible into the vernacular language, the Gallo-Provencal idiom. With the help of three other scholars, the entire New Testament, Psalms and many books of the Old Testament were made accessible to the bulk of the people. (Blackwell D. The Plain Truth About The Waldensians. Ambassador College Library, 1974, p. 17)

Waldensians ... translated the Scriptures into the vernacular, criticized clerical wealth and corruption, and ... formed their own churches; despite persecution. ... (Fanning S. Mystics of the Christian Tradition. Routeldge, New York. 2001, reprinted 2006, pp. 256)

While subject to persecutions (officially, such as edicts issued by Roman Catholics from the 1184 Synod of Verona), the Fourth Lateran Council of 1215, and the 1487 Bull by Pope Innocent VII), many Waldenesian writings were stolen and ended up in the hands of Roman supporters.

It was not just the Waldenses that suffered persecution. Notice that Rome issued edicts against their lay members having the Bible:

"Canon 14. We prohibit also that the laity should be permitted to have the books of the Old or the New Testament; unless anyone from motives of devotion should wish to have the Psalter or the Breviary for divine offices or the hours of the blessed Virgin; but we most strictly forbid their having any translation of these books." (The Council of Toulouse, 1229.) ...

The councils that prohibited vernacular translations were Toulouse (1229), Trier (1231), Tarragona (1233), and Béziers (1246). Rheims (1230) also banned translation into Gallic (French). ... The council of Trier in 1231 is poorly reported, but it condemned heretics with Scripture translated into German; this is likely to have been aimed at the Waldensians. (Nowell P. Burning the Bible: Heresy and Translation in Occitania 1229-1250. Academia.edu undated, but prior to 2018, pp. 1,7)

These councils did not stop all the Waldenses as they still held on to reading scripture in languages they could understand. The New Testament praises lay people reading the scriptures (cf. Acts 17:11; 2 Timothy 3:14-17), while also showing that the ministry should be consulted on matters that may be misunderstood (Acts 8:3-31; 2 Timothy 3:14; Ephesians 4:11-16). That has been the Church of God position throughout history, not that lay people should be forbidden to read scriptures in their native language. The Waldenesians had essentially the same view.

Dr. Frederick Nolan asserted after 28 years of research he had traced the *Textus Receptus* back to the apostles through "early translations made by the Waldenses, who were the lineal descendants of the Italick Church" (Nolan F. An Inquiry into the integrity of the Greek Vulgate, or received text of the New Testament, etc. F.C. and J. Rivington, 1815, pp. xvii-xviii), which seemingly came from Antioch (Ibid pp. 125-126). The Italick, seems to have come from Old Latin. "Old Latin (*Itala*) NT translated from apostolic Greek NT (ca. 157)" (Coulter, p. 1412).

Some, but not all or most, of the Waldenses held Church of God doctrines. Others outside the COG have also claimed that the faithful among the Waldensians had "the pure ... text" (Grady WP. Final Authority. Grady Publications, 1993, p. 36).

Certain Latin Texts Corrupted

Now Jerome, despite being informed what the books were, had issues with the manuscripts he was working with. Notice what he wrote Pope Damasus related to the Gospels:

You urge me to revise the Old Latin version, and, as it were, to sit in judgment on the copies of the scriptures and, inasmuch as they differ from one another, you would have me decide which of them agree with the Greek original. ... readings at variance with the early copies cannot be right. For if we are to pin our faith to the Latin texts, it is for our opponents to tell us *which;* for there are almost as many forms of texts as there are copies. (Jerome. The Four Gospels Addressed to Pope Damasus, a.d. 383. In Horn A. The Writings of Jerome. New Apostolic Bible Covenant, 2020, p. 293)

Notice that Jerome attested to the corruptness of the Latin forms. His letter then immediately continued with:

If, on the other hand, we are to glean the truth from a comparison of *many,* why not go back to the original Greek and correct the mistakes introduced by inaccurate translators, and the blundering alterations of confident but ignorant critics, and, further, all that has been inserted or changed by copyists more asleep than awake? (Ibid, p. 293)

Notice also the following:

Jerome himself used manuscripts of the Alexandrian type-preserved and copied in *Egypt*. Again, he *did not use* the official text which God had preserved. ...

Jerome attested to the corruptness of the Latin forms. ...

"During all this time the original text of the Vulgate *became greatly* CORRUPTED. Again and again it was 'revised' back to the favorite rendering of the Old Latin Text." (Henry Thiessen, *Introduction to the New Testament*, p 60)

There you have it! The texts that the Catholic Church preserved were the *most corrupt* They *did not follow* the true readings of the divinely preserved Greek manuscripts. Its revision was dependent on *Egyptian manuscripts*-again corrupt. The revised Vulgate also became corrupted. (Kroll, p. 21)

So, yes there were issues with the Latin and other writings that Rome tried to preserve and use.

Notice the following:

> 1520, Prierio, one of the first theologians of Leo X., had said, "*He is a heretic whosoever does not rest on the doctrine of the Roman Church, and of the Roman pontiff, as the infallible rule of faith, from which Holy Scripture itself derives its force and its authority.*" (Bungener F, McClintock F, Scott DD. History of the Council of Trent. Harper, 1855, p. 82)

But the authority of the Bible comes from God. Furthermore, scripture does not say God gave that authority to a Roman pontiff (the term "pontiff" is not in the Bible).

Despite what the Bible teaches, some Roman Catholic writings basically claim that since they allege that "it is through the Church that the Bible was given to the world," "the Bible is a Catholic book," they gave the world the Bible, and they alone, through their "Magisterium" are the ones to interpret it (e.g. Akin J. The Bible is a Catholic Book. Catholic Answers Press, 2019, pp. 8, 166-169).

But God gave the Bible and finalized it in Asia Minor.

Regarding interpretation, the Church of Rome, itself, asserts:

> The task of interpreting the Word of God authentically has been entrusted solely to the Magisterium of the Church, that is, to the Pope and to the bishops in communion with him. (Catechism of the Catholic Church, p.30)

Yet, nothing in the Bible suggests that the Church of Rome would be the true arbitrator of what the word of God is or what it means (for more on early church history, check out the free book, online at ccog.org, titled: *Continuing History of the Church of God*).

10. Language of the New Testament

What language was the New Testament originally written in?

The document and linguistic evidence has concluded that it was Greek. Furthermore, while Jews were reached with the gospel, the Book of Acts repeatedly points out that many Greeks listened and believed. (Acts 14:1, 17:4,12, 18:4, 19:10,17-18, 20:21)

Scholars of ancient *koine* Greek have consistently concluded that the literary quality of the Greek of the NT books (including Matthew and Mark) point to Greek being the original language and not being a translation (Bromiley GW, ed. International Standard Bible Encyclopedia. Wm B Eerdmans, 1979).

But some people have claimed that the Greek is a translation from either Aramaic or Hebrew.

Aramaic

The ancient Aramaic language originated among the Arameans in northern Syria and became widely used under the Assyrians. While the Old Testament was mainly written in Hebrew, a few passages in the Old Testament were written in Aramaic. Generally recognized Aramaic phrases include Genesis 31:47; Ezra 4:8-6:18, 7:12-26; Jeremiah 10:11; Daniel 2:4b-7:28; plus possibly one or more words in Job 36:2a and Psalm 2:12. There are two other questioned places, that have also been proposed, with possibly one word each: Genesis 15:1 and Numbers 23:10 — presuming that someone like Ezra made minor edits for clarity (and, likely, changed some text from proto-Hebrew characters to more contemporary Hebrew letters).

Various ones have compared the relationship between Hebrew and Aramaic to that between the modern versions of Spanish and Portuguese: the two are distinct languages, but sufficiently related that a reader of one can understand much of the other (see Isaiah 36:11). The pronunciation can be another matter, however (see Judges 12:6).

Some claim that the New Testament was originally written in Aramaic. It has been stated that the position of the Assyrian Church of the East is that the Syriac Peshitta (a Bible version which is written in a vernacular form of Aramaic), used in that church, is the original of the New Testament. For instance, the patriarch Shimun XXIII Eshai declared in 1957:

> With reference to... the originality of the Peshitta text, as the Patriarch and Head of the Holy Apostolic and Catholic Church of the East, we wish to state, that the Church of the East received the scriptures from the hands of the blessed Apostles themselves in the Aramaic original, the language spoken by our Lord Jesus Christ Himself, and that the Peshitta is the text of the Church of the East which has come down from the Biblical times without any change or revision. (April 5, 1957). (Aramaic original New Testament theory.

The basic claim that advocates of this tend to make is that since Jesus and others in Judea spoke Aramaic, some of the translations into Greek do not appear to be logical, and the disciples would not have known Greek, therefore the entire New Testament was written in Aramaic. Yet, Jesus normally would have spoken Semitic Aramaic (sometimes also called Jewish Palestinian Aramaic), not the form used in the Peshitta text. He also spoke Hebrew and had some knowledge of Greek.

P52 and P66

The earliest New Testament manuscripts that we know of are in Greek. The Rylands Library Papyrus P52 is dated from A.D. 90-125 A.D., with c. A.D. 100 considered as being the more likely date. This document, which is shown on the front cover of this book, is clearly in the Greek language. And if the New Testament had not been originally written in Greek as some claim, it fairly quickly was being communicated in Greek. P52 predates the earliest manuscripts found in Hebrew or Aramaic.

Another early manuscript is called Papyrus 66 (P66) and has been claimed to be from the early to mid-2nd century (others have different views). It contains much of the Gospel of John and uses the Greek abbreviations for certain names. P66 often abbreviates the names of the Father, God, and Jesus Christ to two or three letters in which the last letter changes according to the grammatical use with the name shown highlighted with a line over the abbreviation:

Jesus is abbreviated as Iη-, (transliterated into English as Je- or Ye-). Christ is abbreviated as Χρ- (literally Chr-). The word God is recorded as Θ- while Father is shown as Πρ- and Lord as K-. These abbreviations clearly derive from the Greek terms and not the Hebrew. (Nathan P. Early Manuscripts Answer Modern Question about Sacred Names. http://firstfollowers.vision.org/first-followers/ --- accessed 06/15/2010)

This author personally reviewed photographs of P66 and saw the highlighted abbreviated names on it. It is in Greek, not Hebrew or Aramaic.

A Greek fragment from Mark, known as P137, looks to be from the latter half of the 2nd century.

P137 comprising Mark 1:7–9, 16–18

Perhaps it should be noted that there are over 5,800 ancient manuscripts of the New Testament in Greek (Holden, p. 103). The bulk of the original New Testament was written in Greek.

The overwhelming consensus of scholars is that the Old Testament of the Peshitta was translated into Syriac from Hebrew, probably in the 2nd century A.D., and that the New Testament of the Peshitta was translated from the Greek:

> The Peshitta Old Testament was translated directly from the original Hebrew text, and the Peshitta New Testament directly from the original Greek. (Brock SP. The Bible in the Syriac Tradition. St. Ephrem Ecumenical Research Institute, 1988, page 13)

What has been believed to be the oldest dated Peshitta (Syriac Aramaic) manuscript is dated to "464 CE" (Lasater R. Was the New Testament Really Written in Greek? A Concise Compendium of the Many Internal and External Evidences of Aramaic Primacy. 2008, p. 199). The same source claims that the New Testament was "completed around 100 AD" (Ibid, p. 208) — about when the Rylands Library Papyrus P52 was written.

A pro-Aramaic NT source has claimed, "That the Peshitta dates back to 175 AD at the very latest" (Ibid, p. 208). But even if 175 A.D. is correct, it simply was not the original text. It should also be noted that Lasater's book is very misleading with what it tries to indicate—like that the oldest major texts are in Aramaic. The reality is that entire codices of the Greek and Aramaic New Testaments that exist are of similar ages. Furthermore, fragments like Rylands P52 are in Greek and older than any known Aramaic texts.

There are additional problems for the original Aramaic hypothesis.

For one, it originally did not include all the books of the New Testament. The traditional New Testament of the Peshitta had only 22 books — --it was missing the Second Epistle of John, the Third Epistle of John, the Second Epistle of Peter, the Epistle of Jude and the Book of Revelation. The missing books were later reconstructed by the Syriacist John Gwynn in 1893 and 1897 from alternative manuscripts, and included them in the United Bible Societies edition of 1905. The 1997 modern Aramaic New Testament has all 27 books. But the fact that it originally missed 5 should raise flags.

But that is not its only major flaw.

Westcott and Hort noted that there were different forms of Aramaic, and the Peshitta form differed from Jewish Aramaic which they referred to as "Jerusalem Syriac" (Westcott, pp. 84-85).

Notice also the following from Steve Caruso, who was a professional Aramaic translator for 15 years, concerning the commonly claimed

Aramaic Peshitta language of the New Testament:

160

The Wrong Language

Many Peshitta Primacy advocates claim that the Peshitta dates back to the first few centuries AD. Since it's written in Classical Syriac, and Syriac was spoken at that time, it seems logical that the text could be that old. The problem, however, is that not *all* Syriac is equal.

If the Peshitta was written right after Jesus' lifetime, one would expect the dialect to match up with other inscriptions from the first few centuries. This particular dialect of Syriac is known as Old Syriac, and is attested in about 80 different inscriptions. So when we compare the two what do we find are some very curious and telling differences. ... **the Peshitta, at the earliest, represents fourth century Syriac. It cannot be from the first or second centuries AD as some proponents claim.** (Caruso S. Problems With Peshitta Primacy. http://aramaicnt.org/articles/ problems-with-peshitta-primacy/ --- accessed 06/01/20)

There is no way that a 4th century language was used for the original New Testament. The type of Aramaic pointed to as original could not possibly be used for the New Testament:

There are numerous dialects and Aramaic has continually changed over the centuries of its existence, with unique dialects in Palestine, Samaria, Galilee, etc. Edessan Aramaic/Eastern Aramaic, differed from Western dialects. There was also 100-200 years between the time of the apostles and the Syriac, which brought even more changes.

Lamsa's Pe-shi-tta (dashes included to bypass the forum filter) is inaccurate. Odessa, the focus of Syriac and its major New Testament versions was not evangelized, much less established in Christianity, until after A.D. 116, which was long after the NT had been written. Lamsa used unidentified Aramaic texts to supply missing portions of the texts he chose, and in some places merely copied from the King James Version. The forms of Aramaic he used are not the Aramaic from the time of Jesus. Aramaic spoken today, called the Eastern group of dialects, is different from the Aramaic spoken by Jesus Christ, which was the

Western group, a branch that is considered extinct. ('Embrachu' Tom. The "AENT" and the Khaboris Codex. www.survivalist boards.com/showthread.php?t=168313&page=2)

The Aramaic dialect used in Galilee during the time of Jesus was not the same as the "dialect used in the Peshitta New Testament." (DeFrancisco JJ. Which Language Did Jesus Speak – Aramaic, Hebrew, or Greek? http://godward.org/hebrew%20roots/which_language_did_jesus_spe ak.htm --- retrieved 03/32/19)

Notice also the following from Paul Stevenson, who is a translator, editor, and linguist:

Was Syriac "The Language of Jesus"?

Today you can find various books written in Syriac or teaching Syriac or translated from Syriac, in which the author claims that this is "Aramaic, the language of Jesus." Well, it is true that Syriac is one of the many dialects of Aramaic, and it is true that Jesus spoke Aramaic. However ... (sorry to burst any bubbles) Jesus did not speak Syriac. Jesus spoke a rather different dialect of Aramaic. (Stevenson P. Was Syriac "The Language of Jesus"? The Language Fan, March 8, 2008 http://syriacspanish.blog spot.com/2008/03/was-syriac-language-of-jesus.html --- accessed 06/01/20)

So, no, despite adamant statements from Aramaic proponents, it is not possible that Aramaic was the original language of the New Testament.

There is also the fact that the New Testament is clear in areas that it is directly specifying Aramaic.

Matthew 27:46 reads:

Peshitta — And about the ninth hour Jesus cried out with a loud voice and said: "Ēl, Ēl, why have you forsaken me?"

Greek — And about the ninth hour Jesus cried with a loud voice, saying: "Eli, Eli, lamma sabacthani?" that is, "My God, my God, why hast thou forsaken me?"

The parallel verse in Mark 15:34 has Christ's quoted Aramaic words with a translation in both the Greek and Peshitta texts:

> Peshitta — And in the ninth hour, Jesus cried out in a loud voice and said: "Ēl, Ēl Imānā shvaqtāni" that is "My God, my God, why have you forsaken me?"

> Greek — And at the ninth hour, Jesus cried out with a loud voice, saying: "Eloi, Eloi, lamma sabacthani?" Which is, being interpreted, "My God, my God, why hast thou forsaken me?"

Having to repeat certain statements twice in Aramaic, as opposed to Aramaic and the Greek translation, in places like Matthew 27:46 and Mark 15:34 seems to disprove the Aramaic hypothesis. It makes sense to have the Greek translation of Aramaic in a Greek text, but not the other way around if Aramaic was the original language.

The fact that Jesus spoke in a version of Aramaic accounts for seemingly unusual translations into Greek — the so-called "bad idiom transfers," poetry, grammatical issues, and "split words" that the Aramaic primacy advocates point to as proof (e.g. Lasater, pp. 13, 147-151). So does the fact that Greek was not the native language of the apostles. Therefore, certain grammatical awkwardness is not proof of an Aramaic original New Testament.

Consider also the following from Mark:

> [41] Then He took the child by the hand, and said to her, "Talitha, cumi," which is translated, "Little girl, I say to you, arise." (Mark 5:41 NKJV)

> [41] And he took the hand of the girl and said to her, "Talitha cumi (Young girl arise)." (Mark 5:41 Aramaic New Testament)

Why would Mark quote and translate from Aramaic while leaving the Aramaic in? Because his account was not originally written in Aramaic!

Let it be noted that the *Aramaic English New Testament* also does not properly handle 2 Corinthians 6:2, and hence gives a misconception related to salvation (details are in the free book, online at ccog.org,

Universal OFFER of Salvation, Apokatastasis: Can God save the lost in an age to come? Hundreds of scriptures reveal God's plan of salvation).

One 'proof' given in the book *Ruach Qadim* regarding why the Aramaic should be trusted is the assertion that Mark was in Egypt and died in Alexandria in A.D. 63 (Roth AG. Ruach Qadim: Aramaic Origins of the New Testament. Tushiyah Press, 2005, p. 97). However, Mark's New Testament travels are shown and never have him going anywhere near Alexandria. The view *Rauch Qadim* points to that Mark died in Egypt is consistent with neither the biblical nor the historical reports of Mark near that period. That author then tries to tie that in with Clement of Alexandria — yet he was one who blended Gnosticism with his version of Christianity and should not be considered to have followed faithful presbyters as *Rauch Qadim* points to on page 98.

Ruach Qadim states that it took centuries for the Greeks to catch up to the ending of Mark 16:9-20 on page 100 that the Aramaic supposedly already had. Yet, the Greeks already knew of it in the 2nd century: specifically, Papias, Justin, and Irenaeus (see the article at www.ccog.org: *Should Mark 16:9-20 be part of the Bible?*).

Some Aramaic supporters have pointed to a statement from Papias related to Matthew (Eusebius. The History of the Church, Book 3, Chapter XXXIX). He did not write that Matthew was written in Aramaic, but Hebrew. Here is the actual Greek word Papias used: Ἑβραΐδι (Hebrew) not Αραμαϊκή (Aramaic). Papias did not write that Matthew was originally written in Aramaic.

Note that one 'proof' that Aramaic is supposedly correct is that Gabriel Roth, author of the *Ruach Qadim*, asserts his language is sacred (Roth, p. 113). That is a false and unbiblical assertion.

Translation Biases in Many Lands

It should also be noted that there are translation errors in the Aramaic showing bias. Like most biased translators of Greek, the two translations of the Syriac/Aramaic this author has seen have both mistranslated John 14:17 and John 15:26:

"He is The Spirit of Truth, whom the world cannot receive, because it has neither seen him nor known him; but you know him, for he dwells with you and he is in you." (John 14:17, Aramaic Bible in Plain English)

The Spirit of Truth, He who the world is not able to receive because it has not seen Him, nor does it know Him. But you know Him for He dwells with you and He is in you. (John 14:17, Aramaic English New Testament)

"But when The Redeemer of the accursed comes, him whom I shall send to you from the presence of my Father, The Spirit of Truth, he who proceeds from the presence of my Father, he shall testify concerning me." (John 15:26, Aramaic Bible in Plain English)

'Spirit' is not a masculine term in Aramaic. Those who do not believe that there are biases in the Aramaic translation are in error. 'Spirit' is a gender neuter term in Greek—and has also been improperly translated by most Greco-Roman-Protestant scholars as well into the male gender in opposition to rules of Greek grammar.

Here are two correct translations of these two verses from the Greek to the English:

Even the Spirit of the truth which the world cannot receive because it perceives it not, nor knows it; but you know it because it dwells with you, and shall be within you. (John 14:17, A Faithful Version)

The helper whom I will send to you from the Father will come. This helper, the Spirit of Truth who comes from the Father, will declare the truth about me. (John 15:26, God's Word Translation)

Translations are done by humans and subject to error. The Aramaic translations into English are as well as these few examples point out.

It also should be pointed out that political and theological biases are real. Related to that, a recent Danish translation of the New Testament left out the word "Israel" at least 74 of the 75 times it is in the Greek, apparently to appease/support certain Palestinian concerns (Berkowitz AE. Lutherans Publish New Version of Bible Without the Word 'Israel' in It. Breaking Israel News, April 20, 2020).

The Communist Chinese Party (CCP) has been looking for its own edited translation of scripture. "To accomplish this goal, passages that have been ruled to violate the 'core socialist values' of the CCP would be removed from texts like the Bible and the Quran" (Churches in China Must Preach 'Patriotism' to Reopen After Coronavirus. National Catholic Register, June 5, 2020). The word of God is sharper than any two-edged sword (Hebrews 4:12)—ignoring parts does not change the truth. Scripture cannot truly be broken (John 10:35b). No one is supposed to add to or take away from the word of God (cf. Revelation 22:18-19, Deuteronomy 4:2,12:32). Yet, for political, theological, and other reasons, translators and others have attempted to do so.

Greek Text Contradictions?

The book *Was the New Testament Really Written in Greek? A Concise Compendium of the Many Internal and External Evidences of Aramaic Primacy* claims that "split words" is one of the "most convincing proofs" of "Peshitta primacy".

But is it really?

No.

Having read the arguments, they simply are not proof. They are assertions of opinions. One of which was that certain words would not coincidentally be the same — thus this proves an Aramaic origin. Yet, we see this clearly happening with the New Testament and Greek translations of the Old Testament, plus we see this when early church writers quoted the New Testament. We also do not seem to have any early post-NT church writer who quoted Aramaic (other than if they quoted a Greek translation account that included it).

Now the "big one" proof in *Was the New Testament Really Written in Greek? A Concise Compendium of the Many Internal and External Evidences of Aramaic Primacy* supposedly has to do with a "QUADRUPLE split word" in Philemon 1:1 (Lasater, p. 59-62). But again, there was no proof, just assertions that this existence and the book's explanation was proof. Actually, it is much more logical to conclude that Paul, the Apostle to the Gentiles, wrote to the Greek-speaking Gentile Philemon in Greek.

The same source claims that the Greek text is in contradiction for Jesus' genealogy that supposedly is solved by the Aramaic. (Lasater, p. 214-216)

Steve Caruso also addressed this and explained why that Peshitta/Aramaic argument is in error:

> Hundreds of theologians have spilled rivers of ink taking on this apparent "problem" trying to find different ways to harmonize it, but in the end, Matthew's genealogy only has 13 actual generations in its last set rather than the 14 described.
>
> Now within the Peshitta Primacy movement, the argument goes that in the Syriac Peshitta, the word for "husband" or *gavrā* can also mean "guardian," and therefore the Joseph listed here is Mary's *father* or *legal guardian*. This would make Mary the next generation on the list, and round out the third set of 14 evenly.
>
> **Unfortunately *gavrā* has no such meaning.**
>
> There is not a *single* ancient lexicographer in any dialect of Aramaic that attests to this, nor a single ancient Syriac-speaking theologian who brought this possibility up, nor a single modern lexicographer that attests to this meaning either. However, plenty of ancient sources attest to the fact that *gavrā* — in the relational context of a genealogy — exclusively means "husband" (just like the word ἄνδρα *andra* does in Greek). (Caruso S. Problems With Peshitta Primacy. http://aramaicnt.org/articles/problems-with-peshitta-primacy/ --- accessed 06/01/20)

Here is one explanation of the 13 vs. 14 generations:

> In the listing of Jesus' forefathers, there is a name missing. Excluded from the list is Jehoiakim (a.k.a. Eliakim), who was Josiah's son and Jeconiah's father (1 Chronicles 3:15-16). The reason for his exclusion may be that he was a puppet king, given

his rule by the Pharaoh of Egypt. The first phase of the captivity of Judah by Babylon began at the end of Jehoiakim's reign, prior to his son Jeconiah coming into power. Thus, the 3 groupings of 14 generations would include: 1. Abraham to David; 2. Solomon to Jehoiakim (he is not mentioned, but was among the first to be carried off into Babylon); 3. Jeconiah to Jesus. (Is there an error in the counting of the generations in Matthew chapter 1? www.gotquestions.org/14-generations.html---accessed 06/01/20)

There is no contradiction in the Greek text. This issue also does not prove that the New Testament was not written in Greek — plus the Aramaic also does not list 14 generations — despite the claim based on a forced-mistranslation.

Notice also another possible explanation:

c. 1. Abraham; 2. Isaac; 3. Jacob; 4. Judah; 5. Perez; 6. Hezron; 7. Ram; 8. Aminadab; 9. Naasson; 10. Salma; 11. Boaz; 12. Obed; 13. Jesse; 14. David.

II. 1. Solomon; 2. Rehoboam; 3. Abijah; 4. Asa; 5. Jehoshaphat; 6. Joram; 7. Uzziah; 8. Jotham; 9. Ahaz; 10. Hezekiah; 11. Manasseh; 12. Ammon; 13. Josiah; 14. Jechoniah (ἐπὶ τῆς μετοικεσίας, Matthew 1:11).

III. 1. Jechoniah (μετὰ τὴν μετοικεσίαν, Matthew 1:12); 2. Salathiel; 3. Zerubbabel; 4. Abiud; 5. Eliakim; 6. Azor; 7. Zadok; 8. Achim; 9. Eliud; 10. Eleazar; 11. Matthan; 12. Jacob; 13. Joseph; 14. Jesus.

In the third division we have to notice that in any case Jesus also must be counted, because Matthew 1:17 says ἕως τοῦ Χριστοῦ, in keeping with Matthew 1:1, where Ἰησοῦς Χριστός is announced as the subject of the genealogy, and consequently as the last of the entire list. If Jesus were not included in the enumeration, we should then have a genealogy of Joseph, and the final terminus must have been said to be ἕως Ἰωσήφ. (Meyer's NT Commentary)

The generational count is not some error that Aramaic fixes. Aramaic claimers need to understand that their explanation is not possible according to the Aramaic. There are various possible explanations and two have been shown. It is wrong to conclude that an Aramaic original text resolves this, as it does not.

Another so-called Greek NT contradiction listed was related to the treatment of eunuchs by the children of Israel and in the church era (Lasater, pp. 222-223). Yet, the OT verses simply do not apply to NT Christians like R. Lasater cites.

He also makes the claim that because the Greek NT says that Jeremiah SPOKE something (Matthew 27:9-10), that is written in Zechariah and not found written in Jeremiah, that this too is a contradiction (Lasater, pp. 225-226). Well, when checking with the Greek, one sees that the Greek term transliterated as *légontos* in Matthew 27:9 does not mean written (Interlinear Transliterated Bible. Copyright © 1994, 2003, 2006 by Biblesoft, Inc.). So, this is not a contradiction nor proof that Aramaic was the original language of the NT.

For the sake of space this book will not rebut every one of R. Lasater's claimed contradictions, but he is flat-out wrong on all his 'proofs' this author looked into.

He also claims that "conjunction usage" is proof that the NT was not originally written in Greek as the usage of conjunctions seems too consistent with Semitic writings (Lasater, pp. 263-269). However, since most of the writers of the NT had a version of Aramaic as their native language, it is reasonable to conclude they would have been expected to have a Semitic bias in their use of Greek conjunctions.

Of course, since the Aramaic Peshitta text used was not the language of Jesus or His disciples this eliminates Aramaic. Yet, various ones with less interest in the actual truth, prefer to believe a lie (cf. 2 Thessalonians 2:10-11; Revelation 22:15).

What About Hebrew?

While the Old Testament was written in Hebrew, and scholars and some others in Jesus' time knew how to read Hebrew, it is not likely that much, if any, of the New Testament was written in Hebrew.

Furthermore, Isaiah prophesied "For with ... another tongue He will speak to this people" (Isaiah 28:11), which indicates that Hebrew would not be retained.

Now there is something speculated to once have existed that has been called "Q." "Q" has been claimed by some modern scholars to include some facts about, and statements from, Jesus in either Hebrew or Aramaic. Some claim that Matthew and Luke (or Mark) essentially used this to assist them in writing. If such a document existed, it no longer seems to. All the earliest manuscripts we have of the New Testament are written in the Greek language.

The following is from the Book of Acts:

> 26:14 And when we all had fallen to the ground, I heard a voice speaking to me and saying in the Hebrew language, 'Saul, Saul, why are you persecuting Me? It is hard for you to kick against the goads.' (Acts 26:14)
>
> 21:40 So when he had given him permission, Paul stood on the stairs and motioned with his hand to the people. And when there was a great silence, he spoke to them in the Hebrew language, saying,
>
> 22:1 "Brethren and fathers, hear my defense before you now." 2 And when they heard that he spoke to them in the Hebrew language, they kept all the more silent. (Acts 21:40-22:2, NKJV)

If the Book of Acts was originally written in Hebrew, then there would have been no need to point out something being communicated in the Hebrew language.

Consider also that the synoptic gospels (Matthew, Mark, and Luke) have large overlaps in Greek. This would suggest that one or more of the gospel writers had access to one of the other gospels in Greek. While that would not preclude one of them being originally in Hebrew/Aramaic, it does show they all cannot have been in Hebrew/Aramaic originally. Consider also that some of the Old

Testament scripture quotations in the New Testament are identical to those found in some versions of the Greek Septuagint. This would not be the case if they were simply translated from Hebrew or Aramaic.

It could be that the Book of Hebrews was initially written in Hebrew. Eusebius reports the following claim from Clement:

> 2. He says that the Epistle to the Hebrews is the work of Paul, and that it was written to the Hebrews in the Hebrew language; but that Luke translated it carefully and published it for the Greeks, and hence the same style of expression is found in this epistle and in the Acts.

> 3. But he says that the words, Paul the Apostle, were probably not prefixed, because, in sending it to the Hebrews, who were prejudiced and suspicious of him, he wisely did not wish to repel them at the very beginning by giving his name.

> 4. Farther on he says: "But now, as the blessed presbyter said, since the Lord being the apostle of the Almighty, was sent to the Hebrews, Paul, as sent to the Gentiles, on account of his modesty did not subscribe himself an apostle of the Hebrews, through respect for the Lord, and because being a herald and apostle of the Gentiles he wrote to the Hebrews out of his superabundance." (Eusebius. Book 6, Chapter XIV)

If this is accurate, it explains why Hebrews is of a different style than other writings from the Apostle Paul.

Some have claimed that because the New Testament writers often quoted from the Hebrew Masoretic Text, as opposed to the Septuagint (a translation of the Old Testament into Greek), that this proves a Hebrew or Aramaic origin of the New Testament. But, no it does not.

Consider the following from an Eastern Orthodox Priest:

> Already two centuries before the advent of our Lord Jesus Christ, the Jews living both in Palestine and those scattered throughout the Roman Empire found it necessary to have translations of the Hebrew Old Testament. This was because the

Hebrew language, while still used in worship and perhaps in some rural villages, was no longer a widely spoken language. In the synagogues, the Scriptures were still read in the Hebrew original ... (Barriger L. The Septuagint. © 2019 by the American Carpatho-Russian Orthodox Diocese of the U.S.A.)

Others agree that the scriptures were still read in the Hebrew original in the synagogues (e.g. What Bible Version Did Jesus Read? www.christianitytoday.com/ct/1999/april26/9t5098.html).

The fact is that the Old Testament scriptures were read in Hebrew at synagogues in Jesus' area, would make the New Testament writers more familiar with those as opposed to the Septuagint. Hence, it is natural that they would have translated from the Hebrew text.

We do not have any truly ancient Hebrew New Testament documents. Some of those who assert that the NT was written in Hebrew claim, for example, that this is because the Roman Church destroyed/burned them all. But that is mainly an assertion.

Asia Minor was part of the Eastern Roman Empire. It makes no sense for the two-thirds of the New Testament written to Gentile churches to be in Aramaic or Hebrew. There are no known Aramaic or Hebrew manuscripts of the New Testament that compete with the earliest Greek manuscripts of the New Testament for chronological primacy. The Apostle Paul's ministry was to minister to the Gentiles (Galatians 2:7). Greek was the Gentile language, spoken and understood by many within the confines of the Roman Empire, as that was the common tongue.

Jesus said for his followers to "make disciples of all nations" and teach all things He commanded (Matthew 28:19-20). That necessitated using a language people outside of Judea could understand. Back then, it was Greek.

The New Testament was basically written in Greek, not Hebrew or Aramaic.

Perhaps it should be pointed out that Greek was so common, a study involving Jewish "funerary inscriptions {noted }that most of them are IN

172

GREEK -- approximately 70 percent; about 12 percent are in Latin; and only 18 percent are in Hebrew or Aramaic" for the period 300 B.C.E.– 500 C.E. (van der Horst PW. Jewish Funerary Inscriptions—Most Are in Greek. Biblical Archaeology Review 18:5, September/October 1992). Greek was in common usage by the Jews in Judea and elsewhere.

More details on why the New Testament was originally written primarily in Greek can be found at the following link: www.cogwriter.com/greek-aramaic-hebrew-new-testament.htm.

Key Points on the Language of the New Testament

- The earliest New Testament manuscripts are in Greek. The Greek Rylands P52 is from 90-125 A.D., with A.D. 100 the apparent date that document was written.
- There are no known truly ancient New Testament manuscripts in Hebrew.
- An Aramaic New Testament was not around until later centuries — with the Syriac dating to the 4th century.
- What seems to be the earliest Aramaic manuscript dates from 464 A.D. (Lasater, p. 199)
- Those in Jesus' time did not speak the form of Syriac which the Aramaic translations are predominantly based upon.
- Having to repeat certain statements twice in Aramaic, as opposed to Aramaic and the Greek translation, in places like Matthew 27:46 and Mark 15:34 seems to disprove the Aramaic hypothesis. It makes sense to have the Greek translation of Aramaic in a Greek text, but not the other way around.
- The author of *Rauch Qadim* points to his language being "sacred." The Bible does not teach that.
- The fact of Jesus speaking in Aramaic and Greek not being the native language of most of the NT writers accounts for seemingly unusual translations into Greek — the so-called "bad idiom transfers."
- Scholars of ancient Greek have consistently concluded that, the literary quality of the Greek of the NT books (including Matthew and Mark) point to Greek being the original and not a translation.
- The Jews stopped using YHWH centuries before Jesus and switched to using the term Adonai, meaning Lord.

- This is also consistent with the Septuagint version of the Old Testament which uses the term Kurios, Lord, in the Greek.
- Luke and Paul clearly knew Greek (Acts 21:37-39) and we have reasons to see that other New Testament writers did as well.
- The fact is that Greek was the language used in the Eastern Roman Empire. Most of the books of the New Testament were written to those who were Greek-speaking Gentiles. It would not be logical that Aramaic (or Hebrew) would have been used as the original language when Jesus' followers were intended to reach the world. (Matthew 24:14; 28:19-20)
- Nearly all (at least 19 – 24) of the books of the New Testament were written to people in predominantly Greek speaking areas.
- The vast bulk of early post New Testament writings were written in Greek and they quoted the Greek New Testament.

11. English Translations

There are dozens of translations of the Bible into the English language. This author has read several completely through as well as parts of dozens of them.

One of the earliest English translations was done by John Wycliffe, an Oxford professor, scholar, and theologian. In the 1380s, Wycliffe (also spelled 'Wycliff' & 'Wyclif') produced dozens of handwritten English language manuscript copies of the scriptures. They were translated from the Latin Vulgate, which was the only source text available to Wycliffe.

> Until John Wycliffe translated the New Testament, only small portions of the Bible had been translated into English. The English language traces its roots back to approximately AD 600.
>
> What is the significance of the Wycliffe translation?
>
> 1. It was the first complete Bible in English — in fact, the first complete Bible in any modern European language!
> 2. It indirectly began to break down the power structures of the political-religious machinery of the Roman Catholic church. (1. From Wycliffe to King James (The Period of Challenge). Bible.org, March 21, 2001)

In 1525, William Tyndale went to Germany and translated Erasmus' 1516 Greek text into the English language. In 1525-1526 the *Tyndale New Testament* became the first printed edition of the scriptures in the English language. King Henry VIII of England and various Roman Catholic bishops burned any copies they could get their hands on. Tyndale was tried for heresy and treason. After conviction, he was strangled and burnt at the stake in the prison yard, Oct. 6, 1536. Many later translators, including those associated with the KJV, used many parts of his translation (over 80% of the New Testament and over 70% of the Old Testament).

In 1539, something known as the Great Bible was produced. In 1568, a revision of the Great Bible known as the Bishop's Bible was introduced. Despite 19 editions being printed between 1568 and 1606, this Bible was referred to as the "rough draft of the King James Version."

Myles Coverdale, John Foxe, Thomas Sampson, and William Whittingham in association with John Calvin and John Knox put together an English translation in Geneva, Switzerland. The New Testament was completed in 1557, and the complete Bible was first published in 1560. It became known as the Geneva Bible. The Geneva Bible itself retains over 90% of William Tyndale's original English translation.

Before going further, perhaps it should be mentioned that Protestant Reformer Martin Luther translated the New Testament into German, which was published in 1522 and then a Bible with the Old Testament and the Apocrypha was published in 1534. However, he mistranslated parts and admittedly added to it to support some of his pet doctrines, as have many other translators (for more details, check out the free book, online at ccog.org, *Hope of Salvation: How the Continuing Church of God differs from Protestantism*).

The King James Version

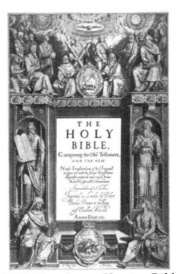

1611 King James Version Bible

The Protestant clergy approached King James I in 1604 and announced their desire for a new translation to replace the Bishop's Bible. King James authorized the translation. The first edition came out in 1611. Textually, it was about 95% the same as the Geneva Bible, which means that despite having a large team of translators, it relied heavily on the original work done by William Tyndale. Many Protestants have considered the KJV to be the best English translation.

Is the original *King James Version* (KJV) of the Bible, often also called the *Authorized Version* (AV), the one you can completely trust?

Some Protestants view the *King James Version* as essentially inspired by God and to be relied on above all others for scripture.

Notice something from a 'holiness' Methodist church:

> We wholeheartedly endorse the use of the Authorized Version of the Bible as the final authority in our English-speaking churches and schools. (Manual of the Bible Missionary Church, Inc. Bible Missionary Church. 2015, p. 138)

While that church is entitled to do that as opposed to considering the original language as divinely inspired, is that biblically wise?

Some others, however, agree that it is. Notice something from a Protestant group called Chick Publications:

> The King James Bible is a true and direct translation from the original languages. ... What if you found out it's the one English Bible that deserves your complete trust? ... the King James ... should be the only Bible that you need — and can completely trust. ... trusting the KJV. Build your faith in God's Word by learning why you can trust the KJV alone and why it is the most accurate translation in English. (Daniels DW. Yes You Can Read the King James Bible. Chick Publications, www.chick.com/products/item?stk=1425 --- accessed 06/02/20)

> The King James Bible was translated by men whose agenda was to give the exact meaning of the Greek or Hebrew originals without injecting their personal biases. Amazingly, Puritan members of the Church of England ... had to come together and agree on each verse of the 1189 chapters of the Bible, going over the text at least 14 times. God used that process to take out personal and denominational bias. What was left was a true interpretation, stripped of personal opinions or interpretations. (Daniels DW. New Book. Chick Publications, 2020, p. 7)

> Every new Bible version that rolls off the press is an insult to our Lord. (Ibid, p. 5)

Because in **1611** the most *important* event happened: **GOD'S PRESERVED WORDS were published**, perfectly translated into **English!** Soon King James held THE BOOK ... (Daniels DW. Did the Catholic Church Give Us the Bible? Chick Publications, 2013, p. 111)

Is that view of the KJV accurate?

No.

While the KJV is superior in several ways to many translations, it was translated by men. Despite claims of going over the texts at least 14 times, doctrinal bias was included, not eliminated.

Humans are fallible. It was not an insult to God for humans to try to improve translation errors with later translations.

Yet, Protestant Dr. Jack Hyles asserted "that the King James is not **A** version, but **THE** Bible" (Grady, p. iii). No, the King James Version is a translation, hence a version, and not the actual Bible.

Dr. William Grady pushes "the King James Bible as *the* true Bible for English-speaking people" (Ibid, p. v). And from the United Kingdom, "King James Bible ... translation was ordained by God and not man." (Denny H. The Final Destination of Man. WestBow Press, 2015)

That last statement that indicates God ordained and made the KJV a perfect translation of His word is false.

As pointed to earlier, various writings from Chick Publications indicate that because of God's inspiration and because so many men checked and rechecked it (e.g. Daniels DW. Yes You Can (and You Should) Read the King James Bible. Chick Publications, 2020, p. 28), that the KJV had no bias and is completely accurate.

But that simply is not true.

The unbiased/inspired KJV arguments remind this author of the arguments that the Eastern Orthodox have about the Septuagint. The Eastern Orthodox basically claim that God inspired the translators to correct and improve the Old Testament when they translated the original text from Hebrew to Greek. That is blasphemous. God did not need His word corrected.

Nor is it correct to state that you can completely trust the KJV translation or that God inspired/ordained it to be perfect.

Furthermore, consider that even a Protestant KJV supporter wrote that "the 1611 KJV was edited several times to correct minor translation errors or changes in spelling in 1612, 1613, 1616, 1629, 1638, 1660, 1683, 1727, 1762, 1769 and 1873." (Urick S. False Teachings and Divisive Movements: Schisms in Modern-Day Christendom. AuthorHouse, 2013, p. 251).

The *King James Version* was originally written over 400 years ago. In the time since, the English language has undergone many changes. Someone gave this author an original leaf from the 1611 KJV Bible that was printed in the early 1600s—a part of which is pictured here (with a modern font clarification below it):

Obferbe the moneth of Abib, and keep the paffeover unto the LORD thy God; for in the moneth of Abib the LORD thy God brought thee forth out of Egypt by night. (Deuteronomy 16:1, Original KJV)

Yes, the picture shown above is the original KJV. It simply is not in modern English. Even the updated KJV's, which are not written as the original, also do not fully use modern English.

Furthermore, sometimes those texts which are vague and unclear in the King James can be cleared up very easily by just reading a more modern translation. Plus, the KJV contains many errors.

Errors in the King James Version

Consider also the following about KJV errors from the late Richard Nickels:

> **Genesis 1:2** should read "And the earth **became** without form . . . " The word translated "was" is *hayah*, and denotes a condition different than a former condition, as in **Genesis 19:26**.
>
> **Genesis 10:9** should read " . . . Nimrod the mighty hunter **in place of** [in opposition to] the LORD." The word "before" is incorrect and gives the connotation that Nimrod was a good guy, which is false.
>
> **Leviticus 16:8, 10, 26** in the KJV is "scapegoat" which today has the connotation of someone who is unjustly blamed for other's sins. The Hebrew is *Azazel*, which means "one removed or separated." The Azazel goat represents Satan, who is no scapegoat. He is guilty of his part in our sins.
>
> **Deuteronomy 24:1**, "then let him" should be "and he." As the Savior explained in Matthew 19, Moses did not command divorcement. This statute is regulating the permission of divorce because of the hardness of their hearts.
>
> **II Kings 2:23**, should be "young men", not "little children."
>
> **Isaiah 65:17** should be "I am creating [am about to create] new heavens and new earth . . . ."
>
> **Ezekiel 20:25** should read "Wherefore I permitted them, or gave them over to, [false] statutes that are not good, and judgments whereby they should not live." God's laws are good, perfect and right. This verse shows that since Israel rejected God's laws, He allowed them to hurt themselves by following false man-made customs and laws.
>
> **Daniel 8:14** is correct in the margin, which substitutes "evening morning" for "days." Too bad William Miller didn't realize this.

Malachi 4:6 should read " . . . lest I come and smite the earth with utter destruction." "Curse" doesn't give the proper sense here. Same word used in **Zechariah 14:11**.

Matthew 5:48 should be "Become ye therefore perfect" rather than "be ye therefore perfect." "Perfect" here means "spiritually mature." Sanctification is a process of overcoming with the aid of the Holy Spirit.

Matthew 24:22 needs an additional word to clarify the meaning. It should say "there should no flesh be saved **alive**."

Matthew 27:49 omits text which was in the original. Moffatt correctly adds it, while the RSV puts it in a footnote: "And another took a spear and pierced His side, and out came water and blood." ...

Matthew 28:1, "In the end of the sabbath as it began to dawn toward the first day of the week . . ." should be translated literally, "Now late on Sabbath, as it was getting dusk toward the first day of the week . . . ." The Sabbath does not end at dawn but at dusk.

Luke 2:14 should say, "Glory to God in the highest, and on earth peace among men of God's good pleasure or choosing." That is, there will be peace on earth among men who have God's good will in their hearts.

Luke 14:26 has the unfortunate translation of the Greek word *miseo*, Strong's #3404, as "hate", when it should be rendered "love less by comparison." We are not to hate our parents and family!

John 1:17 is another instance of a poor preposition. "By" should be "through": "For the law was given by [through] Moses . . . ." Moses did not proclaim his law, but God's Law.

John 13:2 should be "And during supper" (RSV) rather than "And supper being ended" (KJV).

Acts 12:4 has the inaccurate word "Easter" which should be rendered "Passover." The Greek word is *pascha* which is translated correctly as **Passover** in Matthew 26:2, etc.

I Corinthians 1:18 should be: "For the preaching of the {stake} is to them that **are perishing** foolishness; but unto us which **are being saved** it is the power of God", rather than "perish" and "are saved." Likewise, **II Thessalonians 2:10** should be "are perishing" rather than "perish."

I Corinthians 15:29 should be: "Else what shall they do which are baptized for **the hope of** the dead, if the dead rise not at all? Why are they then baptized for **the hope of** the dead?"

II Corinthians 6:2 should be "**a** day of salvation", instead of "**the** day of salvation." This is a quote from **Isaiah 49:8**, which is correct. The day of salvation is not the same for each individual. The firstfruits have their day of salvation during this life. The rest in the second resurrection.

I Timothy 4:8 should say, "For bodily exercise profiteth **for a little time**: but godliness is profitable unto all things . . . ."

I Timothy 6:10 should be, "For the love of money is a [not the] root of all evil . . . ."

Hebrews 4:8 should be "Joshua" rather than "Jesus", although these two words are Hebrew and Greek equivalents.

Hebrews 4:9 should read, "There remaineth therefore a **keeping of a sabbath** to the people of God."

I John 5:7-8 contains additional text which was added to the original. "For there are three that bear record in *heaven, the Father, the Word, and the Holy Ghost: and these three are one. And there are three that bear witness in earth*, the Spirit, and the water, and the blood: and these three agree in one." The italicized text was added to the original manuscripts. Most modern translations agree that this was an uninspired addition to the Latin Vulgate to support the unscriptural trinity doctrine.

Revelation 20:10, "And the devil that deceived them was cast into the lake of fire and brimstone, where the beast and the false prophet are [correction: should be 'were cast' because the beast and false prophet were mortal human beings who were burned up in the lake of fire 1,000 years previous to this time, Revelation 19:20], and shall be tormented day and night for ever and ever." The point is that Satan will be cast into the **same** lake of fire into which the beast and false prophet were cast a thousand years previously. (Nickels R. Errors and Mistranslations in the KJV Written by: Richard Nickels. www.angelfire.com/hi2/graphic1designer/errors.html --- accessed 06/02/20)

(Note: The AFV is in agreement with most of Richard Nickel's statements.) It is not that the KJV is always a terrible translation, or that others are perfect, it is just people should not insist that God inspired the translators to do a perfect job. Because obviously, He did not. THE KJV CANNOT BE COMPLETELY TRUSTED AS IT IS NOT THE ORIGINAL INSPIRED TEXT.

The mistranslation of Genesis 1:2 has resulted in many not understanding about the age of the world and various aspects of prehistory. This has resulted in many Protestants making scientifically unsound statements that have turned many against the reliability of scripture.

The KJV translators intentionally mistranslated the Greek term *sabbatismos* (ςαββατισμός) which is actually found in Hebrews 4:9 (Green JP. The Interlinear Bible, 2nd edition. Hendrickson Publishers, 1986, p. 930: translated as "there remains, then, a Sabbath rest to the people of God" by the LSV). This mistranslation by the KJV translators has resulted in many people not realizing that the New Testament enjoins the seventh-day Sabbath. Hence, the KJV translators have misled many to violate the fourth commandment. They also intentionally mistranslated some scripture related to the biblical Holy Days (for details, see the free online book at ccog.org, *Should You Keep God's Holy Days or Demonic Holidays?*) – this has resulted in many NOT understanding God's true plan of salvation. (See also the free online book *Universal OFFER of Salvation, Apokatastasis: Can God save the lost in an age to come?* – Hundreds of scriptures reveal God's plan of salvation).

As far as the word "Easter" goes, does any thinking person really believe that God wanted the word for Passover changed to the name of a pagan goddess in His word? That is absurd. EVERY TRANSLATOR IN THE KJV WHO 'CHECKED' THAT PART OF THE 'TRANSLATION' HAD TO HAVE KNOWN THAT WAS IN ERROR – PARTICULARLY SINCE THAT SAME WORD IS TRANSLATED FROM THE GREEK IN THE KJV 28 TIMES AS 'PASSOVER'! God did not inspire this or other KJV translation mistakes.

Notice also that the Latin Vulgate was mentioned related to 1 John 5:7-8. It needs to be understood that the *original* Latin Vulgate (known as the *Codex Amiatinus*) as translated by the Roman Catholic saint and doctor Jerome did NOT have this error – it was added later and should not be part of the original text. Those interested in the truth should accept that.

Jesus Spoke of Hades and Gehenna

Now, one of the things that Chick Publications likes about the KJV is that it often uses the word 'hell.' Chick Publications indicates that using the actual Greek words of the New Testament transliterated into English results in people not understanding about God's punishment. But it is the opposite—using "hell" without distinguishing its original Greek term, confuses people about the grave, burning up in Gehenna, and that the only place of restraint was for fallen angels.

Jesus often is quoting using the Greek word Gehenna. Notice some of how Chick Publications views that:

> **Question:** Gehenna is not hell, is it? It was a valley where outcasts, thieves and infected people where thrown when they died. The Bible refers to "Gehenna" as the place of death and pain. The word "hell", as you so often use, where eternal pain and fire awaits is actually "Gehenna". If you have read a bible written before 1400, you will notice a very important thing: "HELL" is missing. Instead it says "Gehenna". There is no fire breathing eternal pain demon hell!! In fact YOU are committing a sin here. Telling people, or lying to people about hell, when

184

you should know about "Gehenna". There is no hell. Only the valley of "Gehenna". A graveyard!!

Answer: The word "Gehenna" is properly translated "hell" in the King James Bible. …

Even though the word "Gehenna" comes from the Valley of Hinnom, simply rendering it as "garbage dump" or "valley of waste disposal" or "burning garbage" could not be an accurate translation, because that's not what Jesus and the apostles **meant** when they used the word. It meant "the place where people go when they die." That's what we mean when we say "hell". …

Not until Young's Literal Translation in the late 1800s, followed by the Catholic New American Bible of 1970 was the untranslated "Gehenna" put in. … And "hell" accurately translates the **meaning** of the word "Gehenna." "Gehenna" is not a translation; it is just a transliteration (translating letters, but not meaning). (Daniels DW. Should "Gehenna" be Translated as "Hell'? Answers to Your Bible Questions. Chick Publications, 2002)

In other words, Chick Publications is saying that IT KNOWS BETTER WHAT THE WORD IS SUPPOSED TO MEAN THAN THE WORD JESUS HIMSELF USED. Furthermore, Gehenna does NOT mean "the place where people go when they die"—Chick Publications is flat out wrong!

Now, we in the *Continuing* Church of God rarely use the word "hell." The word "hell" originally meant to cover or to hide. Another old meaning of that word was "a tailor's receptacle" according to *Merriam-Webster*. In time, it tended to mean being underground.

Furthermore, consider that the KJV IMPROPERLY TRANSLATES THREE DIFFERENT WORDS TO MEAN THE SAME THING!

There are three different words in the New Testament – Hades, Gehenna, or Tartaroosas – which the King James Version of the Bible translated as "hell." And not one of them means what most people think the word hell means.

The fact of the three different Greek words, as well as various understandings and traditions, has resulted in confusion and false doctrines concerning what hell means.

Now, since the term has become highly used in cursing and in various vulgarities it is often not appropriate to use.

Furthermore, because of influence from Dante's book *The Divine Comedy*, the area he called the Inferno/Infernus resulted in many people getting the wrong impression that God has a place of torturing that would last forever. And later the term hell got attached to it, and that is how most Protestants (including Chick Publications as its tract *Some Like It Hot* shows) and Roman Catholics now view it.

Yet, Chick Publications and others should know better. Even in its post against Gehenna, it had the following:

> "And fear not them which kill the body, but are not able to kill the soul: but rather fear **him which is able to destroy both soul and body in <u>hell</u>**" (Matthew 10:28). No power on earth can destroy a soul. The soul is a part of a person that exists beyond physical death (Revelation 20:4). "Gehenna" has to be a place to destroy both the body **and the soul.** (www.chick.com/information/article?id=does-gehenna-mean-hell --- accessed 06/02/20)

Note: Chick Publications admits that the body and soul are destroyed in Gehenna—hence that is not where people immediately go when they die. In Jesus' time what was tossed into Gehenna burnt up and was no more. In the Gehenna to come, the same thing will happen.

Chick Publications also has the following:

> "Hades" has a big pagan meaning that is completely divorced from the Bible. "Sheol" is a Hebrew word without any meaning at all to an ordinary reader. Have you ever heard people say they don't want to "go to gehenna?" ... We need a Bible with a lot of hell in it. We need to know where we are not going. The whole purpose of evangelism is to save people from hell. ... That forceful warning word, "hell," is found in the King James

Bible. (www.chick.com/information/article?id=Who-Needs-Hell --- accessed 06/02/20)

No, Hades is NOT completely divorced from the Bible. The New Testament shows JESUS USED THE WORD HADES 5 TIMES IN THE *TEXTUS RECEPTUS* (the text that the bulk of the KJV was translated from). Jesus was NOT trying to teach a pagan concept. Hades means the 'grave.' It does NOT mean an ever-burning hell fire of torture — that is a pagan concept that places like Chick Publications wants to perpetuate! Consider also that the Bible teaches that the time will come when "Death and Hades were cast into the lake of fire" (Revelation 20:14)— Hades, translated as "hell in the KJV in this verse" cannot possibly mean the lake of fire as it is *cast into the lake of fire*!

Furthermore, no, the whole purpose of proclaiming the good news of the Bible is not to save people from the type of punishing hell that Chick Publications wants to believe in. God has a plan that Chick Publications does not understand (for details, see the free online book: *The MYSTERY of GOD's PLAN: Why Did God Create Anything? Why Did God Make You?*).

One of the main purposes of evangelism, ***according to Jesus,*** is to have the "gospel of the kingdom … preached in all the world as a witness to all the nations" (Matthew 24:14) and to "make disciples of all the nations, baptizing them in the name of the Father and of the Son and of the Holy Spirit, teaching them to observe all things that I have commanded you" (Matthew 28:19-20). Note: One of the reasons to use the proper Greek New Testament manuscripts is that some have improperly claimed that the preceding verses are not part of the Bible— they are found in the Greek manuscripts, including the *Textus Receptus*.

Through proper teaching, those converted will build godly character so that they will be able to give love in a unique way to make eternity better for themselves and all who ultimately will accept Jesus (see also our free online book at ccog.org: *The MYSTERY of GOD's PLAN: Why Did God Create Anything? Why did God make you?*)

What about Gehenna? This Greek word represents "the Valley of HINNOM which lay just outside of Jerusalem and was the place refuse was constantly being burned up" (Lesson 15 - What is Hell? 58 Lesson:

187

Ambassador College Bible Correspondence Course, 1966). It is first referred to in scripture in Joshua 15:8. It was also associated with pagan fire practices in 2 Kings 23:10; 2 Chronicles 28:3, 33:6; Jeremiah 7:31-32, 19:2-6, & 32:35.

Trash, filth, and the dead bodies of animals and DESPISED CRIMINALS were thrown into Gehenna. Ordinarily, everything thrown into this valley was DESTROYED by fire. Christ used it to picture the terrible fate of UNREPENTANT SINNERS! Please understand that JESUS USED THE WORD GEHENNA 11 TIMES IN THE *TEXTUS RECEPTUS*. Jesus knew what it meant! But instead, Chick Publications (and others) want you to not comprehend what Jesus was really teaching!

Now the NKJV and MEV also fail as they translate the word Gehenna as hell as well. But the AFV and YLT get it right. Yet, all four of those, however, do not translate Hades as hell.

Now, consider that Chick Publications asserted that Hades has a pagan meaning, but apparently it also overlooked the true meaning of the word Easter (the name of one or more pagan goddesses – Ishtar and Eostre). That being said, on the use of the word 'hell' in the New and Old Testament, let's read what an old Bible dictionary, edited by James Hastings, a leading authority on such technical matters, says:

> In our Authorized Version the word 'hell' is unfortunately used as the rendering of three distinct words, WITH DIFFERENT MEANINGS. It represents, 1. The 'sheol' of the Hebrew Old Testament, and the 'hades' in the New Testament … It is now an entirely misleading rendering, especially in the New Testament passages. The English revisers, therefore, have substituted 'Hades' [going back to the original Greek word] for 'hell' in the New Testament …. In the American revision the word 'hell' is entirely discarded in this connexion ….
>
> The word 'hell' is used 2. As equivalent to [the Greek word] 'tartaros' (II Peter 2:4), … and, 3. More properly as the equivalent of [the Greek word] 'gehenna.' (Hastings J., ed. Dictionary of the Bible, Vol. 2. 1900, pp. 343-344)

So, we see that the real MEANINGS of three different Greek words – 'hades' ('sheol' in Old Testament), 'tartaros,' and 'gehenna' – have been confused with each other because translators, like those of the KJV, have attempted to make the ONE English word 'hell' cover all THREE meanings! But now let us amplify the foregoing facts.

The original Old Testament HEBREW word 'sheol' and the New Testament Greek word 'hades' mean basically the same thing. These original words have been translated 'grave' in many places in the Bible.

> THE WORD "SHEOL,"... It is never used by Moses or the Prophets in the sense of a place of torment after death; and in no way conflicts with the statement already proved, that the Law of Moses deals wholly in temporal rewards and punishments.

> This position, also, I wish to fortify by the testimony of Orthodox critics, men of learning and candor. They know, and therefore they speak.

> 1. CHAPMAN. "Sheol, in itself considered, has no connection with future punishment." *Cited by Balfour, First Inquiry.*
> 2. DR. ALLEN, quoted above, says: "The term *sheol* does not seem to mean, with certainty, anything more than the state of the dead in their deep abode."
> 3. DR. CAMPBELL. "Sheol signifies the state of the dead without regard to their happiness or misery."
> 4. DR. WHITBY. "Sheol throughout the Old Testament signifies not the place of punishment, or of the souls of bad men only, but the grave only, or the place of death." (Thayer TB. THE ORIGIN AND HISTORY OF THE Doctrine of Endless Punishment. 1855; Universal Publishing House 1871)

Sheol is a reference to the grave, as is the word hades.

Note that the Greek word TARTAROS, which has also been translated into the English word 'hell' in the KJV, occurs only once in the New Testament (2 Peter 2:4) and does not refer to humans, but to the RESTRAINED condition of fallen angels. Its meaning, translated into English, is 'darkness of the material universe,' or 'dark abyss,' or 'prison.'

It is disappointing, but the KJV translators often failed to properly translate the preserved Greek NT manuscripts.

More on 'Hell' can be found in the following at https://studythebible course.org/lesson-15-what-is-hell/: *Study the Bible Course Lesson 15: What is "Hell"?*

Other KJV Issues

Here are some comments from Dr. Daniel Wallace, Professor at the Dallas Theological Seminary, about issues in the KJV:

> I can have no scriptural warrant for arguing that the King James has exclusive rights to the throne. … the Greek text which stands behind the King James Bible is demonstrably inferior in certain places. The man who edited the text was a Roman Catholic priest and humanist named Erasmus. He was under pressure to get it to the press as soon as possible … Consequently, his edition has been called the most poorly edited volume in all of literature! It is filled with hundreds of typographical errors which even Erasmus would acknowledge. (Wallace D. Why I Do Not Think the King James Bible Is the Best Translation Available Today. Bible.org, accessed 03/25/20)

Furthermore, it should be mentioned that the KJV erred by assigning the male gender to the Holy Spirit in the New Testament. This is a major and intentionally biased error.

The Hebrew term for spirit in the Old Testament is grammatically female, and the Greek term in the New Testament is grammatically neuter – this is noted by even trinitarian scholars, such as Dr. Daniel Wallace of Dallas Theological Seminary (Wallace D. Greek Grammar. Pp. 331-332).

This MISTRANSLATION by the KJV translators has resulted in a major misunderstanding of the Godhead and has resulted in many believing differently about the Godhead than early Christians did (see also the free online book: *Continuing History of the Church of God*).

Now, getting back to the KJV Bible itself, many do not realize that it originally also included, basically as an appendix, what the Roman and Eastern Orthodox Catholics called the deuterocanonical books (otherwise known as the Apocrypha) – these books were NOT inspired by God and should not have been in the Bible. Yet, for about two centuries they were part of some printings of the KJV.

But since the Old Testament Apocrypha has not been in it for about two hundred years, many people do not realize that flaw with the original KJV.

Do not be deceived by men who do not want to hold to what the original biblical text teaches. The KJV has real errors and most certainly CANNOT BE COMPLETELY TRUSTED as an accurate portrayal of the words of God.

Let it also be understood that various words have changed in meaning in the English language since 1611. For example, one would not say, "Suffer the little children" in the 21st century, but instead would say "Allow the little children" (AFV) or "Permit the little children" (NKJV) for Mark 10:14.

Furthermore, modern native English speakers simply no longer use 'King James English" as many words common in the 17th century are not used, or even understood, by many today.

Speaking of the 17th century, Dr. Peter Chamberlain, who seemed to hold COG doctrines, did not seem to quote the KJV when (in 1677) he used expressions such as "he that sinneth in one point is guilty of all" when referring to James 2:10 (Clarke H. A History of the Sabbatarians Or Seventh Day Baptists, in America; Containing Their Rise and Progress to the Year 1811, with Their Leaders' Names, and Their Distinguishing Tenets, etc. Utica, 1811, pp. 12-13). On the other hand, COG leader William Saller/Sellers did seem to quote the KJV in his writings (e.g. Sellers W. An Examination of a late book published by Doctor Owen ... A Sacred Day of Rest. 1671, p. 6). It is NOT inappropriate to cite the KJV, but it is inappropriate to claim its translation is 100% accurate or is completely approved by God.

1 John 5:7-8

Here are some comments from Dr. Daniel Wallace, Professor at the Dallas Theological Seminary, about the KJV using an expanded version of 1 John 5:7-8:

To date, only a handful of Greek MSS have been discovered which have the Trinitarian formula in 1 John 5:7-8, though none of them is demonstrably earlier than the sixteenth century. (Wallace D. Why I Do Not Think the King James Bible Is the Best Translation Available Today. Bible.org, accessed 03/25/20)

In 1 John 5:7-8, the King James Bible speaks of three that bear witness in heaven – the Father, the Word, and the Holy Spirit (or Holy Ghost) – and these three are one.

In 1516, Desiderius Erasmus, a Dutch humanist scholar, published the first printed Greek New Testament—on March 1, 1516. When it came out, he did not have this verse, 1 John 5:7 in there, affirming the Trinity. There were Catholic scholars who got very upset with him for not putting it in there. And in his second edition of 1519, he didn't have it. What he mentioned in his notes in that second edition is "I did not put it in because I did not see it in any Greek manuscripts." ... his third edition of 1522 now has 1 John 5:7-8 in it with that Trinitarian formula.

That is something that has plagued English readers of the Bible, but not German readers. Because Martin Luther based his New Testament on the 1519 edition that didn't have that. So, in 1519 Luther was using that edition and it didn't have that Trinitarian formula. German Christianity has never had a problem {as its version of} the Bible, never had the Trinitarian formula in 1 John 5:7-8. As stated, it made it into Erasmus' 1522 text and then in the King James Version Bible after that. Erasmus basically puts it in under protest. ... It seems that this particular reading was never part of the Greek New Testament until after there was a protest. ... It never affected Christians through any of the church councils. They never pointed out that verse, because it did not exist in the Bible. So, they came up to the doctrine of the Trinity on some other basis. (Wallace D. What are Some Passages You Interpret Differently than Dr. Ehrman?, 1 John 5:7-8. YouTube video. Jan 15, 2011)

Erasmus reportedly was concerned about self-preservation, so he compromised on purpose (Whitmore DM. Yielding to the Prejudice of

His Times: Erasmus and the Comma Johanneum. Church History and Religious Culture, Vol. 95, No. 1, 2015: 19-40).

So obviously, "the Trinitarian formula in 1 John 5:7-8" was not part of the true *Textus Receptus*. And yes, the trinitarian doctrine came from somewhere else.

Some wish to believe the expanded passage of 1 John 5:7-8 was real because early heretics seem to have possibly referred to it. One popular online source falsely claims that Tertullian, who followed the trinitarian heretic Montanus, quoted the omitted words in *Against Praxeas*. However, this is not true as I have read that writing and it is not a quote of 1 John 5:7-8. Yet, even if it was true, Tertullian was a heretic who did not seem to have the proper canon.

The reality is that unbiased scholars realize that 1 John 5:7-8 additions were added centuries after the New Testament was originally written.

Here is a copy of the relevant section of the *Codex Sinaiticus* c. 350:

Here is a translation of 1 John 5:7-8 as shown in the *Codex Sinaiticus* from a scholastic source:

> [7] For they that testify are three, [8] the Spirit, and the water, and the blood, and the three are one. (CodexSinaiticus.org accessed 07/02/20)

Notice also:

> 1 John 5:8 … Ambrose, a Latin … quotes the passage thus:
>
>> "But the same Evangelist, that he might make it plain that he wrote this concerning the Holy Spirit, says elsewhere: 'Jesus Christ came by water and blood, not in the water only, but by water and blood. And the Spirit beareth witness, because the Spirit is truth; for there are three witnesses, the Spirit, the water, and the blood; and these three are one,'" (Ambrose of Milan, On the Holy Spirit, Book 3, Chapter 10).
>
> Again, the phrase "these three are one" refers here to the Spirit, water, and blood. Further, the passage is quoted fully here and it is absolutely clear that the Comma is not in the text. (Wayne L. 1 John 5:7-8 and King James Onlyism. CARM.org, October 31, 2018)

Yes, it should be absolutely clear that the "trinitarian formula" was never part of the biblical text.

Notice also the following related to the improperly added text:

> (1) The text is missing from all Greek manuscripts except eight and these contain the passage of in what appears to be a translation of the Latin Vulgate …
>
> (2) The passage is quoted in none of the Greek Fathers, who, had they known it, would most certainly have employed it in the Trinitarian controversies (Sabellian and Arian). Its first appearance in Greek is in a Greek version of the (Latin) Acts of the Lateran Council in 1215.
>
> (3) The passage is absent from the manuscripts of all ancient versions (Syriac, Coptic, Armenian, Ethiopic, Arabic, Slavonic), except the Latin; and it is not found (a) in the Old Latin in its early form (Tertullian Cyprian Augustine), or in the Vulgate (b) as issued by Jerome … or (c) as revised by Alcuin...

The earliest instance of the passage being *quoted as a part of the actual text of the Epistle* [italics added] is in a fourth century Latin treatise entitled *Liber Apologeticus* (chap. 4), attributed either to the Spanish heretic Priscillian (died about 385) or to his follower Bishop Instantius. (Metzger B. A Textual Commentary on the Greek New Testament, 2nd ed. Hendrickson Publishers, 2005, pp. 647-648)

What some seem to want to do is claim that because some writers wrote statements similar to the extra words added to 1 John 5:7-8 that this proves that they were originally in the inspired manuscripts of scripture (e.g. Rogers J. Why Creeds and Confessions? Lulu.com, pp. 98-99).

Instead, if that proves anything, it proves that a monk who read non-biblical texts (probably the late 4th century document known as the *Latin Liber Apologeticus* by the gnostic Priscillian) decided to insert a comment he read elsewhere—not the other way around. Accepting that the added words to 1 John 5:7-8 are divinely inspired is believing a lie (cf. 2 Thessalonians 2:10-11; Revelation 22:15).

It is partially because of intentional errors like including those verses that Muslims claim that the New Testament cannot be trusted because 'Christians' (so-called) changed it. The Apostle Peter warned, "there will be false teachers among you, who will secretly bring in destructive heresies ... And many will follow their destructive ways, because of whom the way of truth will be blasphemed" (2 Peter 2:1-2). Certainly that warning applies to any who intentionally changed the Bible on their own.

The Protestants Did Not Give the World the Bible

Some Protestants believe that they have taken over as the guardians of the Bible:

> PROTESTANTS CLAIM that: "The guardianship of the Greek New Testament passed from the Greek Church to those who were MORE FAITHFUL to its teachings, namely, to evangelical Protestants.

"Consistently Christian textual criticism, therefore, is truly Protestant. In the Protestant Reformation, God summoned men to return to the holy scriptures" (Edward Hills, *The King James Version Defended!*, pp. 19, 21). ...

Erasmus-a humanist scholar-who *was neither doctrinally Protestant nor Catholic*, was the editor of the first printed Greek New Testament (1516) (Kroll P. Is the Bible a Protestant Book? Good News magazine, April 1964, p. 13, 20)

It should be pointed out that Erasmus, who put together texts used by the translators of the King James version, was originally trained as a Roman Catholic priest and, although he had doctrinal differences with Rome, he remained a Roman Catholic all his life.

Erasmus rejected the manuscripts of Origen, as did Lucian. Lucian prevailed over Origen, especially in the East. "The Bibles produced by the Syrian scribes presented the Syrian text of the school of Antioch, and this text became the form which displaced all others in the Eastern churches and is, indeed, the Textus Receptus (Received Text) from which our Authorized Version is translated." (Wilkinson, The Truth Triumphant)

Lucian emphasized the need for textual accuracy and sought to limit the allegorical interpretation of the Alexandrian Christian tradition, which incorporated pagan philosophy. Lucian's edition ... became the basis of the textus receptus from which most of the Reformation era New Testament translations were made. (Lucian. New World Encyclopedia, 2018)

Notice also:

Westcott and Hort ... believed that from the very beginning the Traditional (Byzantine) Text was an official text with official backing and that this was the reason why it overcame all rival texts and ultimately reigned supreme in the usage of the Greek Church. They regarded the Traditional Text as the product of a thorough-going revision of the New Testament text which took place at Antioch in two stages between 250 A.D. and 350 A.D. They believed that this text was the deliberate creation of certain scholarly Christians at Antioch and that the presbyter Lucian (d. 312) was probably the original leader in this work. (Hills EF. The King James Version Defended! 1956)

Lucian of Antioch's textual work lies at the basis of the *Textus Receptus* (Westcott BF, Hort JA. The New Testament in the original Greek introduction and appendix [to] the text revised by Brooke Foss Westcott and Fenton John Anthony Hort. Harper, 1882, p. 138). Some have dismissed Lucian's involvement "because early Church Councils and Church Fathers are completely silent on the matter" and because there are papyri that pre-date Lucian (Gordon RL. A History of Biblical Transmission. Written April 1997, Updated September 2020). But Lucian did have involvement. Leaders with beliefs like Lucian's did not attend the Greco-Roman councils (Bagatti, The Church from the Gentiles in Palestine, pp. 47-48) and were often condemned, not praised, by those councils (Bagatti, The Church from the Circumcision, p.35). The fact of pre-Lucian documents, of course, does not mean that Lucian was not involved with the Bible, because he was.

The version associated with Lucian was essentially supreme in the East, whereas Rome preferred a Latin text (Westcott, pp. 138-143). "Receiving the literal sense alone he {Lucian} laid stress on the need of textual accuracy and himself undertook to revise the Septuagint on the original Hebrew. His edition was widely used in the fourth century (Jerome, De Vir. III. Lxxvii Praef. Ad Paralip.; Adv. Rufium xxvi, Epis., 106). "He also published a recession of the New Testament" (Healy, P. Lucian of Antioch. The Catholic Encyclopedia. New York: Robert Appleton Company, 1910). "During the Dark Ages, the Received Text was practically unknown outside of the Greek Church ... It is altogether too little known that the real editor of the Received Text was Lucian ... Lucian's unrivaled success in verifying, safeguarding, and transmitting the divine writings left a heritage for which all generations should be thankful. ... Lucian and his school produced and edited a definite and complete Bible" (Wilkinson, The Truth Triumphant, pp. 50,59). The "chain of custody" of the received text reportedly passed through Lucian who was NOT Protestant.

In the early 19th century, it was reported:

Let us now take this circumstance into account, together with the critical reputation of Lucianus: let us consider, that the place and period in which he made his revisal, was the region where the inspired writings were deposited, and within a short distance of the period when they were published: ... while the Byzantine text has confessedly retained its integrity for full eleven hundred {years}. We may thence form a just estimate of the conclusiveness of that evidence which still exists in attestation of the purity of the text of Lucianus. In fine, a very short process enables us to prove, that the tradition which supports the authority of this text, has continued unbroken since the age of the apostles. The coincidence of the Vulgar Greek of our present editions with the old Italick translation, enables us to carry up the tradition ... to the times of Lucianus, in whose age the Byzantine text equally constituted the Vulgate or common edition. (Nolan, pp. 125-126)

The Rome supporting Jerome was opposed to a lot of the theology that the school Lucian had founded taught (Westcott, p. 138). Yet, his contacts with Lucian's works appear to be one of several reasons he rejected the Apocrypha (Wilkinson, The Truth Triumphant, p. 51). Being a semi-arian/binitarian (Newman, JH Cardinal. The Arians of the Fourth Century. Longmans, Green, & Co., New York, 1908, p. 7) and Sabbatarian (Wilkinson, The Truth Triumphant, pp. 55-57; cf. Newman, p. 9; Kohen E. History of the Byzantine Jews. University Press of America, 2007, p. 53), Lucian would have been neither a Roman Catholic nor Alexandrian Orthodox, but held to more Church of God doctrines.

Despite early Protestant scholars knowing about Lucian, beginning no later than the late 19th century, many Protestant scholars began to reject various of the Byzantine texts. Notice the following report:

True Manuscripts Rejected

It may come as a shock for you to know that *scholars have rejected ninety-five per cent* of all extant Greek manuscripts of the Bible. These are the VERY MANUSCRIPTS which have been preserved by the Greek-speaking world – those to whom *God gave the responsibility* for copying and preserving His Word. Instead, modern Protestant translators and critics turn to the

CORRUPTED five per cent of manuscripts found in *Egypt and the Latin-speaking world!* These Byzantine manuscripts have been rejected due to the false ideas and theories of men. (Kroll, p. 21)

Why?

Basically Protestants Wescott and Hort believed that because various Egyptian (Alexandrian) texts were older copies than many of the Byzantine ones, that the older ones were more likely to be reliable:

> **Modern Scholarship** ... scholars began to recognize there were other versions of the Greek text, some of them in much older manuscripts. Things came to a head in the late 1800s. At this time two British New Testament scholars, Westcott and Hort, produced a new edition of the Greek New Testament with a defense of it. ...
>
> The last century has seen a number of new discoveries ...
>
> Most of these finds have been basically of the Alexandrian or the Western text-types. Thus, the picture painted by Westcott and Hort from fourth and fifth-century manuscripts has not been appreciably affected by the work done and the material discovered since their time. A few scholars did advance the idea that the Western text might be the most original, but this idea is almost totally rejected now. (Grabbe LL. Good News, October 1976)

The reality is that the Byzantine Greeks had followed the Jewish practice of destroying older deteriorating manuscripts. That is one reason they are not the oldest. Another reason is the fact that 'Western' manuscripts in relatively drier Egypt deteriorated slower and hence lasted longer. Thus, age of the Alexandrian texts, of itself, is in no way proof of their superiority over the Byzantine manuscripts.

Consider also that Dr. Fenton Hort reportedly stated, "I am so ignorant of the Hebrew and, what is worse, of the Greek text of the N.T. that I have all but discarded them" (Grady, p. 245). He also reportedly referred to the *Textus Receptus* as "villainous" (Ibid, p. 245).

Perhaps it should be pointed out that some Protestants have asserted that Dr. Hort (Ibid, p. 248-249) and Dr. Brooke Westcott had an 'Alexandrian/allegorical' view of scripture and that Dr. Wescott accepted certain apocryphal gnostic texts (Sightler, pp. 112-114).

"Although Wescott was not the first man to use the minority Alexandrian texts, he was the man, more than any other, who gave academic respectability and a false sense of sanction to what has become known as the critical text" (Ibid, p. 313). There are hundreds of differences and omissions as compared to the *Textus Receptus* (Fowler EW. Evaluating Versions of the New Testament. Maranatha Baptist Press, 1981, pp. 32-66).

Anyway, since the 1900s, most Protestant translations have been mainly based upon the inferior non-Byzantine texts and some Byzantine texts. Such as one by Eberhard Nestle first published in 1898 called *Novum Testamentum Graece*, which was later updated. The 25ᵗʰ edition was highly edited by Kurt Alland, and the joint work has tended to be called the Nestle-Aland Greek Text (NGT).

As far as the Nestle-Aland Greek Text goes, it has missing words and tends to be less doctrinally clear than the *Textus Receptus*. For example, The *Textus Receptus* says Jesus was Mary's "firstborn" son in Matthew 1:25, which implies that Mary had other sons later, whereas the NGT does not use that word. For another example the NGT does not have the word "kingdom" in Mark 1:14, whereas the *Textus Receptus* does. The NGT also leaves out John 7:53-8:11 as well as 19 other verses of the New Testament (Fowler, p. 10).

The NGT is simply not as reliable and there appear to be over 1,000 or so differences from the *Textus Receptus* (Ibid, pp. 10-11, 30-66), though many are not significant—some, however, like the omission of Mark 16:9-20, are (this does NOT mean that the document called the *Textus Receptus* is perfect, but it overall tends to better reflect the original text—which is the text that is preserved in heaven). That being said, some versions of parts of the NGT can at times help provide clarification/insight related to some passages.

Yet, another problem in the New Testament related to the NGT, to cite one example, is that it leaves out of the true word of God the following inspired statement from the Apostle Paul in Acts 18:21: "I must by all means keep this coming feast in Jerusalem." Hence, this discourages people from realizing that the Apostle Paul did keep the Holy Days.

Perhaps it should be mentioned that the "New Agreement" New Testament, a version of which was put out in 2020 by Lutheran supporters, did NOT include the word "Israel" in it, despite it being used in 73 verses of the New Testament (Berkowitz AE. Lutherans Publish New Version of Bible Without the Word 'Israel' in It. Breaking Israel News, April 20, 2020). Apparently, the translators and publishers believed, like certain others before them have, that it was fine to intentionally change the word of God.

There is also sometimes a problem with the Old Testament text in many Protestant translations. Notice something from a couple of Protestant sources:

> "The UBS or Nestle-Aland Greek text is the most reliable and popular, as is the *Bible Hebraica* for the Old Testament. As for Greek dictionaries well, of course, the one translators use most is Kittel's Theological Dictionary of the New Testament. Naturally, before making his many selections, the translator always prays first." (Alworth J. HITLER'S SAY IN YOUR NEW VERSION BIBLE. Day of Christ Ministries, New Zealand, 2012)

> The Biblia Hebraica Stuttgartensia (BHS), which reflects the findings from more than a hundred years of Old Testament textual research, is structured according to this principle. The BHS is in worldwide use today and is esteemed among all denominations as a highly reliable edition of the Hebrew Bible. It provides the basis both for clerical training and for all reputable biblical translations. Since 2004, it has been successively replaced by the Biblia Hebraica Quinta (BHQ), which is initially being published in individual fascicles. (The Biblia Hebraica Stuttgartensia. Academic-Bible.com accessed 03/31/20)

Here is a Protestant criticism of the *Biblia Hebraica*:

So what's wrong with the *Biblia Hebraica*, you ask? Well, according to the authoritative *Encyclopaedia Judaica*, the compiler of the *Biblia Hebraica* rendition of the Old Testament text is none other than Gerhard Kittel's father. Old Papa Rudolf Kittel, was a vehement anti-Semite who, far from being a Christian, was a devout believer in Hellenistic religions. Both father and son Kittel were in fact liberal German scholars and "higher critics" – that is they believed scripture should be understood as scholars interpret and alter it – not as God actually wrote it and preserved it ... Meanwhile an institute founded at Hitler's explicit command rewrote Bible texts under the supervision of Gerhard Kittel, eliminating mention of the special role of the Jewish people. (Alworth, 2012)

Many modern Protestant translators have used Kittel's *Biblia Hebraica* such as the NIV and ESV. It is also the basis of many Bibles put out by the United Bible Societies.

It is not that those translations are never correct, but certainly parts of their foundation are very questionable.

Anyway, while Greco-Roman Catholics and Protestants have had involvement with translations and manuscript preservation, none of them gave the world the Bible. God did.

Translations

ALL TRANSLATIONS by men are subject to error. And while the KJV and the more modern NKJV are fine in many areas, both have translation flaws, many of which are intentional.

So, which translation is best?

In general, we in the *Continuing* Church of God like to quote from the NKJV because it 1) uses modern English and 2) is widely accessible. But, because of the translation flaws it has, as well as occasional clarity issues, we will sometimes use other translations. For example, when referring to the Holy Spirit, we will often quote other translations, like the AFV which always handles related gender issues correctly. Also, in order to specifically make a point to those of a particular group, we will sometimes intentionally use Roman Catholic, Eastern Orthodox, or Jehovah's Witnesses' translations to show that the translation is not biased against their group.

In general, the best translations are based on the Masoretic Text for the Old Testament and the *Textus Receptus* for the New Testament.

Some of the main Bibles that do that are the AFV (A Faithful Version), GNV (Geneva Bible), GLT (Green's Literal Translation), IB (Interlinear Bible), KJV (King James Version), LST (Literal Standard Version), MEV (Modern English Version), NKJV (New King James Version), and YLT (Young's Literal Translation). Of these, the only one that does not make a grammatical pronoun error related to the Holy Spirit is the AFV. Note: The NWT used by the Jehovah's Witnesses tends to get the pronouns correct for the Holy Spirit, but its primary textual bases are not the *Masoretic Text* and the *Textus Receptus* (it uses the NGT for the New Testament), hence there are textual basis issues for some verses in it.

That being said, most Protestants did use some version of the Masoretic Text to translate from for the Old Testament. But most Protestant translations from the late 19th century on did not use the *Textus Receptus* for the NT.

Here are some points about some other translations:

> **American Standard Version Bible** (1901, ASV) Text basis for Old Testament: Masoretic Text (Septuagint influence). Text basis for New Testament: Westcott and Hort (1881), Tregelles (1857).

> **Holman Christian Standard Bible** (2004, HCSB) Text basis for O.T.: B.H.S. 5th edition with Septuagint influence. Text basis for N. T.: Nestle-Aland N.T.G. 27th edition, United Bible Societies' Greek New Testament, 4th corrected edition.

> **New American Bible** (1970, NAB) Text basis for O. T.: Primarily Biblia Hebraica Stuttgartensia (B.H.S.). Has influence of Dead Sea Scrolls along with Septuagint. Text basis for Apocrypha: Primarily Septuagint with Vulgate and Dead Sea Scrolls influence. Text basis for N.T.: Nestle-Aland N.T.G. 25th edition.

New American Standard Bible (1971, NASB) Text basis for O.T.: Primarily B.H.S. with influences from the Septuagint. Text basis for N.T.: Nestle-Aland N.T.G.

New International Version (1978, NIV) Text basis for O.T.: Primarily Masoretic with influences from the Dead Sea Scrolls. Text basis for N.T.: Nestle-Aland N.T.G.

New Revised Standard Version Bible (1989, NRSV) Text basis for O.T.: B.H.S. Also has influence of Septuagint and the Dead Sea Scrolls. Text basis for Apocrypha: Septuagint. Has influence of Vulgate. Text basis for N.T.: Nestle-Aland N.T.G. 27th edition.

New World Translation (1961, NWT) Text basis for O.T.: Primarily B.H.S. and Biblia Hebraica Quinta, with influences from the Dead Sea Scrolls, Septuagint, and other texts. Text basis for N.T.: Nestle-Aland N.T.G., 18th and other editions.

It is NOT that these translations are always wrong, but some parts are not based on the correct text.

Perhaps it should be mentioned that some Bibles are not intended to be word for word translations of the ancient texts. Some are paraphrases. Paraphrase translations use contemporary language to try to capture the essence behind the text in order to convey the paraphrasers' understandings of the text. Some of the better known ones are the Easy–to-Read Version (ERV) which uses the B.H.S. and N.T.G, the Good News Bible (formerly known as Today's English Bible) which uses the N.T.G., and the Living Bible which is a paraphrase of the American Standard Bible. Paraphrases can sometimes help with understanding, but are not reliable enough for many points of doctrine.

Believe the originally inspired word of God. That is what God had recorded in the original languages in the Old and New Testaments.

The inspired language was NOT English. It was NOT the KJV or any other translation.

New Testament Text Reliability

There are over 5,800 ancient Greek manuscripts that have been found that contain at least parts of the New Testament, plus 19,000 early translations of it into other languages (McDowell J, McDowell S. Evidence That Demands a Verdict. Josh McDowell Ministry, 2017, p. 52; Holden JM. The Popular Handbook of Archaeology and the Bible: Discoveries That Confirm the Reliability of Scripture. Harvest House Publishers, 2013, pp. 103,122). "Nothing like this exists for any book in the ancient world ... The next closest book to the New Testament in terms of manuscripts is the *Iliad* of Homer, which is attested to by 643 manuscripts, the oldest of these were made 500 years after the original." (Ibid, pp. 122,126)

Modern readers may be surprised to learn how expensive early book production was. It has been estimated by Randolph Richards that making a copy of just Matthew's gospel cost the equivalent of US$2,238 (Akin, p. 92). So, having 5,800+ Greek manuscripts shows the value of having the scriptures. Plus, since even short books cost so much, accuracy was important.

In terms of the accuracy of the events in the New Testament, it is full of personal, eye-witness accounts (e.g. John 19:35, 21:24; Acts 2:32, 4:19-20, 10:39-41; Hebrews 2:3-4; 1 Peter 5:1; 2 Peter 1:16; 1 John 1:1-4; Revelation 1:1-20, 21:2, 22:8).

Notice some of what John, the last writer of the New Testament, wrote:

> [35] And he who has seen has testified, and his testimony is true; and he knows that he is telling the truth, so that you may believe. (John 19:35)

> [31] but these are written that you may believe that Jesus is the Christ, the Son of God, and that believing you may have life in His name. (John 20:31)

> [1] That which was from the beginning, which we have heard, which we have seen with our eyes, which we have looked upon, and our hands have handled, concerning the Word of life — [2] the life was manifested, and we have seen, and bear witness, and declare to you that eternal life which was with the Father

and was manifested to us — [3] that which we have seen and heard we declare to you, that you also may have fellowship with us; and truly our fellowship is with the Father and with His Son Jesus Christ. [4] And these things we write to you that your joy may be full. [5] This is the message which we have heard from Him and declare to you, that God is light and in Him is no darkness at all. (1 John 1:1-5)

Although Luke was not an eyewitness of what is in his gospel account, he had testimony from eyewitnesses (cf. Luke 1:1-4). Furthermore, he was an eyewitness to many events in the Book of Acts, which it is believed that he wrote. Plus, he accurately referred to various facts and geographical points in that book (Acts 13:4-5,13; 14:6,12, 16:11,14; 17:1; 18:12; 19:9; 21:3; 23:2, 24; 24:27; 27:13; 28:15), which have been confirmed by later researchers (Holden, p. 136).

As far as the Book of Acts itself goes, evidence points to it being written by around A.D. 62 (Hemer CJ. The Book of Acts in the Setting of Hellenistic History. Coronet Books, 1990).

The New Testament does give an accurate account of Jesus and holds many doctrines and prophecies that people should strive to understand today.

Key Points on the New Testament Canon

- The Book of Isaiah prophesied that the disciples would bind and seal the testimony and law (Isaiah 8:16), meaning the books of the Bible.
- The Apostle Paul had Timothy and Mark bring the "the parchments," the custody of which ultimately ended up with the Apostle Peter, who was often with the Apostle John.
- The Apostle John was the last writer of the New Testament, so he was in a position to finalize what the scriptures were.
- The Apostle John passed on the canons to Polycarp of Smyrna.
- In the second century, Polycarp told the Philippians that they were "well versed in the Sacred Scriptures" which points to the fact that in order to do so, they had to know what they were.
- In the 2nd century, Melito, Bishop of the Church of God in Sardis (and a saint even according to Greco-Roman Catholic sources),

verified that list (the so-called protocanonical books) and did not include one book from the additional ones that the Hellenists preserved (sometimes called deuterocanonical books).

- In the late 2nd century, Irenaeus wrote that Polycarp taught what he had been taught by the Apostles and such teachings were handed down.
- In the late 2nd century, Polycrates of Ephesus said he and others had "gone through every Holy scripture."
- In the early 3rd century, Serapion of Antioch stated that the books of the Bible had been handed down.
- The Eastern Orthodox incorrectly believe that the translation from the Hebrew to Greek resulted in a superior Old Testament (the Septuagint) than the original.
- In the early 4th century, Lucian of Antioch was involved with the Old Testament by using the original Hebrew to fix errors in the Septuagint. Lucian was also involved with what later became known as the *Textus Receptus* of the New Testament.
- Nazarene Christians said that God had given them the Bible, presumably through early faithful leaders. There was continuity of the scriptures from the beginning of the church and throughout COG history.
- The proto-Waldenses and the Waldenses were involved with a chain of custody of the scriptures into the late Middle Ages.
- It took the Church of Rome until 1546 to finalize their canon.
- In the 1600's, Church of God leaders cited books in the canon that are the same as we in the CCOG use today.
- It took the Eastern Orthodox until 1672 to essentially finalize their canon — which includes books that the Protestant and Roman Catholics do not accept as canonical.
- In 1830, Joseph Smith first published the Book of Mormon, which allegedly contains materials as far back as 2200 B.C. that no early Christian ever cited.
- The true Church of God never accepted that the deuterocanonical books were inspired scripture, nor that the Book of Mormon was a divinely revealed testament.
- Because of various scriptures, it is theologically improper to believe that God would allow His true Church to not know which books of the New Testament He inspired until centuries after Jesus died.

12. The Canon of the Bible Timeline

Some have wondered about the order of the books of the Bible, when were the books known, what group(s) knew what the best texts of the Bible were, as well as who gave the world the Bible.

Order of the Books of the Bible

As far as the order of the books go, the order we see the books in the Bible currently traditionally listed in was put together by the Catholic saint and doctor of their church, Jerome. Jerome put together what is now considered to be the 'traditional order' as his order has been kept for many centuries. He seems to have been influenced by the order in the Septuagint (a Greek, not Hebrew, language OT Bible).

Jerome's order does not change the fact that neither he nor his church actually came up with the books, though it took the Church of Rome many centuries to finalize their 'canons' of scripture — and when they did so, they added books in the Old Testament that Jerome opposed, but was essentially forced to put in his *Latin Vulgate Bible*.

Jerome's order, however, does not appear to have been the completely truly traditional order, as his was from a later tradition.

Here is what the *Jewish Encyclopedia of 1906* says about the sequence:

Sequence

The classical passage for the sequence of the books is the Baraita in B. B. 14b. With the exclusion of interjected remarks chronicled there, it runs as follows:

> "The sequence of the Prophets is Joshua, Judges, Samuel, Kings, Jeremiah, Ezekiel, Isaiah, the 12 [minor] prophets; that of the Hagiographa is Ruth, Psalms, Job, Proverbs, Ecclesiastes, Song of Solomon, Lamentations, Daniel, Esther, Ezra, Chronicles. Who wrote the books? Moses wrote his book, the section of Balaam and Job; Joshua wrote his book, and the last eight verses of the

Torah; Samuel wrote his book, Judges, and Ruth; David wrote the Psalms, by the hand of the ten Ancients; namely, through Adam (Psalm cxxxix. 16, perhaps also xcii.), through Melchizedek, Ps. Cx.: through Abraham, Ps. Lxxxix. (איתן האזרחי explained to = Abraham); through Moses, Ps. Xc.-c.; through Heman, Ps. Lxxxviii.; through Jeduthun, Ps. Lxii.; perhaps lxxvii.; through Asaph, Ps. L., lxxiii.-lxxxiii.; and through the three sons of Korah, Ps. Xlii. Xlix., lxxviii., lxxxiv., lxxxv., lxxxviii. [The question whether Solomon should be included among the Psalmists is discussed in Tosafot 15a.] Jeremiah wrote his book, the Book of Kings, and Lamentations; King Hezekiah, and his council that survived him, wrote Isaiah, Proverbs, Song of Solomon, and Ecclesiastes; the men of the Great Synagogues wrote Ezekiel, the Twelve Prophets, Daniel, and Esther; Ezra wrote his book and the genealogy of Chronicles down to himself."

From the fact that in this account of the authors Moses is mentioned as the author of the Torah, it may be inferred that in the collection from which the Baraita is cited the sequence also of the five books of the Torah was probably given. (Bible Canon. Jewish Encyclopedia of 1906)

It has been asserted by some that former Worldwide Church of God scholar, Dr. Ernest Martin, did the major scholastic work to determine the original order of the books of the Bible in the late 20th century related to his book *Restoring the Original Bible*.

Here is a list of the books of the Old Testament in what the AFV (put together by a COG leader) says is their original order (starting from the left going down):

Genesis	1 Samuel	Hosea	Habakkuk
Exodus	2 Samuel	Joel	Zephaniah
Leviticus	1 Kings	Amos	Haggai
Numbers	2 Kings	Obadiah	Zechariah
Deuteronomy	Isaiah	Jonah	Malachi
Joshua	Jeremiah	Micah	Psalms
Judges	Ezekiel	Nahum	Proverbs

Job	Lamentations	Daniel	1 Chronicles
Song of Songs	Ecclesiastes	Ezra	2 Chronicles
Ruth	Esther	Nehemiah	

Note: There is a possibility that Daniel originally may have been listed earlier in order than in the above list.

Some have pointed out a seven-fold division of the entire Bible:

> Most people are not aware that if the New Testament is placed side by side with the Old, the Bible is COMPLETE IN SEVEN DIVISIONS: Law, Prophets, Psalms, Gospels, Acts, Epistles, Revelation. Here is an amazing SEVENFOLD DIVISION of the books of the Bible. Seven is God's number for completion. With these seven divisions of the Bible, God's Book is complete. (Do We Have The COMPLETE BIBLE? Ambassador College Publications, 1974)

Here is a list of the books of the New Testament in the order of how they were displayed in the ancient manuscripts (see AFV; see also Scrivener E. A Plain Introduction to the Criticism of the New Testament, Volume 1. Wipf and Stock Publishers, Reprint 1997, p. 124):

Matthew	2 Peter	2 Corinthians	Hebrews
Mark	1 John	Galatians	1 Timothy
Luke	2 John	Ephesians	2 Timothy
John	3 John	Philippians	Titus
Acts	Jude	Colossians	Philemon
James	Romans	1 Thessalonians	Revelation
1 Peter	1 Corinthians	2 Thessalonians	

While the placement order of the books can be debated, knowing the true word of God is what is most important.

Who Gave the World the Bible?

Who gave the world the Bible?

God did.

Did God inspire translators of the Septuagint to improve His own words as many Eastern Orthodox claim?

No.

Were the Apostles Paul, Peter, and John involved?

Yes.

Did God inspire Martin Luther to add words to the Bible that He did not originally have?

No.

Did God inspire translators of the King James Version to be true and without error as some Protestants claim?

No.

Did the Church of Rome give the world the Bible on its own?

No.

Was the Church of God involved in preserving and translating the word of God?

Yes.

How did God give the world the Bible?

Writers throughout the centuries were moved by the Holy Spirit to record the inspired written words (2 Timothy 3:16-17; 2 Peter 1:20-21).

For the last book of the Bible, Jesus instructed John to write what he saw (Revelation 1:11).

As the last writer of the New Testament, and one who knew both Peter and Paul (cf. Galatians 2:9), the Apostle John would be the first person who could have known and possessed the complete canon.

Jesus had the New Testament canon finalized in Asia Minor via John. Rome later accepted that canon.

The Apostle John passed the knowledge of the canon, seemingly along with the books themselves, to people such as Polycarp of Smyrna.

Polycarp demonstrated familiarity with all the books of the New Testament.

Melito of Sardis demonstrated knowledge of the books of the Old Testament, essentially by accepting the canonical books that the Jews of Palestine had recognized — which were consistent with books that Jesus and the apostles quoted from.

Throughout early history, we see that Church of God leaders (like Polycrates) asserted they had the entire Bible. There is also later evidence that various leaders who held to Church of God doctrines were involved in its preservation and its "chain of custody" (like Antiochians Serapion and Lucian), even into the Middle Ages (some of the Waldensians and pre-Waldensians) and later times, as well as a translation into English in the 21st century (AFV).

None of the so-called 'lost books of the Bible,' 'lost gospels,' or Old Testament Apocrypha (sometimes referred to as deuterocanonical books) were part of the original Christian canon. Nor was the *Qur'an* or the *Book of Mormon*. So, no, in the *Continuing* Church of God we do not believe that some group of men conspired to keep any of those writings out of the true canon. Those other books are not scripture.

Timeline

This book has often mentioned the chain of custody of the books of the Bible as well as which manuscripts were best.

Church of God leaders knew the books of the New Testament from the beginning and did NOT need the later councils that many Greco-Roman-Protestant scholars claim were necessary to determine the canon of the New Testament.

212

Now, notice the following improper assertion from the 19th century Roman Catholic Cardinal Gibbons:

> The Catholic Church ... For fifteen centuries the Church was the sole guardian and depository of the Bible, (Gibbons J, Cardinal. The faith of our fathers: being a plain exposition and vindication of the church founded by Our Lord Jesus Christ, 93rd reprint edition. John Murphy Company, 1917, p. 90,91)

It is a fact that Rome had both possession issues as well as a lack of a firm understanding of the New Testament canon for many centuries, plus it also adopted Old Testament books that the original Christian church did not recognize.

Here is a timeline of custody from the view of the *Continuing* Church of God and the Greco-Roman-Protestant churches with many of the early dates approximate:

Timeline of Custody

Church of God	Date	*Greco-Roman-Protestants*
God inspired various ones to write the gospels and other letters, and other parts of the New Testament.	c. 40-92	God inspired various ones to write the gospels and other parts of the New Testament.
Paul writes Timothy to bring Mark and the parchments (2 Timothy 4:11-13).	c. 66	Paul writes Timothy to bring Mark and the parchments (2 Timothy 4:11-13).
Peter has Paul's writings (2 Peter 3:15-16).	c. 66	Peter has at least some of Paul's writings (2 Peter 3:15-16).
John gets writings from Peter.	c. 66	John gets some writings from Peter.
Peter and Paul are killed.	c. 67	Peter and Paul are killed.
In Patmos, John pens the last book of the Bible (Revelation 1:9-11). He is the last disciple	c. 92	In Patmos, John pens the last book of the Bible (Revelation 1:9-11).

to bind and seal the testimony (cf. Isaiah 8:16).		
John moves back to Ephesus.	c. 96	John moves back to Ephesus.
John passes the finalized canons on to Polycarp of Smyrna and others.	c. 98	John passes knowledge to Polycarp of Smyrna.
Papias of Hierapolis shows he accepted Revelation as scripture.	c. 120	
Polycarp quotes or alludes to every one of the 27 books of the New Testament (including Hebrews, 1 & 2 Peter, and James) and notes that those of Philipi are "well versed in the Sacred Scriptures."	c. 135	Polycarp refers to various NT books and notes that those of Philipi are "well versed in the Sacred Scriptures."
	c. 160	*Shepherd of Hermas* and *Gospel of Peter* are considered to be scripture.
	c. 175	*Muratorian Canon* includes *Apocalypse of Peter and Wisdom of Solomon,* but excludes Book of Hebrews, James, 1 Peter, 2 Peter, and one of John's epistles.
Melito of Sardis lists the books of the Old Testament, but does not include any of the Apocrypha. Melito's use of the term 'Old Testament' presupposes that he also knew the New Testament.	c. 175	Melito of Sardis lists the books of the Old Testament, but does not include any of the Apocrypha. Melito's use of the term 'Old Testament' presupposes that he also knew the New Testament. Apocrypha used by some Greco-Romans.
Polycrates of Ephesus said he and others in Asia Minor	c. 192	

had "gone through every Holy scripture."		
Serapion of Antioch condemns *Gospel of Peter* as **pseudepigrapha** (ψευδεπιγραφα) after seeing it for the first time.	c. 209	*Gospel of Peter* still being used.
Serapion says the books were "handed down" to those in Antioch/Asia Minor, as opposed to those he encountered in Egypt.	c. 209	
	c. 180-250	School in Alexandria, with Origen in the 3rd century, classifies Hebrews, 2 Peter, 2 and 3 John, James, and Jude as "contested writings."
	c. 230	Origen sees major problems with the Septuagint texts, but it is still used.
	c. 250	Cyprian of Carthage's "first Latin Bible" fails to include Hebrews, 2 Peter, James, and Jude.
School in Antioch, with Lucian predecessors, then Lucian himself, improves Greek Septuagint by using Hebrew Masoretic documents and also edits the 'Traditional Text' of the Greek New Testament.	c. 250-312	
	c. 320	Eusebius writes that Hebrews, James, Jude, 2 Peter, 2 John, 3 John, and Revelation are disputed.

	367	Athanasius lists the 27 books of the New Testament.
	c. 380	Canon 85 of the *Apostolic Constitutions* includes the "two Epistles of Clement" among its "sacred books."
	382	Damasan catalogue has a canon for the Roman Church with the Book of Hebrews.
Nazarene Christians use the Old and New Testaments without the Apocrypha.	c. 382 - 395	Jerome works on Latin Vulgate Bible, but does not want to include the Apocrypha. He notices that he is often using corrupted texts.
Nazarenes continued with the original canon.	c. 382- 404	Jerome consults with one or more Nazarene Christians on the canon.
	393	Augustine said Hebrews was still disputed.
	c. 405	Pope Innocent I left Hebrews out of his list of the New Testament canon he sent to Exsuperius.
	c.405	Jerome completes his Bible, and, after succumbing to pressure, includes the Apocrypha.
	419	Council of Carthage adopts catalogue of canon.
Nazarenes and Proto-Waldenses preserve the books. Their canon included the whole of the New Testament.	5th-7th centuries	
Constantine of Mananali (Armenia) receives much of	c. 650	

the New Testament in Greek from an Syrian/Antiochian and translates it.		
Proto-Waldenses preserve and translate the books.	7th-11th centuries	
Team led by Peter Waldo translates the entire New Testament and parts of the Old Testament.	12th century	
Waldenses preserve and translate the books.	12th-15th centuries	
Waldensian books taken by supporters of Rome.	12th-15th centuries	Edicts against the Waldeneses issued by Roman Catholics in 1184 (Synod of Verona), 1215 (Fourth Lateran Council), and 1487 (Bull by Innocent VII).
	1522	Martin Luther included Apocrypha in his translation of the Bible.
	16th century	Huldrych Zwingli did not accept Revelation as scripture.
	1546	Martin Luther still doubted the inclusion of Hebrews, James, Jude, and Revelation.
	1546	Rome's Council of Trent declares fixed canon is a dogma that cannot be changed.
	1611	King James Version published with the Apocrypha as part of the appendix.
	1672	Eastern Orthodox finalize their canon, at the Synod of Jerusalem, which includes the Apocrypha.

	19th century	Protestants drop the Apocrypha from the appendix of the edited KJV.
Church of God leaders continued to cite the same canon of scripture from prior to the Protestant Reformation to present. They basically continue to point to the Masoretic Hebrew and a version of the Textus Receptus as the best available scriptural texts.	16th- 21st centuries	

There are basically two views of the canon.

The last column reflects, to a significant degree, the major scholastic view today. It shows a lack of chain of custody of the books of the Bible as the Greco-Roman churches were confused. It is because of Greco-Roman confusion that most scholars do not believe that the true church had the canon from the beginning.

But that scholastic view is not only historically wrong, it essentially goes against scripture (cf. 2 Timothy 3:16-17; Matthew 16:17-18, Hebrews 13:5).

That being said, the first column hopefully provides enough scriptural and historical information to show the honest inquirer that, yes, there is evidence that the Church of God had the canon from the beginning. This is also consistent with scriptures such as Isaiah 8:16, Matthew 16:18, and Ephesians 2:19-22.

The true chain of custody for the Church of God has continued to hold the same books of the canon of scripture to this day.

Because the Greco-Roman churches often included certain books they dropped and did not include others which they added, that would not be considered an unbroken chain of custody.

Although Jesus taught that His church would be a "little flock" (Luke 12:32), most scholars ignore that and accept that the Greco-Romans (and later the Protestants) represent Christianity as a whole. So, they have tended to teach the Greco-Roman view as fact.

Most have overlooked the true chain of custody. Part of the reason is that many aspects of church history have been misunderstood (details on church history can be found in the free book, online at ccog.org, titled *Continuing History of the Church of God*).

The Truth About the Word of God is Important to Know

In the end times, the Bible shows that some will be killed for the word of God:

> [4] And I saw thrones, and they sat on them, and judgment was committed to them. Then I saw the souls of those who had been beheaded for their witness to Jesus and for the word of God, who had not worshiped the beast or his image, and had not received his mark on their foreheads or on their hands. And they lived and reigned with Christ for a thousand years. (Revelation 20:4)

So, this is another reason it is important to know the right books — who would want to die for a lie?

Consider also the following:

> [12] And I saw the dead, small and great, standing before God, and books were opened. And another book was opened, which is the Book of Life. And the dead were judged according to their works, by the things which were written in the books. (Revelation 20:12)

The 'books' mentioned above include the books of the Bible — therefore it is very important to know what they are as people will be judged by what is in them.

The last book of the Bible was written in the late 1st century. Books written after that, despite sometimes purporting to be scripture, are not part of the canon.

Despite scholastic claims to the contrary, the true canon was known by the end of the 1st century, with the Old Testament re-checked in the 2nd century.

Early Church of God Christians, mostly all considered to be saints by the Greco-Roman-Protestants, including Papias, Polycarp, Melito, Polycrates, and Serapion essentially attested to the fact that the Church of God had the full canon in the 2nd century, and that knowledge was basically passed on from the original apostles, like the Apostle John.

This was later confirmed by other groups with at least distant ties to the Church of God (like the Nazarenes) and was a factor in the Roman Catholics and Eastern Orthodox (who were in the areas these saints had lived in and had been affected by them) agreeing to the currently accepted list of the Books of the New Testament.

Seemingly, that is also confirmed by the realization by the Roman and Eastern Orthodox Catholics that their Old Testament Apocrypha was not in the same category as what they call the protocanonical books of the Old Testament — which is the list of books accepted by the Jews, the Church of God, and most Protestants.

There exists proof that in the early 17th century men who held to COG doctrines cited the canonical scriptures authoritatively (Falconer J. A briefe refutation of Iohn Traskes iudaical and nouel fancyes Stiling himselfe Minister of Gods Word, imprisoned for the lawes eternall perfection, or God's lawes perfect eternity. English College Press, 1618). Later in the 17th century, Church of God leaders were clearly citing the canonical scriptures in English in their writings (Clarke, pp. 12-13; Sellers, p. 6). The Church of God has known the scriptures since the Apostle John passed the knowledge to leaders such as Polycarp.

Since Jesus said that God's word was truth (John 17:17), Jesus frequently cited the books of the Old Testament as scripture (but not the Apocrypha), and Jesus taught that Christians needed to have a rock-solid foundation (Matthew 7:24-27), Christians need to realize it is important to know which books constitute the word of God—and who always knew them.

Furthermore, the New Testament teaches that it is God's true ministers who are tasked with helping people understand what the word of God means (Ephesians 4:11-16).

We in the *Continuing* Church of God are among those that have striven to faithfully do that from the time of Jesus through to the 21st century.

Now it is true that many people, in various faiths, have been involved in copying and translating the Bible. But they, of themselves, did not give the world the Bible.

God gave the world the Bible.

The Bible has been known in its final form by the faithful Church of God since the Apostle John passed on that knowledge of the Old and New Testament canons.

A chain of custody of the knowledge of the books of the Bible has existed in the Church of God from the apostles until the present time.

Bibliography

Akin J. The Bible is a Catholic Book. Catholic Answers Press, 2019.

Alfeyev H. Orthodox Christianity, Volume II: Doctrine and Teaching of the Orthodox Church, New York: St. Vladimir Seminary Press, 2012

Alworth J. HITLER'S SAY IN YOUR NEW VERSION BIBLE. Day of Christ Ministries, New Zealand, 2012

Apostolic Constitutions. From Ante-Nicene Fathers, Vol. 7. Edited by Alexander Roberts, James Donaldson, and A. Cleveland Coxe. 1886

Athanasius. 39th Letter. Nicene and Post-Nicene Fathers, Second Series, Vol. 4. Edited by Philip Schaff and Henry Wace

Bagatti B. Translated by Eugene Hoade. The Church from the Gentiles in Palestine. Nihil obstat: Ignatius Mancini. Imprimi potest: Herminius Roncari. Imprimatur: +Albertus Gori, die 28 Februarii 1970. Franciscan Printing Press, Jerusalem

Bagatti, Bellarmino. Translated by Eugene Hoade. The Church from the Circumcision. Nihil obstat: Marcus Adinolfi. Imprimi potest: Herminius Roncari. Imprimatur: +Albertus Gori, die 26 Junii 1970. Franciscan Printing Press, Jerusalem

Bauer W, Danker FW. A Greek-English Lexicon of the New Testament, 3rd edition. University of Chicago, 2000

Bauer W. Orthodoxy and Heresy in Earliest Christianity, 2nd ed. Sigler Press Edition, Mifflintown, PA, 1996

Barriger L. The Septuagint. © 2019 by the American Carpatho-Russian Orthodox Diocese of the U.S.A.

Berry GR. Interlinear Greek-English New Testament. Hinds and Noble, 1897

Blackwell D. The Plain Truth About The Waldensians. Ambassador College Library, 1974, p. 17

Brock SP. The Bible in the Syriac Tradition St. Ephrem Ecumenical Research Institute, 1988

Bromiley GW, ed. International Standard Bible Encyclopedia. Wm B Eerdmans, 1979

Bruce FF. The Canon of Scripture. InterVarsityPress, 1988

Bruce FF. The New Testament Documents: Are They Reliable? Wm. B. Eerdmans Publishing,

Bungener F, McClintock F, Scott DD. History of the Council of Trent. Harper, 1855

Burgon JW. The Causes of the Corruption of the Traditional Text of the Holy Gospels. Original 1896; reprint Cosimo Classics, 2007

Burgon DJ. Unholy Hands on the Bible. Original, 1871. Sovereign Grace Publishers, Reprint 1990

Carlson K. Hidden in Plain Sight, Part I: The Development of the Canon. Dormition Publishing, 2019

Catechism of the Catholic Church. Imprimatur Potest +Joseph Cardinal Ratzinger. Doubleday, NY 1995

Clarke H. A History of the Sabbatarians Or Seventh Day Baptists, in America; Containing Their Rise and Progress to the Year 1811, with Their Leaders' Names, and Their Distinguishing Tenets, etc. Utica, 1811

Conybeare F.C. The Key of Truth: A Manual of the Paulician Church of Armenia. Clarendon Press, Oxford, 1898

Coulter F. The Holy Bible in its Original Order. York Publishing, 2011

Daniels DW. Did the Catholic Church Give Us the Bible? Chick Publications, 2013

Daniels DW. Should "Gehenna" be Translated as "Hell'? Answers to Your Bible Questions. Chick Publications, 2002

Danielou, Cardinal Jean-Guenole-Marie. The Theology of Jewish Christianity. Translated by John A. Baker. The Westminister Press, 1964

Dehandschutter B. Polycarpiana, Selected Essays. Leuven University Press, 2007

Denny H. The Final Destination of Man. WestBow Press, 2015

Dines JM. The Septuagint. Michael A. Knibb, Ed., London: T&T Clark, 2004

Do We Have The COMPLETE BIBLE? Ambassador College Publications, 1974

Drummond J. What Is the Oldest Hebrew Bible? Biblical Archeaology Society, January 10, 2021

Duchesne L. Early History of the Christian Church: From Its Foundation to the End of the Third Century, Volume 1, 4th edition. Longmans, Green & Co., 1912

Duffy E. Saints & Sinners: A History of the Popes. Yale University Press, New Haven (CT), 2002

Ehrman B. Lost Christianities. New York: Oxford University Press, 2003

Elpenor's Bilingual (Greek / English) Old Testament. English translation by L.C.L. Brenton

Eusebius. The History of the Church, Book IV, Chapter XXVI. Digireads.com Publishing, Stilwell (KS), 2005

Falconer J. A briefe refutation of Iohn Traskes iudaical and nouel fancyes Stiling himselfe Minister of Gods Word, imprisoned for the lawes eternall perfection, or God's lawes perfect eternity. English College Press, 1618

Fanning S. Mystics of the Christian Tradition. Routeldge, New York. 2001

Fonck, Leopold. "St. John the Evangelist." The Catholic Encyclopedia. Vol. 8. New York: Robert Appleton Company, 1910

Fowler EW. Evaluating Versions of the New Testament. Maranatha Baptist Press, 1981

Francis, Pope. APOSTOLIC LETTER SCRIPTURAE SACRAE AFFECTUS OF THE HOLY FATHER FRANCIS ON THE SIXTEEN HUNDREDTH ANNIVERSARY OF THE DEATH OF SAINT JEROME. Copyright - Libreria Editrice Vaticana, September 30, 2020
Gibbon E. The History of the Decline and Fall of the Roman Empire, Volume 7. London, 1809

Gibbons J, Cardinal. The faith of our fathers: being a plain exposition and vindication of the church founded by Our Lord Jesus Christ, 93rd reprint edition. John Murphy Company, 1917

Gordon RL. A History of Biblical Transmission. Written April 1997, Updated September 2020

Grabbe LL. Good News, October 1976

Grady WP. Final Authority. Grady Publications, 1993

Green JP. Interlinear Greek-English New Testament, 3rd edition. Baker Books, 2002 printing

Healy, P. Lucian of Antioch. The Catholic Encyclopedia. New York: Robert Appleton Company, 1910

Hemer CJ. The Book of Acts in the Setting of Hellenistic History. Coronet Books, 1990

Hills EF. The King James Version Defended! 1956

Hirsch EG, et al. Jewish Encyclopedia, Funk and Wagnalls, 1906, Volume 2, 'Bible Canon'

Holden JM. The Popular Handbook of Archaeology and the Bible: Discoveries That Confirm the Reliability of Scripture. Harvest House Publishers, 2013

Holmes M.W. The Apostolic Fathers: Greek Texts and English Translations, 2nd ed. Baker Books, Grand Rapids, 2004

Hudleston G.R. St. Melito. The Catholic Encyclopedia, Volume X Copyright © 1911 by Robert Appleton Company, NY. Nihil Obstat, October 1, 1911

Irenaeus. Adversus haereses. Ante-Nicene Fathers, Volume 1. Edited by Alexander Roberts & James Donaldson. American Edition, 1885

Jerome, Epistula CXXV, Chapter 12. Patrologia Latina (22, 1079). The edition by J. P. Migne, c. 1886

Jerome. The Four Gospels Addressed to Pope Damasus, a.d. 383. In Horn A. The Writings of Jerome. New Apostolic Bible Covenant, 2020

Josephus. Complete Works. Translated by W. Whiston, Kregel Publications, 1960

Kelly R. Ambassador College Notes and Course Outlines Church History. Ambassador College, 1987

Kohen E. History of the Byzantine Jews. University Press of America, 2007

Kroll P. Is the Bible a Protestant Book? Good News magazine, April 1964

Kruger MJ. Question of Canon, InterVarsity Press, 2013

Lasater R. Was the New Testament Really Written in Greek? A Concise Compendium of the Many Internal and External Evidences of Aramaic Primacy. 2008

Life of Polycarp, Chapter 24. In: J. B. Lightfoot, The Apostolic Fathers, vol. 3.2, 1889

Manual of the Bible Missionary Church, Inc. Bible Missionary Church. 2015

Martin EL. Restoring the Original Bible. A.S.K., 1994

Matthew Henry's Commentary on the Whole Bible: New Modern Edition, Electronic Database. Copyright (c) 1991 by Hendrickson Publishers, Inc.

McDonald LM, Sanders JA. The Canon Debate. Baker Academic, 2002

McDowell J, McDowell S. Evidence That Demands a Verdict. Josh McDowell Ministry, 2017

Melito. From the Book of Extracts. Cited in Eusebius. The History of the Church, Book IV, Chapter XXVI. Digireads.com Publishing, Stilwell (KS), 2005

Methodius. Banquet of the Ten Virgins. Translated by William R. Clark. Ante-Nicene Fathers, Vol. 6. Edited by Alexander Roberts, James Donaldson, and A. Cleveland Coxe. Buffalo, NY: Christian Literature Publishing Co., 1886

Metzger, Bruce M. The Canon of the New Testament: Its Origin, Development, and Significance. Clarendon Press. Oxford. 1987

Metzger B. The Text of the New Testament: Its Transmission, Corruption, and Restoration, 3rd ed., Oxford University Press, 1991

Metzger BM, Ehrman B. The Text of the New Testament: Its Transmission, Corruption, and Restoration, 4th ed. Oxford University Press, 2004

Mihăilă A. The Septuagint and the Masoretic Text in the Orthodox Church(es) Download Date | 9/18/19.

Nelson R. What Is the Masoretic Text? The Beginner's Guide. © 2018 OverviewBible

Newman JH, Cardinal. The Arians of the Fourth Century. Longmans, Green, & Co., New York, 1908

Nolan F. An Inquiry into the integrity of the Greek Vulgate, or received text of the New Testament, etc. F.C. and J. Rivington, 1815

Nowell P. Burning the Bible: Heresy and Translation in Occitania 1229-1250. Academia.edu undated, but prior to 2018

Ogwyn J. Do You Know the Real Jesus? Tomorrow's World. September-October 2004

Ogwyn J. How Did We Get The Bible? Tomorrow's World. January-February 2002

Origen. De Principiis. Ante-Nicene Fathers, Volume 4. Edited by Alexander Roberts & James Donaldson. American Edition, 1885

Ott L. Fundamentals of Catholic Dogma, 4th ed . Imprimatur: + Cornelius, 7 October 1954, Printed 1974, TAN Books

Philip JC. Reliability of The Canon. Indus School of Apologetics and Theology Textbook No -004A1, version used in 2006

Pines S. The Jewish Christians of the Early Centuries of Christianity according to a New Source. Proceedings of the Israel Academy of Sciences and Humanities, Volume II, No.13; 1966. Jerusalem

Petrovich D. The World's Oldest Alphabet: Hebrew As The Language Of The Proto-Consonantal Script. Carta Jerusalem, 2016

Polycarp. Letter to the Philippians. Ante-Nicene Fathers, Volume 1. Alexander Roberts & James Donaldson. American Edition, 1885

Polycarp/pseudo-Polycarp. Fragments from Victor of Capua. Translated by Stephen C. Carlson. 2006

Pritz R. Nazarene Jewish Christianity. Magnas, Jerusalem, 1988

Reid G. Canon of the Old Testament. The Catholic Encyclopedia, Volume III. Copyright © 1908 by Robert Appleton Company.

Roth AG. Aramaic New Testament, 5th ed. Netzari Press, 2012

Roth AG. Ruach Qadim: Aramaic Origins of the New Testament. Tushiyah Press, 2005

Sáenz-Badillos A. A History of the Hebrew Language. Cambridge University Press, 1996

Schaff P. Ante-Nicene Christianity, A.D. 100-325, Volume 2. Wm. B. Eerdmans, 1910

Schaff P. Theological Propaedeutic, A General Introduction to the Study of Theology. Wipf & Stock, 1892

Segal M., et al. "An Early Leviticus Scroll from En Gedi: Preliminary Publication," Textus 26, 2016

Sellers W. An Examination of a late book published by Doctor Owen ... A Sacred Day of Rest. 1671

Septuagint, Jamnia, the Masoretic Text and the Qumran discoveries. St. Michael's Media, Inc., © 2010

Serfes D. Holy Scripture In The Orthodox Church. Boise, Idaho, USA. August 20 2000. 'The Bible'

Sightler JH. A Testimony Founded For Ever, 2nd ed. Sightler Pubs., 2001

Smith, H.B., Jr. 2018. The case for the Septuagint's chronology in Genesis 5 and 11. In Proceedings of the Eighth International Conference on Creationism, ed. J.H. Whitmore, pp. 117–132. Pittsburgh, Pennsylvania: Creation Science Fellowship

Stevenson P. Was Syriac "The Language of Jesus"? The Language Fan, March 8, 2008

Stowe CE. Apocryphal Books of the Old Testament. Bibliotheca sacra: a theological quarterly, Volume 11. Dallas Theological Seminary and Graduate School of Theology, April 1854

Sullivan F.A. From Apostles to Bishops: the development of the episcopacy in the early church. Newman Press, Mahwah (NJ), 2001

Sundberg AC, Jr. The Septuagint: The Bible of Hellenistic Judaism. In: The Canon Debate. Baker Academic, 2002

Tenney MC. The Zondervan Encyclopedia of the Bible, Volume 1: Revised Full-Color Edition--Kindle. Zondervan Academic, 2010

The New Catholic Encyclopedia, McGraw Hill, Copyright 1967, Volume 3, 'Canon, Biblical.'

The Gospel According to Mary Magdalene. THE GNOSTIC SOCIETY LIBRARY, Gnostic Scriptures and Fragments

The Gospel of Philip. THE GNOSTIC SOCIETY LIBRARY. James M. Robinson, ed., The Nag Hammadi Library, revised edition. HarperCollins, San Francisco, 1990

Theissen G. Fortress introduction to the New Testament. Fortress Press, 2003

Thiel B. Polycarp's Letter to the Philippians with New Testament Scriptural Annotations. Trinity Journal of Apologetics and Theology, June 2008

Urick S. False Teachings and Divisive Movements: Schisms in Modern-Day Christendom. AuthorHouse, 2013

van der Horst PW. Jewish Funerary Inscriptions—Most Are in Greek. Biblical Archaeology Review 18:5, September/October 1992

Wallace D. Why I Do Not Think the King James Bible Is the Best Translation Available Today. Bible.org

Ware T. The Orthodox Church. Penguin Books, London, 1997

Weidman, Frederick W. Polycarp and John: The Harris Fragments and Their Challenge to Literary Traditions. University of Notre Dame Press, Notre Dame (IL), 1999

Westcott BF, Hort JA. The New Testament in the original Greek introduction and appendix [to] the text revised by Brooke Foss Westcott and Fenton John Anthony Hort. Harper, 1882

Whitmore DM. Yielding to the Prejudice of His Times: Erasmus and the Comma Johanneum. Church History and Religious Culture, Vol. 95, No. 1, 2015: 19-40

Wilkinson BG. Our Authorized Bible Vindicated. 1930, reprint TEACH Services, 2014

Wilkinson BG. Truth Triumphant, ca. 1890. Reprint: Teach Services, Brushton (NY) 1994,

Williams HD. The Received Text for the Whole World. Williams, 2007

Wooden C. American's donation lets pope peruse oldest copy of St. Luke's Gospel. Catholic News Service. POPE-PAPYRUS Jan-23-2007

Worth Jr, RH. Bible Translations: A History Through Source Documents. McFarland Publishing, 1992

Continuing Church of God

The USA office of the *Continuing* Church of God is located at: 1036 W. Grand Avenue, Grover Beach, California, 93433 USA.

Continuing Church of God (CCOG) Websites

CCOG.AFRICA This site is targeted towards those in Africa. **CCOG.ASIA** This site has focus on Asia and has various articles in multiple Asian languages, as well as some items in English. **CCOG.IN** This site is targeted towards those of Indian heritage. It has materials in the English language and various Indian languages. **CCOG.EU** This site is targeted toward Europe. It has materials in multiple European languages. **CCOG.NZ** This site is targeted towards New Zealand and others with a British-descended background. **CCOG.ORG** This is the main website of the *Continuing* Church of God. It serves people on all continents with literature and sermon videos. **CCOGCANADA.CA** This site is targeted towards those in Canada. **CDLIDD.ES** La Continuación de la Iglesia de Dios. This is the Spanish language website for the *Continuing* Church of God. **CG7.ORG** This is a website for those interested in the Sabbath and churches that observe the seventh day Sabbath. **PNIND.PH** Patuloy na Iglesya ng Diyos. This is the Philippines website with information in English and Tagalog.

News and History Websites

COGWRITER.COM This website is a major proclamation tool and has news, doctrine, historical articles, videos, and prophetic updates. **CHURCHHISTORYBOOK.COM** Has articles and books on church history. **BIBLENEWSPROPHECY.NET** This is an online radio website which covers news and biblical topics. **STUDYTHEBIBLECOURSE.ORG** An online course covering parts of the Bible.

YouTube Video Channels for Sermons & Sermonettes

BibleNewsProphecy channel. CCOG sermonette videos. **CCOGAfrica** channel. CCOG messages in African languages. **CDLIDDSermones** channel. CCOG messages in the Spanish language. **ContinuingCOG** channel. CCOG video sermons.

Made in the USA
Columbia, SC
23 August 2023

21945796R00128